Cosmology of Evil

THE ORIGIN OF EVIL AT
THE COSMIC LEVEL

KIM MICHAELS

Copyright © 2014 Kim Michaels. All rights reserved. No part of this book may be used, reproduced, translated, electronically stored or transmitted by any means except by written permission from the publisher. A reviewer may quote brief passages in a review.

MORE TO LIFE PUBLISHING

www.morepublish.com

For foreign and translation rights,

contact info@ morepublish.com

ISBN: 978-87-93297-02-9

The information and insights in this book should not be considered as a form of therapy, advice, direction, diagnosis, and/or treatment of any kind. This information is not a substitute for medical, psychological, or other professional advice, counseling and care. All matters pertaining to your individual health should be supervised by a physician or appropriate health-care practitioner. No guarantee is made by the author or the publisher that the practices described in this book will yield successful results for anyone at any time. They are presented for informational purposes only, as the practice and proof rests with the individual.

For more information:

www.ascendedmasterlight.com
www.transcendencetoolbox.com

Making Evil Visible, vol 2

Cosmology

of

Evil

CONTENTS

Introduction: The Challenge of Evil 9
1 | Why the Cosmos Was Created 17
2 | The Progressive Creation of the Spheres 25
3 | The Momentous Shift in the Fourth Sphere 35
4 | The Fifth and Sixth Spheres 49
5 | The Creation of Our Sphere 63
6 | The Process of Taking Embodiment 83
7 | The Levels of Human Consciousness 101
8 | The Subtle Workings of Free Will 117
9 | The Existence of an Evil Force 133
10 | Types of Evil Forces 143
11 | Control Through the Physical Body 163
12 | Control Through the Emotional Body 179
13 | Control Through the Mental Body 189
14 | Control Through the Identity Body 197
15 | How the First Beings Fell 217
16 | Separation, Duality and Fallen Consciousness 233
17 | The Mindset of Fallen Beings 241
18 | Understanding how a planet rises or falls 253
19 | The Problem of Evil 267

20 | Fighting Evil Will Not Remove Evil 277
21 | Clearing the Physical Octave 289
22 | Clearing the Emotional Octave 307

INTRODUCTION: THE CHALLENGE OF EVIL

Evil is a challenge for human beings. Evil is by nature aggressive, invasive and it forces itself upon us. Evil forces us to make choices, and we have two basic options:

- To ignore evil.

- To take a closer look at it.

The option we choose depends on what we believe about our ability to do something about evil. Again, we have two options:

- We can do *nothing* about evil.

- We can do *something* about evil.

If it is true that we cannot do anything about evil, then there is no point in writing or reading books about evil. People who believe this will typically seek to ignore evil and hope it ignores them, meaning they are not open to taking a closer look at evil. It can therefore be assumed that since you are reading this, you are open to the possibility that we can do *something* about evil. The question now becomes what we might do.

For thousands of years, human beings have done many things to either protect themselves from evil or combat evil more directly. Yet evil is still around. This gives rise to two new options:

- What people have done so far will one day work. It is just a matter of refining our methods and applying them with more determination.

- What has been done so far has no chance of ever removing evil. A new approach is needed.

If you believe the first option, this book has little to offer you. If you are open to the second option, this book will offer a new approach to evil by giving a deeper understanding of evil than has ever been offered on this planet.

This book is based on the realization that evil is not fundamentally different from so many other problems we have solved. Many diseases can be cured today that were considered incurable in the past because we have acquired new knowledge about the cause and nature of such diseases. New knowledge has also empowered us to solve many other problems. When you increase your knowledge about a problem, you may indeed come to see solutions that you did not see with less knowledge. Solving the problem of evil is a matter of how much we know about evil.

If you are open to this possibility, the conclusion is that we need to look for knowledge or understanding about evil that we do not currently have. This leads us to consider where such knowledge might come from, and again we have two options:

- Our existing thought systems have already given us all of the knowledge we *can* have or are allowed to have about evil.

- There may be knowledge that we do not have, at least not within mainstream thought systems.

If you accept the first option, then we are back at being powerless to do anything. Obviously, none of our existing thought systems have empowered us to remove evil. If there is new knowledge to be found, it will have to be found *outside* the mental boxes defined by our existing thought systems. If the knowledge had been *inside* the borders of existing systems, we should have found it and made progress towards removing evil.

This leads to a conclusion. Those who will play a part in removing evil from this planet, will be those who are willing to look for knowledge outside their existing thought system.

The ego wants you to remain ignorant

Before we can look for knowledge outside existing systems, we need to recognize that there is an element of the human psyche that seeks to prevent us from seeking such knowledge. This book is the second in the series about evil. In the first book, *Psychology of Evil*, I discussed a mechanism in the human psyche that gives rise to evil on the personal level. This element is the separate or localized self, and the core of it is the ego. Let me summarize the conclusions from the first book.

The localized self is by nature separate, meaning it is mortal. This gives it a fear of death, and one of the ways people seek to overcome this fear is by creating a thought system that they elevate to the status of being absolute and infallible. By following this system, your continued existence is supposedly secured. Once you have done this, you will be reluctant to look for explanations outside the system.

When a new idea comes to you, your intellect will immediately compare it to the ideas from your thought system. Your ego will be suspicious of anything that goes beyond or contradicts the system. You may accept a new idea, but only if you think it has some unquestionable authority. Traditionally, this means the idea must be based on an infallible religious scripture or be proven by materialistic science.

If traditional religion or scientific materialism had been able to give us the knowledge we need in order to transcend evil, then we should already have freed ourselves. Given that we have not risen above evil, we must reason that if we are to find new knowledge about evil, it will not come from traditional religion or scientific materialism. People who are attached to either system are likely to reject this new knowledge because it does not have what they see as authority.

In the first book, I attempted to avoid any knowledge that went too far beyond what most people know and believe. While this did give us a deeper understanding of the psychological cause of evil, it could not answer all of our questions about evil. In this book, it is my intent to answer, or at least address, all of these questions. In order to do this, I will have to go very far beyond traditional thought systems.

The criteria I will employ is that I will evaluate ideas based exclusively on their explanatory power. It is irrelevant whether the ideas can be supported by the authoritarian claims of traditional systems. We have made progress because we have considered new ideas, and new ideas have never been supported by the authority of existing systems.

In the following chapters I will present a number of ideas that go far beyond traditional beliefs. My only criteria is: Can these ideas explain something new and useful about evil? I think that if you consider the ideas with the attitude of seeking a deeper explanation, you will find many answers. You might even come to see that evil is not nearly as big of a mystery as it seems to most people. After all, when you see what has been hidden where is the room for mystery?

A brief introduction to a new world view

In the previous book, I started from below and worked my way up. I started with what is commonly known about the psyche and then worked towards higher layers. In this book, I will go in the opposite direction. I will start with the highest level and work my way down. There are several reasons for this, but the main one is that when you have an overall understanding of how the universe works, it becomes so much easier to explain some of the baffling things we observe with our senses.

In order to give you a sort of on-ramp to what I will present, I will sketch the world view that has been necessitated by the latest developments of science. As also described in the previous book, this begins with the theory of relativity. Einstein proved that matter is energy that has taken on a different form and thus appears solid to us. Matter truly does not have an objective existence; it is a product of our perception. We live in a world of vibrating energy—not a world of solid matter.

There are levels or realms of energy beyond the material universe. Visible light is made up of light rays that fall within a certain spectrum of vibrations. There are light rays of lower and higher vibrations than visible light, and there are realms made of higher and lower energies than the material universe.

Everything is connected at a deeper level. Locality, separateness, is another illusion produced by the senses. We live in a universe where nothing is separated from the whole. There is a level of reality that is below the vibrations of the material universe and there is a level that is above it. The material world is one level or octave in a continuum of vibrations.

Visible, physical phenomena can have invisible, even non-physical causes. If we are to explain evil, we cannot confine our inquiries to the material frequency spectrum. We must look for causes in the other realms, both the lower and the higher. Our minds are part of the process of creating the material universe. All visible matter is made from atoms, but atoms are made from subatomic entities. At this most fundamental level of matter, we human beings are not mere observers. Instead, we are so intimately involved that a subatomic entity does not become a particle or a wave until we make an observation. What we make is not an observation but an act of co-creation.

There is a level of reality that is beyond what we normally call the material universe. Our minds can interact with this realm, and this interaction can result in the manifestation of a subatomic particle or an energy wave. In the past, most physicists believed there was a barrier between the level of subatomic particles and what we see with our senses, the so-called macroscopic world. As with the matter-energy duality, the latest research and theories have caused at least some scientists to question this separation. Given that all matter is made from subatomic entities, it is clear that consciousness is present at every level of the universe and that our consciousness is part of the process of determining what will be manifest here on earth. The cause-effect sequence seems to be: Consciousness—energy—matter.

You do not have to accept these ideas in order to read the following chapters. However, it will be easier to read this book if you are open to the possibility that these ideas can explain something about evil that traditional thought systems cannot explain. Once again, we will look for ideas based exclusively on their explanatory power.

Many will wonder where the ideas I present come from. This will be explained as we go along. We first need to set a foundation that will make it possible to explain where this knowledge comes from and why it is given.

1 | WHY THE COSMOS WAS CREATED

The universe, the cosmos, in which we live is much more than what we call the material world. This cosmos is a created world, meaning it had a beginning and will have an end. The cosmos was created by a being whose consciousness is so far beyond ours that we cannot (yet) fathom the totality of this being. The beginning of the cosmos was determined by a mind that is far beyond ours, but the end of the cosmos will be determined – at least in part – by our minds.

Our cosmos has a boundary, and there is an aspect of reality that is outside of that boundary. In order to understand the purpose behind the creation of our cosmos, we need to know something about the reality that is outside our world. This presents a difficulty, and we first need to consider our own state of consciousness.

Our minds are completely adapted to living inside our cosmos, which means it is extremely difficult for us to fathom or envision what reality is like outside our cosmos. The words we use and the way we use them are not very well suited for describing reality outside our cosmos.

We live inside a cosmos that is characterized by forms. We see many forms around us, and they all appear to be distinct from one another. They may even appear to be separate forms, meaning we cannot easily see any underlying reality from which all forms sprang or any connecting link between them. From our perspective on earth, we see material forms that appear to have an independent or self-sufficient existence. We see these forms as existing independently of our own minds, even as being independent of any mind.

These impressions of distinct and separate forms are the products of our perception, and our perception exists only inside our minds. Because we are living inside our cosmos, our present perception is a natural stage in our growth. Our present perception makes it difficult for us to grasp the reality that is outside our cosmos.

This reality has no separate forms and it has nothing that appears to be separate from mind. In the external reality, it is obvious that everything is created from mind. There is only one mind, but this one mind has expressed itself as many individual minds. These minds can only see themselves and each other as expressions of the one mind.

In the external reality, the perception of distinct and separate forms is not possible. The perception of forms that exist independently of mind is not possible. The perception that: "My mind is separate from my environment and from other minds" is not possible. The perception of time, of a beginning and end, is not possible in the external reality.

This reality is characterized by unity, oneness, timelessness and ongoingness. These are concepts that our minds find it difficult to deal with. For example, when told that there is an external reality outside our cosmos, we tend to immediately form questions, such as: "Where did this reality come from? When did it start? When will it end? Who created it?" These questions make sense from inside our cosmos, but they make no sense whatsoever in the external reality.

Our cosmos is a created world. It had a beginning, it will have an end and it was created by a self-aware being. The external reality was not created and it has no beginning or end. We can say it has always existed and will always exist, or we can say it is beyond time. Almost any question we can formulate based on our current perception is meaningless when it comes to the external reality.

The reason it is important to know about this external reality, which could be called the "Allness," is that it explains the purpose of our cosmos. The Allness has always existed, but it does not exist alone. It has always existed in a polarity with a level of reality where there is at least one temporary cosmos.

There are individual beings in the Allness, but because of the nature of the Allness, they experience no contrast to the Allness. When nothing can be seen as separate, there can be no contrast. This does not mean that there is no individual growth in the Allness; it means that such growth is beyond what we can fathom from inside our cosmos. Because there is no contrast in the Allness, the Allness exists in a polarity with the created world, meaning a level of reality where it is possible to experience separateness and contrast. Before a being finds its permanent place in the Allness, it first goes through an evolutionary process in the created world. Only when it has had enough of experiencing what we experience, meaning separateness and limitations in time, does a being permanently become part of the Allness. Joining the Allness must be an entirely free choice where a being has achieved complete inner unity. Our created world is a kind of cosmic educational institution that provides contrast and perspective for beings in the Allness.

The two aspects of the mind

You might notice that upon reading this, your mind begins to formulate questions. These are some examples: Where did the Allness come from, who created it? If there was always a created world, there must have been a first created cosmos—so when was that created and who created it? If a being joins the Allness only by going through the created world, where did the first being in the Allness come from?

This demonstrates the two aspects of our minds. We first have an aspect of our minds that is completely geared towards this world, which is a temporary cosmos. This linear part of our minds is what gives rise to questions that always want to find some beginning and some first cause. It cannot fathom that there could exist a level of reality where questions about cause, beginning and ending simply have no meaning.

There is also a part of our minds that wants to find something non-changing in or beyond the ever-changing world in which we are seemingly stuck. This is what gives us an inner longing to find ultimate answers, to understand the world in which we live. This is what has driven humankind to seek ever-more sophisticated explanations, whether it be in the field of religion (or rather mysticism) or in the field of science (which in its pure form is also a type of mysticism).

We have two aspects of our minds. One is adapted to the ever-changing, linear world that has a beginning and an end, meaning nothing is ever ultimate. The other compels us to seek for something non-changing, something ultimate or final.

The deeper explanation is that ultimately there is only one mind. You have self-awareness because you are an individualized extension of the one mind. Deep within you – for most people this is beyond the boundary of conscious awareness – there is a longing to experience the one mind that is your source. This experience is only possible when you join the Allness.

Even though you are ultimately created out of the one mind, you were created inside this cosmos. This means you were not created as part of the Allness; you were created as a being who is on its way to joining the Allness. Joining the Allness is your highest potential, but it can be accomplished only by going through the evolutionary process for which this cosmos is designed. You have to graduate before you can leave the school.

You have a dual nature. One part of you wants to find something ultimate. This is your longing for the Allness. Another part of you wants to progress through a linear process of gradually higher steps. One part if spherical, non-localized, the other is localized and designed to look for linear progression.

The challenge we face is to balance these two aspects. This challenge is particularly difficult on a planet like earth, but why this is so will be explained only after we have set the necessary foundation. At this point, it is important to be aware of the two aspects so we do not get trapped in seeking linear answers to questions about the non-linear world.

An overall definition of evil

Right now, we are inside a created cosmos, and it is designed to offer us a linear progression towards higher levels of self-awareness. The ultimate level of self-awareness can be achieved only by joining the Allness. Although we are following a linear process towards an ultimate experience, the process itself can never offer us an ultimate experience. Nothing in a created cosmos is the ultimate experience. The ultimate experience is the end goal of growth in our cosmos. The longing for it is part of our minds in order to give us the motivation to always go beyond any level we encounter in the created world.

At this point, an overall definition of evil can be offered. The purpose of our cosmos is that we go through a linear process of starting out with a very localized sense of self and then gradually expanding it. When we have completed this process (which is not possible while on earth as there are many levels of our cosmos above the earth), we reach the highest level of self-awareness possible in this cosmos. We then have the option to go beyond this level and join the Allness.

Evil on the personal level is when you stop your own growth and attempt to stay at a certain level of the linear progression. Evil on a collective level is when you seek to manipulate other self-aware beings to stay at your level or even go towards lower levels of self-awareness instead of going up from where they are.

Evil is caused by an imbalance between the two aspects of the mind. It happens when a being looks at the temporary, relative and possibly undesirable nature of its environment and then becomes obsessed with finding something ultimate. It now takes its longing for something ultimate (which is a longing for the Allness beyond the created cosmos) and transfers it to something in this relative world. It defines something in this cosmos as being ultimate, and then it seeks to make other self-aware beings accept and live by this definition. It takes something *relative* and seeks to make it *absolute*.

This is evil in the sense that the entire purpose of the created cosmos is to lead all self-aware beings towards the Allness. Each self-aware being has free will and this will is individual. It is not within the laws governing this cosmos to manipulate or neutralize the free will of any other being. Each being should ideally be allowed to pursue its own growth towards its ultimate goal without interference from any other being.

This is a very general definition of evil, and more specific definitions will be given later. It will also be explained why our cosmos, or at least planet earth, no longer has ideal conditions for growth and why some beings are indeed seeking to limit the free will of others.

2 | THE PROGRESSIVE CREATION OF THE SPHERES

Our cosmos had a beginning, however it does not make sense to say that our cosmos had a beginning in time or that it started in a certain location in space. Science currently promotes the Big Bang theory in which the universe supposedly started in a single point and has expanded outward from there. The linear mind wants to take this model and "turn back the clock" until it can establish exactly when the universe began and where this happened. Scientists are aware that before the Big Bang happened, time and space as we know it did not exist. Time only began after the Big Bang and space has been created by the expansion of the universe.

Our cosmos is more than the material universe and thus the Big Bang theory cannot explain the creation of the cosmos. The process of the creation of our cosmos began with a being that existed in the Allness. This being decided that it wanted to experience a contrast to the Allness, and it decided to enter the realm of created forms. This being became the Creator of our cosmos.

In order to create a cosmos of distinct forms, the Creator first had to create a realm in which such forms can exist. In the Allness, everything is made from energy of a much higher vibration, or intensity, than what is found in our universe. In such an intensity of light, no form can appear to be separate from another.

The Creator first formulated the intent to create a cosmos and then it defined a boundary around its own mind and being. Inside this spherical boundary was now only the consciousness and energy of the Creator itself. The Creator then withdrew itself, withdrew its energy and being, into a single point in the center of the sphere, leaving the rest of the space empty or void.

After having withdrawn itself into what we can call a singularity, the Creator then defined an energy that was lower than the energy of the Allness. This energy would be the base energy for creating the new cosmos. This energy has no form, but it has the ability to take on a wide range of vibrations and forms. It is often called the Mother Energy or the Ma-ter Light.

The Creator now expanded itself and defined a sphere around the singularity. This sphere did not fill up the entire void but only a small portion of it. This first sphere was filled with a base energy that was one variant of the Ma-ter Light. The energy had a certain range of vibration, a range that was much higher than the energy we find in our universe.

The Creator now formulated a mental image of the structures it wanted to create in the first sphere. It then used the powers of its mind to project or superimpose these thought matrices upon the base energy. This caused the energy to take on the form of the matrices projected upon it. The first sphere was populated with structures that could serve as the basis for self-aware beings, as the galaxies, stars and planets in our universe serve as our basis.

The first co-creators

After the basic structures had been created, the Creator created a large number of self-aware beings. These beings were created out of the Creator's own consciousness, yet they were individualized extensions of the Creator. This means each being had a localized sense of self and an individual free will. It also had the same ability as the Creator in terms of envisioning a thought matrix and projecting it upon the base energy. We will call such beings co-creators.

While a co-creator had the ability to formulate a thought matrix and project it upon the base energy, it did not have this ability with the same power as the Creator. The Creator could create the structures in the first sphere from nothing whereas co-creators could build upon and add to the structures defined by the Creator. The imagination of a co-creator was limited by its sense of self.

The Creator has an omnipresent sense of self-awareness, meaning it experiences its own creation from every point within it at the same time. It also experiences its creation from an overall vantage point. A co-creator has a localized sense of self-awareness, meaning it experiences its environment from a specific vantage point and does not have an overall awareness. This is comparable to our situation where we see our world from the vantage point of a human being on a small planet in a large universe.

The co-creators in the first sphere exercised their co-creative abilities by building upon the structures defined by the Creator. They multiplied the talents they were given. These co-creative abilities had several basic elements:

- Self-awareness gave them the ability to know that they existed, to be conscious of their environment and to know that they could do something to change it. This self-awareness is possible because each co-creator is an extension of the mind of the Creator who is an extension of the One Mind of the Allness.

• Imagination gave them the ability to envision or formulate thought matrices.

• Free will gave them the ability to decide which thought matrix to project upon the base energy.

• Mental projection gave them the ability to superimpose thought images upon the base energy. This ability was possible only because co-creators constantly received a stream of mental energy from their Creator. This mental energy was of a higher vibration than the base energy used to create the structures in the first sphere. That is why the mental energy directed by the co-creators was able to fashion the base energy into structures and add on to the structures defined by the Creator.

By exercising their abilities, the first co-creators accomplished three things at the same time:

• They built up their own environment by making the structures more and more elaborate, intricate and sophisticated.

• They added to the total amount of energy in the first sphere.

- They raised the vibration of the base energy until the entire sphere was filled with light that vibrated at the highest possible level.

The base energy that was defined for the first sphere had a starting value, meaning that it had a certain vibration and there was a certain level of intensity. As the co-creators used their abilities, they added to the amount of energy and they started raising the base energy from its starting value towards the maximum value that had been defined by the Creator.

This eventually (over a very long period of time as measured by our time), raised the first sphere to the point where it could ascend to a higher level. Before the ascension point, the first sphere had been a temporary world in which nothing was permanent. Had the first co-creators failed to fulfill their highest potential, the structures they had created could easily have been erased. After the ascension point, the first sphere became permanent and the ascended co-creators could now create permanent structures.

It may sound as if the purpose of the work of co-creators was to raise their sphere to the ascension point. However, the real purpose was that by experiencing a predefined environment, by learning how it worked and then by changing it through their own powers, the co-creators expanded and raised their own sense of self. They attained mastery over their environment and over their own powers, and this took them from a localized sense of self to a much broader sense of self in which they knew all aspects of how the first sphere worked. They had experienced everything they wanted to experience within that first sphere and they were ready to take the next step.

The first co-creators had become aware that each of them was an extension of the Creator and therefore had the potential to reach the same level of self-awareness as that of their source. They also knew that all other co-creators were extensions of the Creator, and this had given rise to a deep sense of unity and oneness among all co-creators in the first sphere. It was this unity – the vertical oneness with their Creator and the horizontal oneness with each other – that brought the first sphere beyond the ascension point. Only when the co-creators in a sphere have reached this total unity, can the sphere become permanent. Before unity is attained, impermanence will remain.

The growth stages of co-creators

When a new co-creator starts its journey, it has a localized sense of self. This is perfectly natural, and it is also natural that the co-creator goes through a phase where it is completely focused on its own growth. Its goal is to expand its sense of self so it attains some mastery over its co-creative abilities and over its environment. There is, however, a limit to how far a co-creator can go by focusing exclusively on its own growth.

The goal of a co-creator is to expand its sense of self to the same level as its Creator. The Creator is the ultimate selfless being. The Creator creates co-creators out of its own consciousness, creates an environment for them out of its own energy and then allows them complete free will as to what they do with those gifts. This explains why co-creators start out in an environment that is not permanent. If a co-creator decides to continue seeking power only for itself, then it cannot create any permanent structures. This is a safety mechanism necessitated by free will.

2 | The Progressive Creation of the Spheres

In order to ascend, a co-creator must go through a shift in awareness from being focused on its own growth to being focused on the growth of its sphere and all other co-creators in it. It is by completing this shift, from localized to all-encompassing self-awareness, that a being becomes an ascended master and can ascend when its sphere ascends.

The growth of a co-creator is driven by two factors, namely its sense of self and the amount of creative energy that it has at its disposal. The more the co-creator expands its awareness of its environment and how it works, the greater will be its creative potential. Its actual creative power is also linked to the amount of creative energy at its disposal. This is determined by how it has used its co-creative abilities.

There are two forms of energy, namely the base energy and the mental energy that co-creators use to project thought images upon the base energy. As a co-creator projects thought images in order to expand its sense of self, it will receive more mental energy from its source. The mental energy you use for creative purposes is multiplied. As you use more energy, you will receive more and this increases your creative powers.

During the first phase of its growth, the phase where the co-creator is focused on itself, its mental energy will be increased by a certain factor. As the co-creator grows in self-awareness and begins working to raise other co-creators and its environment, its mental energy will be multiplied by a greater and greater factor.

As long as the co-creator is focused on itself, it might (inadvertently or deliberately) use its mental energy in a way that benefits itself while hurting others or its environment. It is therefore safer that the co-creator's power is limited until it has proven that it will not misuse its power. As the co-creator demonstrates more selflessness, its power is increased. Because the growth process is entirely guided by the free will of individual co-creators, there will be differences in how they exercise their powers. As a result, some will rise to leadership positions and others will find roles where they exercise no power over others. This will tend to create a hierarchy before a sphere ascends. In an ascended sphere, there is also a hierarchy ranging from lower to higher self-awareness.

The creation of the second and third spheres

Becoming an ascended master does not mean that growth stops; it means that the being has risen to a higher level of service. When the co-creators from the first sphere had ascended, they were given the opportunity to accelerate their growth by serving in the creation of the second sphere.

The sphere itself was created by the Creator, as the newly ascended masters did not have the power to create a new sphere. The second sphere had a base energy that was denser than the base energy of the first sphere.

The ascended masters from the first sphere envisioned the structures in the second sphere. They used their own accumulated mental energy to project their thought matrices upon the base energy of the second sphere. The ascended masters now created new co-creators out of their own consciousness and sent them to populate the structures in the second sphere.

In the first sphere, the co-creators had received some guidance directly from the Creator. In the first sphere, not much guidance was needed because its base energy was at a high level. Compare this to our experience on earth. A rock seems very dense and it seems that it can exist on its own. A light bulb seems less dense, and we know that it can radiate light only because energy comes from a source outside itself. In the material universe, matter is so dense that we can believe it has an independent existence. If the base energy of our cosmos was higher, all structures would appear translucent. When a structure radiates light, it is easy to see that the light must come from a source beyond the environment.

In the first sphere, co-creators could directly see that there had to be a source beyond the structures in their environment, meaning their sphere was not self-contained or self-sufficient. This made it easier for them to avoid being trapped in their environment.

Because the base energy of the second sphere was more dense, the co-creators in that sphere needed more guidance from a source outside their environment. They received this from the ascended masters who existed in the first sphere, the ascended sphere. These ascended masters knew what it was like to grow from a localized self to a spherical self and were therefore the natural teachers. Since the co-creators in the second sphere were created out of the beings of the ascended masters, these masters had a strong interest in helping the unascended co-creators grow. The masters would grow in self-awareness by helping unascended co-creators.

This was reinforced by the fact that the unascended co-creators were using the energy that the ascended masters had used to create the structures in the second sphere. The unascended co-creators also received their mental energy from the ascended masters who were their spiritual parents. When unascended co-creators made selfless use of their creative powers, they would receive more mental energy from their ascended parents, and the ascended masters would receive more mental energy from the Creator. In this way all levels of creation were magnified.

The second sphere now went through the same process as the first sphere. The co-creators expanded upon the basic structures, increased the amount of energy and raised the vibration of the base energy. They raised their self-awareness until they were ready to ascend and become ascended masters. This brought the second sphere to the ascension point and the sphere ascended, meaning the sphere became permanent.

At this point, the third sphere was created. This sphere was created by the ascended masters from the first sphere. They defined its base energy as slightly more dense than the base energy of the second sphere. The newly ascended masters in the second sphere then created the structures in the third sphere and they created (out of their own beings) the co-creators who populated the third sphere. The third sphere followed the same track as the previous two and ascended.

3 | THE MOMENTOUS SHIFT IN THE FOURTH SPHERE

The fourth sphere was created in a similar manner as the previous ones, only it was once again created with a slightly denser base energy. It was the ascended masters from the second sphere who created the fourth sphere and who defined the base energy. It was the ascended masters from the third sphere who created the structures in the fourth sphere and who sent extensions of themselves as the co-creators who populated the fourth sphere.

Because the evolution of a sphere is guided by free will, there is no predefined course for a sphere. It was theoretically possible that some of the co-creators in the first sphere would not have ascended. As the base energy for the spheres became gradually more dense, it became increasingly likely that some beings in a new sphere would not ascend, and this is what happened in the fourth sphere. There is no law or necessity that says some beings will not ascend. It is quite possible that all beings can ascend regardless of how dense the base energy is, but this is not what happened in our cosmos.

In the first sphere, the co-creators expanded their self-awareness at different speeds. When the first co-creators were ready to ascend, there were still a few that were some distance away from having reached the necessary level of self-awareness. The more advanced co-creators then started helping the others and waited until all were ready to ascend. Then the entire sphere ascended as a coherent unit.

In the second sphere, there was a greater range. When the first co-creators were ready to ascend, many were still below the necessary level. In the second sphere, those who were ready to ascend could theoretically have ascended to the first sphere before the rest were ready to ascend. They chose to wait for the others and all ascended at the same time. The same scenario repeated in the third sphere.

In the fourth sphere, there was an even broader range from the more advanced to the less advanced co-creators. When the first were ready to ascend, the vast majority were not yet ready. Those who could have ascended, chose to wait for the majority. As the fourth sphere progressed further, there came a point when the vast majority of co-creators were ready to ascend or were close to the critical point. It then became clear that there was a relatively small group of co-creators who were lagging quite far behind.

For the first time in the evolution of our cosmos, it became necessary for the ascended masters to discuss how to help the co-creators who were behind. In the previous spheres, a small group had waited for the majority, but now the majority was waiting for a small group. This meant that the sphere as a whole was ready to ascend but some co-creators were not ready.

The first self-centered leaders

It was determined to make a special effort to help the co-creators who were lagging behind the majority. This included a number of special initiatives by the ascended masters who oversaw the fourth sphere. It also included that some of the more advanced co-creators made their ascension ahead of the majority.

These newly ascended masters had the advantage of knowing the conditions in the fourth sphere from within, from personal experience. They could serve as teachers, but because they had ascended from the fourth sphere they also had the authority to release more mental energy into the fourth sphere, thereby increasing the amount of light in the sphere.

A sphere can be compared to a dark room where the light is turned up very gradually. The more the light is increased, the easier it becomes for the inhabitants of the room to see everything that is happening. In the fourth sphere, this meant it became easier for all to see who was lagging behind and who was sincerely overcoming the focus on self. The lifestreams who were resisting their own growth in order to hold on to a position for themselves could no longer hide behind a facade.

Some of these lifestreams now used their free will to do something that had not been done in previous spheres. In these spheres, no co-creator had done anything that we would label as evil. Some co-creators had been quite focused on their own growth, but not to the point of seeking to prevent the growth of others. As a result of this, there had been developed an awareness of the need to serve the whole, to serve others, instead of only raising oneself. This awareness was promoted by the ascended masters who oversaw the fourth sphere.

A new co-creator starts with a point-like sense of self and then gradually expands it. The first stage of this process is that the co-creator is focused on expanding its sense of self in order to have greater power in its environment. The co-creator is competing with itself but not with others. In the first three spheres, the growth in creative power happened in parallel with an increased awareness of the need to serve the whole. No co-creator attempted to stop the growth of others in order to seemingly raise itself in comparison. As the base energy for the spheres became denser, it became increasingly likely that some co-creators would fail to develop their awareness of the whole.

The denser the energy of a sphere, the more believable it becomes that a localized being is also a separate being. A new co-creator does experience itself as a being who is distinct from its source, from its environment and from other co-creators. As it expands its sense of self, the co-creator is likely to overcome this sense and instead develop a sense of oneness with all life, but there is no guarantee that this will happen.

In the fourth sphere, a number of co-creators held on to, and even expanded, their sense of self as separate beings. These co-creators became very focused on expanding their creative power in order to glorify themselves and in order to be able to control their environment. In the beginning phases, these co-creators seemed to be more advanced than the average, and they started setting themselves up as leaders. Because they did seem powerful, many of the less powerful co-creators started following the leaders. The leaders then built empires in their sphere, somewhat comparable to what we have seen on earth where an entire nation is centered around one powerful leader.

The exposure of selfish leaders

Because of the nature of the Law of Free Will, this development was allowed even though it was not the ideal scenario for raising the whole. It is always natural that some co-creators will develop their abilities beyond the majority and they will become leaders. The ideal scenario is that these leaders will also raise their awareness of the whole and become what we know as servant leaders.

In the fourth sphere, a group of co-creators became very powerful in terms of controlling their environment and those co-creators who followed them. There even emerged a rivalry between some of them, leading to the definition of groups who saw themselves as separated from and in competition with others. These forceful leaders believed that by attaining superior positions in their unascended sphere, they would be given special positions after their sphere ascended. They were so obsessed with power and the sense of superiority that they wanted to retain it even in the ascended realm. Although they saw the ascension as a goal, their primary motivation was to increase their power and become even more superior compared to their followers.

This was an illusion because you can ascend only by overcoming all selfishness. No being can become an ascended master, which means an immortal being, without overcoming all traces of self-centeredness. The illusion that you are a separate self and that you are superior must be left behind.

It had not been possible for the ascended masters overseeing the fourth sphere to help the forceful leaders overcome their illusion. Because the Law of Free Will allows co-creators to outplay their free will to the ultimate extent, these forceful leaders had been allowed to set themselves up in powerful positions. Because they had gathered many followers, they had been allowed to outplay their quest for power. It was hoped that they would eventually have had enough of experiencing themselves as powerful separate beings (or as followers of such beings) and would then start becoming more aware of the whole.

Up until the ascended masters started releasing more light into the fourth sphere, the forceful leaders had been able to hide behind a facade that made them appear as genuine and benign leaders to their followers. As the light was increased, it became obvious to these leaders that they would no longer be able to maintain their illusion.

The ideal choice would have been to give up their positions as separate leaders and join the upward movement of the whole. In that case, they would have received all possible help to raise their consciousness beyond selfishness, and they could have attained positions as genuine leaders. Some of the forceful leaders saw this as a loss because they felt they would have to give up the power, position and privilege they had worked so hard to attain.

They refused to give up their positions, and in order to keep control of their followers, they now had to justify their refusal to join the whole. This attempt to justify the denial of oneness is what led to the emergence of what we can call evil, but which often camouflages itself as the opposite of evil.

The rebellion against growth into oneness

It is now necessary to understand the nature of free will. There is a cosmic law, the Law of Free Will, and it is the absolute law for any unascended sphere. This law basically says that an individual co-creator has unrestricted free will. As we will see

3 | The Momentous Shift in the Fourth Sphere

later, this does not mean that a co-creator can do anything it wants regardless of the consequences for others. It means that a co-creator is allowed to create any kind of separate self and to outplay it until it has had enough of this experience.

Although conditions in the fourth sphere were not the same as what we see on earth, let us illustrate the principle by comparing it to what we know. As we discussed in the previous book, a co-creator is truly a universal spiritual being. The core of your identity was created out of the ascended masters in the sphere above yours. You are meant to experience your sphere until you have had enough of the experiences it offers and you are ready to ascend.

Let us seek to illustrate the process by referring to life on this planet. A co-creator on earth might decide that it wants to experience what it is like to be a pirate. Due to the level of consciousness currently found on this planet, this experience is possible. The co-creator experiences this separate form of self until it has had enough of it and wants something different. It may then choose a different role until it has had enough of that, and this process may go on for a long time.

How is it possible that a co-creator can experience many different scenarios, given that you have to be born in a physical body and there is a limit to how many different roles you can play in one lifetime? The answer is that you are a universal spiritual being who only expresses itself through a physical body. You do not die when the body dies, which means you can come back into embodiment and experience another role in the next lifetime. This is the process that is called reincarnation and which is taught by many of the world's religions.

Reincarnation makes it possible for a co-creator to experience many different separate roles over a long period of time. After some time, most co-creators will have had enough of experiencing themselves as separate beings and will then raise their self-awareness and join the process of growing along with the whole.

The Law of Free Will mandates that a co-creator has a right to define a separate self through which it expresses its co-creative powers. It has a right to define such separate selves until it has had enough of this experience.

It was this aspect of the law that the forceful leaders in the fourth sphere took advantage of. They used it to claim that they had a right to set themselves up as powerful leaders and that their followers had a right to experience what it was like to be followers. They claimed that they were not ready to let go of this kind of experience, and they demanded the right to continue in their positions of power and privilege. They even claimed that the ascended masters overseeing the fourth sphere had no right to expose them and their unwillingness to give up their positions.

In reality, the ascended masters were not seeking to force the leaders in the fourth sphere. These leaders had been given a very long time span (compared to earth time) to have the experience of being separate leaders. They had received ample opportunity to live out their dreams of having ultimate power. They had chosen not to let go of this dream of being separated from the whole, and this is where they ran up against another aspect of the Law of Free Will.

Balancing individual and collective freedom

The Law of Free Will defines growth as the overall purpose of creation. An individual co-creator is allowed complete freedom as to how it will define its individual path. Ultimately, this path leads from a point-like sense of self to the omnipresent, spherical sense of self of a Creator. How the co-creator completes

3 | The Momentous Shift in the Fourth Sphere

this journey – how long it takes and how many twists and turns there are – is left up to the co-creator's choices. However, these choices do exist within the overall framework of the cosmos in which the co-creator exists.

This has an overall implication, meaning that in a created world nothing can last forever. A co-creator can have a time-span to complete its journey that seems unfathomable to a human being; yet it cannot have forever.

The more specific implication is that no co-creator exists in a vacuum. We all exist within a given sphere and there are other co-creators in that sphere. All life is connected, meaning that all co-creators in our sphere form a whole. One co-creator has unrestricted free will but so do all other co-creators. One co-creator does not have the right to take away the free will of another co-creator. Nor does a small group of co-creators have the right to force the will of the majority in their sphere.

When the leaders in the fourth sphere refused to let go of their separate selves in order to ascend with the whole, the question became how to balance the free will of these leaders with that of the majority. The solution was both simple and elegant.

Instead of a simultaneous ascension, the fourth sphere entered a spiral that caused it to ascend in increments. If we compare this to our universe, some galaxies would ascend while others would lag behind. At the same time as the fourth sphere started ascending, the fifth sphere was being created.

As a certain unit (comparable to our galaxies) was ready to ascend, those lagging behind were given one last choice to join with the whole. If they once again refused, they would then descend or fall into the fifth sphere while their unit ascended. This allowed the majority in the fourth sphere to ascend while the rebellious co-creators were given another opportunity to outplay their identity as separate beings.

Why the shift was so momentous

The process that caused the first co-creators to fall was the decisive change that happened for our cosmos and it has many implications that will be explored in the rest of the book. For now, we will stay with the big picture and explain why the shift in the fourth sphere was so dramatic.

The purpose of a created cosmos is to provide perspective for the beings who live in the indivisible oneness of the Allness. This is accomplished by allowing a created cosmos to give the illusion of separateness. Note that this is only an illusion. In reality, there is only one mind. It has expressed itself as many individual beings, but you and I are still extensions of the One Mind. We are right now focusing our self-awareness in a created cosmos that has a fairly dense base energy and is (as far as earth is concerned) not yet near the ascension point. It is therefore possible for us to fully identify ourselves as separate beings, thereby being totally convinced that separation is real.

It is not the purpose of a created cosmos to become a permanent abode for us. The purpose is to give us perspective so we can appreciate the oneness of the ascended realm and beyond that the Allness. In order to get this perspective, we start out with a point-like sense of self in a created cosmos. After the fourth sphere, it has become increasingly likely that this will cause us to identity ourselves as separate beings. In itself, this is not a problem because it also gives us perspective on oneness.

The question is how we can free ourselves from separation once we have entered into this state of illusion. It is not the *identification* as separate beings that gives us perspective on oneness. It is when we *awaken* from the illusion of being separate and realize that we truly are immortal spiritual beings that we gain perspective on oneness. The purpose of a created

3 | The Momentous Shift in the Fourth Sphere

cosmos is not that we become stuck in a separate identity indefinitely but that we go into this finite identity for a time and then awaken to our infinite identity.

The Law of Free Will mandates that we can create any kind of self that we can imagine. Once we are inside that self, what we see (as explained in the previous book) will seem completely real. How can we awaken from this illusion? Only by having a frame of reference from outside the perception filter of the separate self.

In the first three spheres, the awakening was a straightforward process. Even though co-creators created various forms of selves, they always had a frame of reference. This took two forms, one from inside their own sphere and one from the sphere above theirs:

- Co-creators could question their selves by comparing it to their observations of how their sphere worked. This is comparable to what we call the laws of nature, and in the previous book I briefly described the second law of thermodynamics as a force that will break down all closed systems and closed minds.

- Co-creators also received direct guidance from the ascended masters who served as their guides or spiritual teachers. In the first spheres, this link to the sphere above was unbroken. Co-creators could ignore this guidance, but they could not fail to know that it was available.

When the forceful leaders in the fourth sphere rebelled, they refused to use both the internal and the external frame of reference. They ignored the laws of nature and the guidance of the ascended masters. They actively rejected any frame of reference from outside their own perception filter. Instead, they elevated their perception filter (which was an illusion based on the fact that it sprang from a separate self) to the status of being an absolute reality. They now became their own frame of reference, and it had become fundamentally more difficult for them to escape their self-created illusion. The illusion had become self-reinforcing; it had become a closed system. This explains why it has been so difficult for humankind on earth to rise above evil. Evil is based on a very subtle illusion.

There is a symbolic representation of this process in the *Book of Genesis* from the Old Testament. It is described how Adam and Eve lived in an idyllic garden, which is a symbol for the innocent state of consciousness in which they had an external frame of reference. The God in the garden symbolizes the ascended masters who are our external frame of reference.

Adam and Eve were allowed to eat all of the fruits in the garden, symbolizing that they were allowed to try on any kind of self—except a separate self. The forbidden fruit is a symbol for what is the extreme outcome of free will, namely a self that is not only localized but based on the illusion that it is separate. Once we step into such a separate self, we refuse any frame of reference from outside ourselves and define our own frame of reference.

The serpent said to Eve that if she ate the fruit, she would become as a God knowing good and evil. This symbolizes that when we refuse an external frame of reference, we put ourselves in the position of a God, meaning a being who defines ultimate reality. We "know" good and evil in the sense that it is defined by our own perception filter.

By entering this frame of mind, we have died in the sense that we have denied ourselves as spiritual beings who have access to an external frame of reference. Instead, we identify ourselves a separate beings, and as such we can only be mortal.

We can gain immortality by ascending and joining the whole, but as separate beings we must eventually die. Our only way out is to *not* do what Adam and Eve did, namely hide from the teacher. Once we have "fallen" into the illusion that raises the separate self to a god-like status, our *only* escape is to appeal to the ascended masters to once again give us an external frame of reference.

In the fourth sphere, a small group of leaders did what we earlier defined as evil in the broadest sense. They took something in a temporary, created cosmos and elevated it to the status of being absolute. They have since attempted to make all other co-creators believe in their definition of themselves and their perception filter as absolute and infallible. They have attempted to set themselves up as Gods and to make the rest of us follow them. Freeing ourselves from evil means freeing ourselves from the illusions perpetrated by these fallen beings.

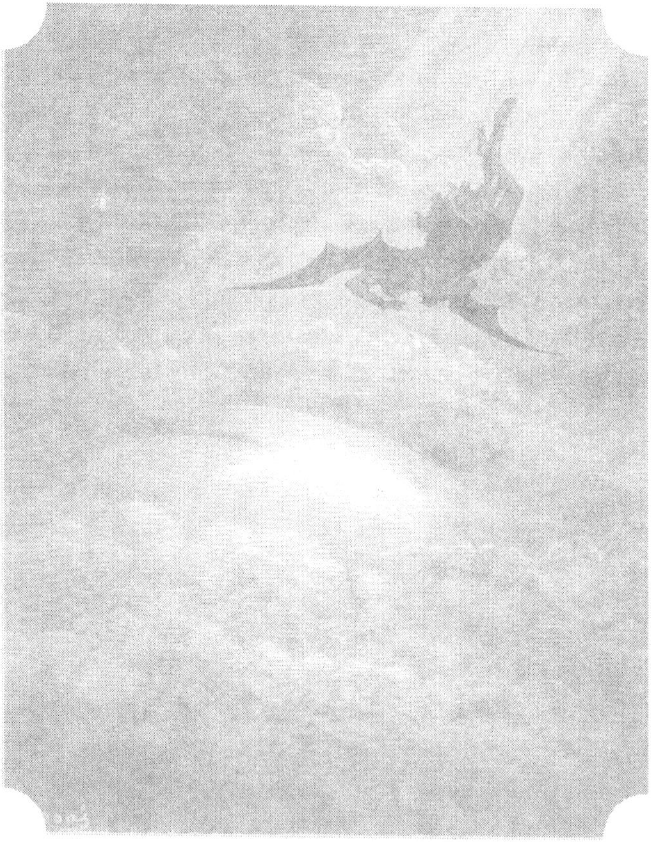

4 | THE FIFTH AND SIXTH SPHERES

The origin of evil in our cosmos was the fall that happened in the fourth sphere. Any attempt to understand evil must incorporate knowledge of this fall or it will be incomplete. Attempting to overcome evil without understanding its ultimate origin and the mindset behind it is like groping in the dark. It can never work, and this explains why evil is still around on this planet.

There is no way we can know about the original fall by observing conditions found in our present universe. We can know about the origin of evil only by receiving this knowledge as direct revelation from the ascended masters who oversee the growth of our sphere.

The fallen beings who are still part of the force of evil will do anything in their power to prevent the majority of the people on earth from acquiring or accepting a complete understanding of the origin of evil. They do not want people to know about their own origin, mindset and methods. If people *did* know, they would not submit to the control of the fallen beings, and the fallen beings are all about control. This is because their rebellion is based on an illusion and they must either rejoin the process of growth or continue to defend their illusion. This includes preventing others from seeing through the illusion.

The creation of the fifth sphere

The ascended masters who created the fifth sphere faced a new situation. In the previous spheres, all of the beings inhabiting them had been new co-creators, meaning they were created in what we can call a state of innocence. They had no prejudice against the process of growth and in the first three spheres, all co-creators had innocently followed the process of growth into oneness.

The fifth sphere would be inhabited by two fundamentally different types of beings. There would be newly created co-creators, but there would also be the beings who had fallen in the fourth sphere. These beings had already proven that they would rebel against the process of growth and that they would attempt to control others in order to get them to join their rebellion. The beings who fell in the fourth sphere can be divided into two groups:

- Some beings were completely convinced that their perception of the cosmos was right and that they were working for a benign cause. They saw it as their role to correct an error in the design of the cosmos, meaning they thought they had to correct an error made by the Creator and errors made by the ascended masters in executing the design of the Creator. They attempted to convince others that they were right, but they were not willing to lie or deceive others in order to convert them. Take note of the subtle distinction. These fallen beings were indeed promoting a lie so everything they said was a lie. Yet they themselves believed in the lie so they were not deliberately deceiving others.

- Some beings had no interest in or allegiance to a specific cause. They were dedicated to having power for themselves. If promoting a cause would allow them to attain power, they were willing to lie and deceive others in order to gather followers. These fallen beings lied deliberately and knowingly.

As a result of this grouping, the fifth sphere was created with two levels or layers, set apart by their base vibration. We will call them "octaves." The octave with the least dense base vibration was for the fallen beings who did not deliberately lie. The octave with the most dense vibration was for those beings who did lie deliberately.

The explanation is that the denser the vibration, the easier it becomes to create illusions of separateness that hide the underlying oneness of all life. In order to give those who were willing to lie the opportunity to outplay their desires, the energy of their octave had to be more dense. Of course, the more dense the energy, the more effort it takes to maintain an illusion. This increases the likelihood that beings will tire of the struggle and decide to rejoin the process of growth.

Each octave had certain base structures. Although they did not have the same design, we can compare them to the galaxies in our universe. In the previous four spheres, all structures had been created as part of a unified whole. Beginning in the fifth sphere (which was larger in spatial extension), the structures were created as distinct units separated by space. This meant they could more easily evolve independently of each other.

Each of the two octaves in the fifth sphere had structural units and in each octave new co-creators incarnated. The following description applies to both octaves. In some of the structural units in the fifth sphere, no fallen beings were allowed to incarnate. They were reserved for new co-creators. Given that there was only a limited number of fallen beings from the fourth sphere, the vast majority of units in the fifth sphere were populated by new co-creators.

The new co-creators innocently pursued the growth towards oneness. None of the new co-creators in the fifth sphere fell on their own. As they grew towards oneness, they started forming a unified mental force, and this force is partly the cause of what scientists on earth call the second law of thermodynamics.

We can compare this force to a magnet that pulls on anything within its field. As the new co-creators in the fifth sphere came closer to oneness, their combined minds formed a magnetic pull. This force pulled on the rest of their sphere, including the units where fallen beings had incarnated. The force pulled on the minds of the fallen beings, pulling them towards oneness.

This pull made it easier for the fallen beings and their followers to overcome the illusion of separation, giving them better opportunities for joining the flow of life. If they resisted, they would have to exert a mental force in order to do so, and this would turn their lives into an even more intense struggle than the struggle they had created by themselves.

When you go into the illusion that you are a separate being, it is inevitable that you will perceive a resistance from your environment and from other co-creators. Your life becomes a struggle. There is nothing inherently wrong with this, and the more intense you make the struggle, the more likely it becomes that you will tire of it and decide to pursue the path towards oneness. The fallen beings in the fifth sphere had already created a struggle in their own units. Although the fallen beings saw their units as being separated, they were part of the whole. As the new co-creators generated a magnetic force, it started pulling on the fallen beings and their resistance intensified their struggle. This was not a violation of the free will of the fallen beings, as they do not have the right to exercise their free will in a vacuum. No co-creator is an island.

The fallen beings in the fifth sphere

The all-important distinction is whether a co-creator stays in the consciousness of innocence or goes into the consciousness of separation. The cosmos is designed to facilitate the growth towards oneness so when you are in innocence, you are going in the same direction as the current of the cosmos. You are flowing with the River of Life. When you go into separation, you are going in the opposite direction of the flow of life, and you can do this only by resisting. Your life inevitably becomes a struggle.

The beings who rebelled in the fourth sphere decided to resist the very purpose and design of our cosmos. On a conscious level, they were saying that they wanted the right to set themselves up as Gods and prove that the One God, the Creator, was wrong. On a subconscious level, they were saying that they wanted to experience more resistance than they had already created for themselves.

The ascended masters have ascended by joining the oneness of the River of Life. Their task, their purpose for being, is to help all other co-creators join oneness, but this will, of course, happen within the framework defined by the Law of Free Will. The ascended masters did not label the first fallen beings as evil and did not condemn them in any way. Their only concern was how they could help the fallen beings rejoin the River of Life. For all practical purposes, the question was: "Which experiences do the fallen beings need to have before they will voluntarily choose oneness over separation?"

Given that separation inevitably leads to a struggle, the question can be formulated this way: "How much struggle do the fallen beings need to experience before they have had enough of it and want a struggle-free life instead?" The answer was very simple: "Give them what they say (consciously and subconsciously) they want."

Any sphere in a created cosmos is designed with certain base structures. The co-creators who incarnate in the sphere are meant to build upon this foundation. Because of free will, it is also possible they can go in the opposite direction and tear down the foundation. A sphere is functioning as a cosmic mirror. Whatever the co-creators project out with their consciousness, the sphere will reflect back in the form of the structures found within it.

As the ascended masters designed the structures in the fifth sphere, they designed certain units specifically for the fallen beings from the fourth sphere. They were designed in order to give these fallen beings exactly the kind of experience they said they wanted—meaning what they said both consciously and subconsciously.

This process was helped by the fact that the base energy of the fifth sphere was more dense than in the fourth sphere. The denser the energy, the easier it becomes for beings in separation to live out the sense that they are separated and that they can attain a state of ultimate power. The denser the energy, the more of a barrier it forms to perception. It becomes more difficult for co-creators inside the sphere to perceive that there

4 | The Fifth and Sixth Spheres

is a reality beyond their sphere. They can believe they really are separated from their source. They can also believe that they live within a small, isolated universe, meaning they can get the sense that they have all-power in this universe. Given how vast our cosmos had become when the fifth sphere was created, awareness of the vastness of creation would have made it clear that the fallen beings could never attain any absolute form of power. Given that this was what they wanted, their experience was possible only if their perception was limited.

The fallen beings also wanted the sense that they were struggling against God and that they had the potential to prove God wrong. The structural units designed for them were set up to give them the sense that they had great resistance from their environment. Again, this was helped by the density of the base energy, but the ascended masters exercised great ingenuity in terms of designing the structural units for the consciousness of the fallen beings.

The separation in the fifth sphere

As in the fourth sphere, there came a point when the vast majority of the co-creators in the fifth sphere were close to ascending and when the entire sphere was close to ascending. The ascended masters overseeing the fifth sphere then made a kind of status:

- None of the new co-creators in the fifth sphere had fallen into separation. They had evolved without any contact with the fallen beings and had not themselves repeated the choices made by those who fell in the fourth sphere.

- Some of the fallen beings in the fourth sphere had tired of resisting and had joined the path of oneness. This was especially true in the higher octave. In the lower octave, only a few had tired of resistance and they had not completely escaped the fallen consciousness. They had transcended the willingness to lie and were now in the state of mind of the beings who believed their illusion without being willing to lie in order to convince others.

- Most fallen beings had not changed but were still pursuing the dream of attaining an ultimate state of power over others or of proving God wrong.

The question now became what could be done to help the fallen beings rise above their state of mind within a time-frame that would not delay the ascension of the entire sphere. Once the majority of the co-creators have created an ascending spiral, the ascension of a sphere cannot be delayed too much.

It was decided to make a change so that it would be possible to mix fallen beings with the co-creators who were created in the fifth sphere. This meant that co-creators who had come close to ascending were given the opportunity to embody in the units designed for the fallen beings.

Naturally, this happened on an entirely voluntary basis. The new co-creators were fully aware of what they were choosing to do. Before actually taking embodiment in a unit ruled by the fallen beings, they were given special instructions about the fallen consciousness. This is symbolized by there being a serpent in the Garden of Eden. Only when their ascended teachers and they themselves decided that they were ready, would they take actual embodiment. Up until that point, the units rules by the fallen beings had not contained anything that

4 | The Fifth and Sixth Spheres

disturbed or challenged the mindset and the perception filter of the fallen consciousness. Except for the few units that had entered an upward spiral, the fallen beings had remained in the same state of consciousness. This had caused their struggle against their environment or against their image of God to intensify, but since all were trapped in the same perception filter, no one had challenged the basic illusion.

When new co-creators took embodiment in units ruled by the fallen beings, this state of affairs changed fundamentally. The newly embodied co-creators challenged the fallen illusions through their words and actions, yet they did so in another way also.

Through their growth, these co-creators had multiplied the mental energy given to them from the ascended masters. They had built a strong momentum on using energy to raise the whole, and they carried this with them into embodiment. They had greater spiritual light than even the seemingly most powerful fallen leaders.

The situation can be compared to having a group of people living in a dark cave. Because no one can see any light, none of the members of the group know that there is an alternative to the darkness. Now you have a bunch of people enter the cave and each is carrying a lamp. The illusion that all is darkness is being challenged, and this causes the original cave dwellers to make a choice. Will they realize that they too have the potential to become a light in the darkness, or will they deny their potential?

The fallen beings who had set themselves up as leaders in their units felt fundamentally threatened by the co-creators who started embodying. Very few of the fallen leaders took the opportunity to let go of their illusions. The vast majority of them attempted to keep their positions of power by doing whatever they could think of in order to counteract the effect of the light and the knowledge brought by the co-creators. What they did varied by octave:

- In the higher octave, the leaders first attempted to convince the newly embodying co-creators that they had been fooled by the ascended masters and that the fallen beings had the only correct view. Some co-creators were convinced by this, but only a small minority. Some of the leaders then decided that they were willing to lie in order to deceive either the co-creators or their own followers. They descended into the state of consciousness that belonged to the lower octave.

- In the lower octave, the leaders first used lies to try to convert the co-creators or keep their followers from listening to them. This did have some effect. Many leaders were able to convince their followers that the co-creators were lying or were a threat. Some co-creators became converted by the lies of the fallen beings. After some time, some fallen leaders invented a new tactic. Instead of simply promoting lies about their own beliefs, they now started using lies to accuse the co-creators. These leaders started falsely accusing the co-creators in all kinds of ways, meaning they now descended to a level of consciousness that was lower than anything seen in the fourth sphere. Quite a few co-creators reacted to this by losing their original vision and harmony, instead starting to struggle against the fallen beings.

After some time, the ascended masters again evaluated the situation. The strategy of mixing new co-creators and fallen beings had been effective in stirring things up in the fallen units. Quite a few fallen beings (especially among the followers) had simply forgotten there was an alternative to their state of consciousness. By seeing that the co-creators were in a higher state of consciousness, they were awakened and started an upward spiral. Others had become even more trapped in the fallen consciousness, and the presence of the co-creators had only given them more to struggle against.

The biggest effect was on the co-creators. A few had indeed reacted to the interaction with the fallen beings by themselves entering separation. The majority had avoided the fallen consciousness but had gained valuable perspective by encountering it. They were ready to ascend from the fallen units and could do so with a wider perspective than if they had not encountered the fallen beings.

There came a point when it was decided to repeat the process from the fourth sphere. The fifth sphere would ascend in increments while the sixth sphere was being created. The beings who refused to rise above the fallen consciousness would then fall into the sixth sphere.

The design of the sixth sphere

The sixth sphere was designed based on similar principles as the fifth sphere, only it had a denser base energy. It also had three levels or octaves instead of two:

- The highest octave was for those fallen beings who genuinely believed in their world view. They sought to convince others without lying.

- The second octave was for those fallen beings who sought personal power and position by controlling others. They were willing to lie, but they were not willing to accuse them directly.

- The third octave was for those who were seeking to control others because they either enjoyed doing so or wanted to prove some cause. These beings were willing to lie in order to convince others, but their most successful strategy was to accuse others falsely in order to pull them into a reactionary pattern.

In the previous book it was explained that the human mind here on earth has four levels, namely the physical level, the emotional, the mental and the identity level. These correspond to the three octaves of the sixth sphere, with the highest being the identity level, the second the mental level and the third the emotional level.

The separation in the sixth sphere

The evolution of the sixth sphere happened in a similar manner as the fifth. Again, no new co-creators entered the fallen consciousness on their own. The new co-creators far outnumbered the fallen beings, and the units with only new co-creators created an upward magnetic pull. There came a time when the sphere was nearing the ascension point, and the ascended masters had to determine how to proceed.

Once again, a few fallen beings had turned around by having had enough of experiencing the struggle. Most had intensified their struggle and were even further from ascending than when the sphere was created.

As with the fifth sphere, it was determined to give new co-creators the opportunity to embody in the units ruled by

4 | The Fifth and Sixth Spheres

the fallen beings. A large number volunteered for this, and the results were similar to the fifth sphere.

The co-creators stirred things up in the fallen units and this caused some fallen beings to awaken. Others became even more determined to resist the growth towards oneness. Again, some in the highest octave descended to the consciousness of the second octave. The same happened in the second octave. In the third octave, some fallen leaders descended to an even lower state of consciousness in which they were willing to forcefully assault, control or even kill those who had greater light. Until this point, no embodied being had experienced having their bodies killed by the fallen beings. This was the watershed change in the sixth sphere.

The number of co-creators who reacted to the fallen beings was greater than it had been in the sixth sphere. Especially in the lowest octave, many co-creators reacted so strongly to being falsely accused that they were pulled into a reactionary pattern with the fallen beings. Those who would not give this up were not able to ascend with the sixth sphere and fell along with the fallen beings into the seventh sphere.

The total number of co-creators who fell in the sixth sphere was large, but still only a very small percentage of the number of co-creators who ascended from the sixth sphere. The overall gain was therefore substantial. Still, a large number of beings fell into the seventh sphere. This is the sphere in which we are presently living. We have in this sphere some beings who are very firmly blinded by the fallen consciousness.

5 | THE CREATION OF OUR SPHERE

Our sphere was created based on similar considerations as the fifth and sixth spheres. It started out with a denser base energy than the sixth sphere and it has four levels or octaves. These are, ranging from the highest to the lowest base vibration:

- The identity octave (also called the etheric realm).

- The mental octave.

- The emotional octave.

- The physical octave.

We live inside the sphere that is the densest of the seven spheres so far created, and our bodies live in the lowest octave of that sphere. The energies we perceive through our physical senses are the densest found anywhere in our cosmos. When we look at life from our vantage point, it is impossible to directly (with our physical senses and outer minds) perceive anything beyond our own octave. This explains many of the theories that human beings have come up with throughout history, be it in the field of religion, science, politics or philosophy. We look at life based on what we perceive directly, and then we use this as a basis for reasoning about what might be or what might *not* be beyond what we see.

When we seek to understand life by using our powers of perception, we are looking through four veils in our own cosmos. The physical, emotional, mental and identity octaves each form a veil to our perception. As will be explained later, our minds have the capacity to go beyond these veils and this is our only hope of escaping the illusions of the fallen beings found at each level of our sphere.

The process of creation did not start at our level but at a level that is so much higher than ours that nothing we perceive on earth can be used to reason about the reality of how the cosmos was created. During the Middle Ages (and also in some other time periods) people believed the earth was the center of the universe. They believed planet earth was so important to God that it was placed at the center of the cosmos and that God took a direct, personal interest in what we do on this planet.

They also believed it was easy for us to understand God and that all we needed to know had been revealed in a few short scriptures. This was a very limited and limiting world view that ignored the basic reality of how the cosmos functions. The most important consequence is that we today do not have a good understanding of the flow of energy.

5 | *The Creation of Our Sphere*

The flow of energy in the cosmos

The energy used to create the physical octave is quite dense. Our physical senses are calibrated to detect the energies that make up what science calls the macroscopic level, meaning what we see as the world of solid matter. When we perceive life only through the physical senses and the level of the mind tied to the senses, we see things formed of a substance we call matter and we see that it exists on its own. It exists in and of itself without being created and sustained by energy from a higher octave. This is an illusion, and it is an illusion that prevents us from knowing the reality of the cosmos and fulfilling our highest potential to ascend beyond the physical octave.

In reality, the entire cosmos is sustained by a flow of energy from beyond our cosmos. Our Creator comes from the Allness and uses the energy of the Allness for its creative efforts. The Creator took energy from the Allness, reduced its vibration and fashioned it as the Ma-ter Light. This is the base energy out of which our entire cosmos is created. This energy is in itself formless and it does not have the capacity to take on form by itself.

In order to be stirred into form, the Ma-ter Light must be acted upon by an external force. This force is a mind that envisions a thought matrix and then uses mental energy to project that matrix upon the Ma-ter Light. Once stirred by this force, the Ma-ter Light takes on the form of the thought matrix.

The matrix must be upheld on a continuous basis. Even though the Ma-ter Light cannot take on form by itself, it can break down form by itself. The Ma-ter Light has a built-in tendency to return to its ground state. This is one aspect of what science calls the second law of thermodynamics that breaks down all structures and returns a closed system to its lowest possible energy state. The other aspect is the upward force created by those co-creators who expand their self-awareness.

Our physical octave appears to be a closed system, but it is being upheld by a constant stream of energy from higher octaves. If this flow of energy stopped, our planet would start disintegrating and our entire galaxy would eventually collapse into a black hole.

Evil truly has no existence or reality in and of itself. Evil is based on an illusion and an illusion can exist only in an unascended sphere. It is the density of the energies of such a sphere that makes it possible to create an illusion. Only when energies are dense, can you create an appearance that hides something else behind it. For example, the dense energies that we see as matter hide the reality that our octave is upheld by a flow of energy from above. Evil can exist only because there is an absence of light in our sphere. The only way to remove evil is to bring more light so the darkness in which evil can hide disappears. The **energy veil** behind which evil hides becomes more transparent.

Our unascended sphere was created by the ascended masters, but they do not have the authority to bring more light in order to eradicate evil. In an unascended sphere, additional light must be brought through the minds of the beings who embody in that sphere. The only way for us to transcend evil is that we use our built-in capacity to let our minds be conduits for energy from a higher realm. The forces that make up evil will do anything to prevent us from doing this.

They have so far taken advantage of the fact that our senses cannot see beyond "solid" matter. This has enabled them to create theories that either deny that there is anything beyond or say that we cannot contact it directly but need a religion on earth. They want us to deny our potential to receive light within ourselves, either by denying that there is anything beyond the material world or by making us believe we can contact a higher realm only through the fallen beings.

We will now take a look at all of the beings who are involved with our sphere.

Ascended masters

Our cosmos is one interconnected whole. It also has levels of energy and this forms a hierarchical structure. Our sphere is the latest and most dense, meaning it is at the lowest level of the structure. Above it is what used to be the sixth sphere, and it now forms the lowest level of the ascended realm, the spiritual world or what many people call "heaven." Above the sixth sphere are the first five spheres. Even though these spheres have ascended, the ascended masters who inhabit them have not been standing still. They have continued to raise their self-awareness after they ascended and this has raised the vibration of their spheres.

There is a huge gap between the first sphere and our sphere. Our sphere is sustained by a flow of energy that originates with our Creator, but this energy is so high that it would instantly burn up our sphere if it came in direct contact with it. The energy must be stepped down, and this happens through each of the spheres above us.

In each sphere we find a number of ascended beings who serve to step down energy to the next sphere down. There are also beings who serve as guides or teachers for the beings evolving in the sphere below theirs. The ascended beings who are directly involved with our sphere are organized into three groupings:

- **Angels and Archangels.** These are ascended beings who serve to step down energy from the sixth sphere to our level. They have in some spiritual traditions been seen as messengers between God and man. This is not entirely correct in the sense that the Creator does not work directly with our octave but only works through the hierarchy in the six ascended spheres. The ascended masters described below are called angels by some spiritual traditions.

- **Elohim.** These beings are often called the creators of form because they are involved with the creation of structures in an unascended sphere. Planet earth was originally created by seven Elohim, and they created this planet in a much higher state of beauty and balance than what we see today. The Elohim create a planet as a foundation, and then co-creators are allowed to embody on that planet. These co-creators can either build upon the foundation created by the Elohim and raise their planet, or they can refuse to do so, causing their planet to descend below its original level. Earth has descended quite far below its original level, and this is part of what gives rise to the concept of a lost paradise found in so many religions and spiritual traditions.

- **Ascended masters.** In the broadest sense, all beings in the ascended realm can be called ascended masters, but we can also use it as a term that refers to those beings who serve as the direct guides or teachers for the inhabitants of an unascended sphere. The ascended masters have it as their role to help unascended co-creators ascend. On a planet like earth, where the presence of fallen beings is allowed, the ascended masters also serve to help us see through and escape the illusions created by the fallen beings. Take note that the ascended masters are not at war with the fallen beings and do not even see themselves as being in opposition to them. Their role is to help all beings rise above the fallen consciousness and their only criteria for helping us is our willingness to transcend our old state of consciousness.

For all three categories mentioned above, we can talk about two groupings. When our sphere was first created, Archangels, Elohim and ascended masters were all beings who had ascended in the sixth sphere. Our sphere has existed for a long period of time, and it has entered the phase where many galaxies have ascended. This means that some of the Archangels, Elohim and ascended masters who now serve planet earth have ascended from our sphere and then taken over the positions from the original masters. Some have ascended from earth but most have ascended from other planets.

The seven spiritual rays

Our sphere is created from seven distinct types of energies. This is logical since it is the seventh sphere in our cosmos. Each sphere has a signature energy that has certain properties. As the entire cosmos forms a hierarchy that steps down the energy of the Creator, it follows that each new sphere is created from the energies of the previous spheres plus its own signature energy.

It may seem as if the progression of the spheres is a process that makes it harder and harder to ascend. This is true in the sense that for each sphere, the base energy is more dense.

This makes it harder to overcome the illusion of separation and come into oneness. At the same time that it is harder, it also carries greater rewards.

In order to ascend from the first sphere, you only had to master one type of creative energy. Ascending from the second sphere meant mastering two kinds of energies whereas ascending from our sphere means mastering seven types of energies. Even though the process has more difficulty, it also leads to greater creative mastery.

Below is a brief description of the seven types of spiritual energies. Each type of energy is normally called a spiritual ray. They are generally named as the First Ray to the Seventh Ray, and this can give rise to some confusion. If you consider the situation of a new co-creator on earth, this being will, as part of its ascension process, be initiated in each of the seven rays. It will begin with the First Ray, which is the signature energy of our sphere. It will end with the Seventh Ray, which is the signature energy of the first sphere. There are, however, other ways to describe the progression of the rays. The spiritual rays are:

- **First Ray.** From our viewpoint, the color of the energy of this ray is electric blue. Its main characteristics (described with our concepts) are will and power.

- **Second Ray.** The color is golden yellow and the characteristics are wisdom and illumination.

- **Third Ray.** The color is pink and the characteristics are love and compassion.

- **Fourth Ray.** The color is white and the characteristics are purity and acceleration.

- **Fifth Ray.** The color is emerald green and the characteristics are vision and healing.

- **Sixth Ray.** The colors are purple and gold and the characteristics are peace and service.

- **Seventh Ray.** The color is violet and the characteristics are freedom and oneness.

Each spiritual ray has both an Archangel, an Elohim and a number of ascended masters. One of these ascended masters is the main teacher for that ray, and this office is called the Chohan. Our only way of rising above the illusion of separation is to be guided by the ascended masters above us. Escaping the fallen consciousness can be done only by coming into oneness with the ascended masters above us. After all, ascending means rising above separation and coming into oneness. We must rise from our level, and this means coming into oneness with the beings at the level of hierarchy immediately above ours.

The spheres are significant because the four octaves of our sphere are made from a combination of the energies of all seven spheres. In order to master your creative energies in our sphere, you have to master the positive qualities of all seven rays. The fallen beings cannot directly absorb the energies of the seven rays. They can only absorb a perversion of the rays whereby the energies are lowered below a critical threshold of vibration.

When the energies of the rays are used to raise up some part of life, they vibrate at the level of love. When they are used to limit life, their vibration becomes lowered into the spectrum of fear. All of the uplifting aspects of life on earth are created from the pure qualities of the rays, and all of the limiting aspects are created from a perversion of the rays. The key to overcoming any limitation is to know from which ray it was created. Once you know the perversion, you can invoke the pure energies of that ray and it will consume or transform the limitation. Tools for invoking the energies of the seven rays can be found on *www.transcendencetoolbox.com*.

Elemental beings

A form is created when a self-aware being, a co-creator, forms a mental matrix and then projects it onto the base energy of its sphere. In the first four spheres, there was no intermediary between thought and manifestation. The moment a co-creator had formed a thought and projected it, at that moment the manifestation was there. After the fall in the fourth sphere, the ascended masters changed the design of the succeeding spheres. This was necessary because once you go into separation, you no longer have the mental power to have your thoughts become directly manifest.

The fifth sphere had two octaves, which meant that the minds of the co-creators who embodied in the lowest octave had two levels. A thought was first formed in the higher level and then descended to the lower level from where it was projected onto the base energy. This meant there was a delay factor, making it possible for co-creators to select which thoughts they projected out. A co-creator could more easily stop an imperfect thought before it was brought into manifestation. The same principle is repeated in our sphere, only we have four levels of our minds:

- The identity mind, corresponding to the identity octave.

5 | The Creation of Our Sphere

- The mental mind, corresponding to the mental octave.

- The emotional mind, corresponding to the emotional octave.

- The physical mind, corresponding to the physical octave.

The physical level of the mind is not necessarily the same as the conscious mind. Some people do have such a low level of self-awareness that their conscious minds are limited to the physical brain and nervous system. Many people have raised their self-awareness to incorporate one or more of the higher levels. Some people also have awareness of the spiritual realm beyond our sphere.

The four levels of the mind provide a delay factor so that our selfish thoughts are not instantly brought into physical manifestation. You may have heard people who are angry with another person say: "Oh, I'm gonna kill him!" If there was no delay factor, such a strong thought could instantly kill the other person. Now, the thought has to descend through the four levels of our sphere before it can become a physical reality. This means two things:

- The person can override or modify the thought before it results in the person taking a physical action to kill another human being.

- The thought can encounter so much resistance as it descends that it will not be manifest as a physical outcome.

We human beings have two ways of manifesting a physical result or form. Because we have lost the full awareness of our creative faculties, most people are not aware of more than one of these, namely that we take physical action. We also have the option of manifesting physical forms as the result of our mental faculties alone.

We can find a hint of this in the Book of Genesis. It is explained that before they partook of the forbidden fruit, Adam and Eve did not have to work in order to survive. They had an abundance of "fruits" available in the garden and everything they needed was right there for the taking. This symbolizes that before the fall, we were able to manifest everything we needed for physical survival through the powers of our minds. We did not have to perform work with our physical bodies. After we fell into the consciousness of separation, we forgot about these abilities and we now had to use our physical bodies, working for a living "by the sweat of the brow." This does not mean we have stopped projecting our thoughts upon the Ma-ter Light, but we no longer do it consciously.

Our mental powers still give rise to physical forms. This happens because at each of the four levels of our sphere there are conscious beings who take the base energy and fashion it according to the thought matrix projected upon the energy. These beings are often called "elemental beings" (or "elementals" for short) in spiritual literature. Throughout the ages, some people have been able to see them as nature spirits or as gnomes, sylphs, elves etcetera. This is what has given rise to the popular myth of various beings, and although the specific form of these myths is usually incorrect, there is a basis of reality in the fact that such beings do exist.

When the seven Elohim created planet earth, they envisioned a thought matrix and projected it into the identity octave. Here, the elemental beings took the matrix and used it to fashion the base energy of the identity octave in the form of the matrix. They then stepped down the energy to the mental level and projected the matrix to the elementals in the mental octave. These took the matrix and built onto it by using the energy of their octave. They then stepped down the energy and projected the matrix into the emotional octave. Here, the elementals did the same thing before they projected it into the physical octave. At the lowest level, the elementals fashioned the energy into what we see as physical forms.

In the first three spheres, there was no delay factor and a thought generated an instant manifestation. In our sphere the four octaves provide a delay factor so even when the seven Elohim created the earth, this took time. It took time for the elementals to fashion the energy around the thought matrix and pass it on to the next level. This design was specifically adapted to the presence of fallen beings in all four levels of our sphere. The fallen beings also have to follow the process of having the elementals serve as intermediaries between thought and manifestation.

As an example, consider a situation where two groups of fallen beings have formed rivaling power elites on a planet. They engage in an all-out war to destroy each other. If their destructive intent would become an instant manifestation, it could easily destroy their planet. With the four levels of delay factors, it is still possible for fallen beings to destroy their planet, but it takes much longer and requires a much larger amount of mental energy. There is a greater chance that fallen beings will see that they are on the way to destroying themselves. Seeing that their actions will lead to self-destruction is often the only way fallen beings can be awakened from their state of delusion.

The elemental beings are conscious beings, but they are not self-conscious and do not have what we call free will. They do have enough awareness to know what is the original matrix for the planet on which they serve. The elementals on earth have a built-in memory of the original design for this planet. They also have a sense of the upward flow of life, meaning they can sense when a thought matrix projected upon them is life-enhancing or life-destroying.

The elementals are servants. Their task is to carry into manifestation whatever matrix is projected upon them by the beings they serve. Originally, the elementals for earth served the Elohim. After co-creators started embodying here, the elementals have been serving these co-creators. It is the task of the elementals to manifest as form whatever is projected through the minds of the co-creators. The elementals will outpicture any form projected, but because of their inner awareness, they do have some flexibility in how they carry out their task.

If a thought matrix is life-supporting, the elementals normally have no hesitation in carrying it out. It will be manifest with the least possible delay of time and the physical form will be very close to the original matrix. If the matrix is not life-supporting, the elementals can resist carrying it out. This can mean a longer delay in time, and it can also mean that the manifest form differs somewhat from the original matrix. The elementals might make the form less destructive than the thought matrix, and the intensity of the intent can be reduced.

The Elohim originally created the earth as a paradise. The first co-creators who embodied on this planet did not have to use their physical bodies to work for a living. They could manifest all they needed for physical survival by using the power of their minds in cooperation with the elementals. At some point in the distant past, the co-creators embodying on earth started to slide downward in self-awareness and became more selfish. This caused human beings to reduce their mental powers so they could no longer consciously manifest a form through the

5 | The Creation of Our Sphere

power of their minds. Today, people have lost the memory of ever having had such mental power. We are now co-creating by projecting images through our subconscious minds. The manifestation takes longer and we do not realize we have created our physical circumstances.

After the downward slide had gone on for a long time, the ascended masters decided to use planet earth in an experiment. This will be explained in greater detail later, but the significance here is that fallen beings were now allowed to embody on this planet. Since then, the collective consciousness has been lowered far below the original level.

This has far-ranging effects because the lowering of the collective consciousness has affected the elementals in profound ways. This has increased the delay factor between thought and manifestation and it has also caused the elementals to be so burdened by imperfect energies that they often produce various imbalances in the physical environment. This accounts for many natural disasters and diseases. Many of the phenomena we call "natural evil" can be explained by the elementals being so burdened by negative energy that they react violently. The rest can be explained by destructive thought matrices being projected upon the elementals by fallen beings.

Fallen beings

From the very beginning, our sphere was designed to accommodate fallen beings. This does not mean that the fallen beings dominated our sphere. The vast majority of planets and even galaxies did not have fallen beings. Throughout the first phase of the evolution of our sphere, innumerable new co-creators built a powerful upward momentum. Our sphere has now entered the phase that is the preparation for the ascension, meaning fallen beings are now allowed to mix with co-creators who were created in this sphere.

Planet earth was originally created to house new co-creators. For a long time, fallen beings have been allowed to embody on this planet. Each octave is designed to accommodate a specific type of fallen beings:

- In the identity octave we find the fallen beings with the most non-aggressive frame of mind. These beings firmly believe in their world view and they are equally convinced that they are working for a noble cause. They are sure that the Creator of our cosmos made a mistake and they are the only ones who are wise enough to see it. It is their responsibility to correct this mistake by seeking to make all co-creators accept the world views they have created. Because they see themselves as working for a noble cause, they do not see it as acceptable to lie, manipulate or force co-creators. This does not mean they are not (in a certain way) lying, manipulating and forcing; it means they themselves are not seeing what they are doing. These are in a sense the most deceived of the fallen beings, yet because they are not as aggressive and self-centered, they are still the ones closest to awakening.

- In the mental octave we find fallen beings who are not as wise or sophisticated as the ones in the etheric octave. These beings seek personal power and position and because they are not as good at persuading others, they are willing to lie in order to directly control others and get them to follow their leadership. As described in the previous book, the mental level of the mind is dominated by the intellect and it can argue for or against any issue or viewpoint. The fallen beings at the mental level have often accepted the world views created by the fallen beings in the identity octave. At the mental level, they add many details and often end up creating such elaborate thought systems that they contain many contradictions and inconsistencies. The mental fallen beings often use confusion as a weapon, and when people do not know what to think, they offer them a seemingly simply solution.

- In the emotional octave we find fallen beings who are not very skilled in using analytical thinking. They may accept a thought system created by the beings in the higher octaves, but they add an emotional component to it. They will seek to stir up people's fear-based emotions so that they will blindly follow their own leadership. At each level, the fallen beings are divided into groups that have rivalry or competition. In the emotional realm you find the greatest division and you also find a kind of open warfare between groups. This warfare is often driven by intense anger and hatred directed at other groups. These beings will often falsely accuse new co-creators in order to force them to react and thus become entangled with the power plays of the fallen beings.

- In the physical octave you find fallen beings with the lowest level of consciousness, meaning the greatest level of aggression and focus on themselves and their immediate situation. These are beings who are willing to openly use aggression and who will use physical force in order to control others. They are also willing to kill those who will not be controlled. We have seen a number of dictatorial leaders on earth who have been and are willing to use physical force in order to control their own people or destroy a group that is defined as their enemy. Wars are always started by such fallen beings, even though they are usually controlled, mentally and emotionally, by fallen beings in higher octaves.

A special note on fallen angels

The concept of fallen angels can be traced back to *The Book of Enoch*, which originated in Old Testament times but was taken out of the official Bible. There is also talk of fallen angels in *The Book of Revelation*. This has led to the use of this concept in many contexts, including modern fantasy novels and computer games.

Again, we need to consider the tendency to look at ourselves here on earth and interpret everything from our perspective. This has caused many spiritual or religious people to reason that any being who came from a realm higher than the material octave must be an angel. This is not necessarily the case.

In an ascended sphere, there are beings who hold the positions of angels, but these angels cannot fall. The reason is that they started in a lower realm as unascended beings and have gone through the process of the ascension. Once you have done this, you cannot be deceived by the illusion of separation and thus cannot fall. If one defines angels as beings who exist exclusively in the ascended realm, then the concept of fallen angels becomes meaningless.

The concept of fallen angels refers to beings who fell as their sphere ascended. For example, the fifth sphere had two levels or octaves. The beings who were created to inhabit the

5 | The Creation of Our Sphere

higher octave were not designed to embody in the most dense octave. These beings had a dual function in the sense that it was their task to secure their own ascensions while helping the beings who embodied in the lowest octave. Because of this, the beings in the higher octave seemed like angels to those in the lower octave. As the fifth sphere ascended, some of the beings in the higher octave fell. From the perspective of the beings in the lower octave, these became fallen angels.

The sixth sphere had three octaves so the beings in the two higher octaves seemed like angels to those in the lowest octave. Some of the beings in the two higher octaves fell when the sixth sphere ascended. This means our sphere has beings from both the fifth and the sixth spheres who can be called fallen angels.

Our sphere has beings in the emotional, mental and identity octaves who are not designed to take embodiment in the physical octave. Their task is to secure their own ascensions, but those in a higher octave can do this only by ministering to those in the lowest octave. This ministry can cause such beings to become frustrated with the lack of progress of those in embodiment, and this can cause them to fall. Take note that unascended angels cannot fall until their sphere ascends, meaning our sphere has not produced any fallen angels although beings from the three higher octaves have taken on and are acting out the fallen consciousness. Technically, they will not become fallen angels until our sphere ascends and they refuse to ascend with it.

In order to avoid the confusion between ascended angels who cannot fall and fallen angels, this book will use the terms "fallen beings." It will use the term unascended beings to refer to those in the three higher octaves who were created for our sphere. Take note that the three higher octaves also contain fallen beings, meaning beings who fell in a previous sphere.

The term co-creator will be used to refer to those who take embodiment in the lowest realm, meaning the physical octave of our sphere.

Co-creators

As explained, the earth was originally created as an environment for new co-creators. The first co-creators to embody here were created specifically to embody on earth. There have been several groups, waves or root races of co-creators who were created for the earth. Most of them have ascended.

At some point a group of co-creators had created a downward spiral on this planet. Most of them had become trapped in a limited perception filter and this had created a self-reinforcing effect. Because all were blinded by the collective perception filter, there was no one in physical embodiment who could challenge the common perception. The co-creators could not pull themselves out of the downward spiral.

The ascended masters then decided to allow the embodiment of co-creators from other planets as well as fallen beings. Because these newcomers had a different background than the inhabitants of earth, they would challenge the collective perception filter of the original co-creators. This had the potential to break the downward spiral, which has happened. Of course, the presence of such different beings on the same planet can also generate conflict, as witnessed abundantly by known history.

From an overall perspective, planet earth has been pulled out of the downward spiral that would have led to the planet's destruction. This planet is now in an upward spiral although it is obviously still facing great challenges.

6 | THE PROCESS OF TAKING EMBODIMENT

In this chapter we will explore how the ascended masters designed us so we have the greatest opportunity to grow from experiencing the conditions in our sphere. Again we need to be careful not to take our limited perception and project it beyond our sphere. We may look at the people living on earth and think that although there are individual differences, many people are still alike. We may think that because we currently have limited capabilities, these limitations are built into our design.

We were all created by the ascended masters, and they have a much broader imagination and knowledge than we do. Each human being was originally created with a unique individuality. This spiritual individuality is far more complex than what we normally call our personality. Each of us has a unique potential for bringing forth a creative effort that will help raise our sphere.

Obviously, this potential is not being fulfilled at present, and we will explore why that is so. In order to explain this, we will first look at the components of self. The explanation given here will be about co-creators designed for this sphere but is with small variations applicable to all co-creators.

Your I AM Presence

Your individuality is completely unique among the seven billion people on earth, and it is even unique among the innumerable beings in the entire cosmos. Creating your individuality is a major effort by the ascended masters who are your spiritual parents. They invest their time, attention and energy. They even invest a part of their own beings in order to give you self-awareness. Their goal is to have you grow to become an ascended master yourself. They do everything possible to design you so that your individuality cannot be lost.

Because of the nature of free will, the potential has always been there that a co-creator could choose not to ascend. This potential has increased as the spheres have become denser and as the presence of fallen beings has been allowed. This explains why your unique individuality is not located in the physical octave.

Your individuality is located in the ascended realm, right above the identity octave. Your individuality is a form of geometric or holographic structure that can be called various names, such as your spiritual self or higher self. The ascended masters often call it your "I AM Presence."

Your I AM Presence has self-awareness, meaning it has the ability to imagine options and to choose among them. It is a creative being, which means it can imagine a thought matrix

6 | The Process of Taking Embodiment

and project it upon the Ma-ter Light. It is a self-sufficient being, meaning it can create by using the energy it obtains from within itself. When we say "from within itself" this means that the I AM Presence does not need to obtain energy from its immediate environment. It obtains energy from the level above itself, from a vertical rather than a horizontal direction.

The I AM Presence is fully aware that its creative energy comes from the ascended masters who are the next link in the spiritual hierarchy right above itself. The I AM Presence could never fall prey to the illusion that it is a separate being and that it produces energy by itself. The Presence always sees itself as one with its source and with all life. Why this is important will become clear later.

The I AM Presence is located in the ascended realm, and this is done to prevent your unique individuality from becoming lost. Your I AM Presence is not created in order to confine itself to the ascended realm and grow from there. Your I AM Presence has a unique individuality, but when it is created, it does not have a particularly wide or sophisticated self-awareness. It is meant to expand its self-awareness, and the way it does so is by sending part of itself to take embodiment in the unascended sphere. It is through the experiences in the unascended sphere that your I AM Presence grows in self-awareness. This growth is, of course, the entire purpose of life.

Because the I AM Presence is the anchor of your individuality, the Presence cannot take embodiment in its totality. It sends only a part of itself into the unascended sphere. Words are often inadequate to describe what actually happens in the ascended realm. We could also say that your I AM Presence focuses itself as a point-like self in the unascended sphere. It is this part we will look at next.

The part of you that takes embodiment

Again we need to be careful not to take our every-day perception and project it upon what actually happens. When I say "you," most people have only an imprecise awareness of what this "you" really is. Many are so identified with their physical bodies and outer personalities that they find it difficult to grasp that they are much more.

Your I AM Presence can be described as a spherical being or a being with spherical awareness. It has a much broader self-awareness than most people have, and this is partly because it exists in a realm where the energies are much higher. It is easier for the Presence to be aware of its source, its creative abilities and its broader environment. When the Presence sends part of itself into this denser realm, it focuses itself as a point-like self.

Let us compare this to a person who is in a completely dark place and has only a small candle as a lighting source. You can see only what is within the very small circle of light created by the candle. This is you when you first took embodiment.

As you experience life in the physical octave, you gradually increase your awareness of the environment, your creative abilities and yourself. This is comparable to a person who gradually acquires a more and more powerful lamp instead of the candle. As the person's circle of light grows, it can see more and more. This is how we grow in self-awareness.

The you that descends into the physical octave is designed in order to minimize the risk that it will become lost. The self that descends does not have an actual individuality in the same way that your I AM Presence does. The unique characteristics that set you apart from all other beings are anchored in the Presence. The you that descends has individuality only in the sense that it starts out being focused in one point. This point is set apart from all other points. As you grow in self-awareness, your individual sense of self becomes wider and more encompassing. At the core of your identity is still a sense of being one individual. Until you ascend, you will have a sense of there being one point from which you perceive the world. We can say that you will always be looking at the world from one point. The question is how wide of a sphere of the world you can see from your particular vantage point. How far beyond the central point is your observation horizon?

The you that descends has no individual characteristics, meaning it can be described as pure awareness. You may have seen technological devices where a long flexible tube has a lens at one end and a screen at the other. A person can stick the tube into a room and can observe what is happening through the lens. The lens, of course, is just a clear pane of glass that does not distort what is seen. The you that descends is the lens whereby your I AM Presence sees into this unascended sphere. Because this self is a form of pure awareness, the ascended masters often refer to it as the Conscious You or the conscious self.

The Conscious You is a two-way street. Your I AM Presence not only observes the world through the Conscious You, it can also send spiritual light into the world through it. That is why you have co-creative abilities and can do something in the physical octave. This is also your potential to help eradicate evil from this planet. Most people have reduced the flow of energy from the Presence, but by becoming an open door you can help increase the light in our sphere and thereby expose evil for more people to see.

The fact that the Conscious You is pure awareness means that it can never come to permanently identify itself with or as anything in this world. The Conscious You can focus its awareness entirely outwardly and can thereby come to identify itself with the physical body and your life here on earth. There will always be some awareness of or longing for something beyond this world.

As you grow in self-awareness, you will become more and more aware that nothing in this world truly satisfies you. The reason is that the Conscious You cannot permanently forget that it is an extension of your I AM Presence. The Conscious You will always have some longing for again becoming aware of the Presence, eventually expanding its self-awareness to the point where it can reunite with the I AM Presence in the process of the ascension.

Because the Conscious You is pure awareness, no matter what you might have identified yourself with or as in this world, you can always pull yourself away from that sense of identity. No matter who you are or what you may have done in the past, you can never lose the potential to leave it all behind by reconnecting to the fact that you are pure awareness. You then see that the Conscious You has not been altered by anything it has experienced in this world. Nor has it become permanently trapped in anything in this world.

It is the very fact that the Conscious You is pure awareness that makes it possible for you to ascend from this sphere. You can always rise above anything in this world. Of course, it is also the fact that the Conscious You is pure awareness that allows you to go into anything, any kind of self, in this world.

Your four lower bodies

The Conscious You is pure awareness, and theoretically it could be floating around in the world and simply observing it. The Conscious You could be a sort of dis-embodied spirit that could observe the world without being able to do anything in the world. The Conscious You might learn something from this, but it would not learn as much as it would by taking actual embodiment.

When we say "take embodiment," we mean a process whereby the Conscious You takes on or enters into "bodies" that are made from the energies that make up the four octaves of our sphere: the identity, the mental, the emotional and the physical octaves. It is only by taking on these "four lower bodies" that the Conscious You gains the ability to perform creative actions in this world.

In order to do something in the physical octave, you need to have a body made from the energies that are dense enough to act on other physical things. Your three higher bodies can move a physical object, but only when you raise your self-awareness beyond a certain level. In the beginning, you can move material things only by using the physical body.

Our cosmos is a hierarchical structure ranging from higher to more dense energies, and your I AM Presence exists on the borderline between the ascended realm and our sphere. The Conscious You is made from the higher energies of the ascended realm. In order for the Conscious You to take embodiment, it must first enter into a "body" formed from the energies in the identity octave. It then enters into a body made of the energies in the mental octave. Then comes a body made of the energies of the emotional octave and only then can the Conscious You enter into and operate a physical body.

There are many profound implications of this process of taking on the four lower bodies. It is important to be aware that each of the for lower bodies forms a veil to the perception of the Conscious You. These veils are in a hierarchical structure. Your identity body contains the definition of how you currently see yourself as a being and how you see yourself in relation to your environment. This sets a matrix for how you think about yourself and the world in the mental body. Your mental body cannot question the identity at the higher level. The mental body sets a pattern for how you feel about yourself and this sets the stage for your physical actions.

Because the Conscious You is pure awareness, it can focus itself totally in the physical body and identify itself here. If it does so, then it will not – from this vantage point – be able to question and transcend any of the definitions found in the three higher bodies. This mechanism is what gives evil an inroad into our four lower bodies and makes it difficult for us to free ourselves from evil.

As explained in the first book, there are some people who are so identified with their physical bodies that they will instantly kill someone if they perceive him or her as being a threat to their physical life. That is why certain groups of people can be in conflict for thousands of years without coming closer to a resolution. The people in both groups are so identified with their physical characteristics that they cannot see beyond them to the fact that we are all spiritual beings who came from the same source.

The path of freeing yourself from the influence of evil means you gradually free the Conscious You from identification with the four lower bodies:

- First, you free it from identification with the physical body.

- You then begin to become aware of the influence of your emotions.

- As you stop identifying yourself with your feelings, you can become more aware of your thoughts.

- Eventually, you can become aware of your limited identity and begin to shed that also.

Because the Conscious You is pure awareness, it cannot lose the ability to step outside the perception filter (the four veils) of the four lower bodies. Many people have had spiritual, intuitive or mystical experiences. These can be explained as instances where the Conscious You momentarily stepped outside one or more of the four lower bodies and experienced what life looks like when not seen through the normal filters.

Such experiences form an invaluable frame of reference. When you become aware that there is a way to look at life without the normal filters, it becomes so much easier to start dis-identifying yourself from the four lower bodies and their perception. These experiences of stepping outside the four lower bodies are the only way for you to become free:

- While you are inside the physical body and looking at life from there, you cannot question what comes to you from the emotional body. Neither can you question what comes from the fallen beings in the physical octave.

- When you are inside the emotional veil, you cannot question what comes from the mental body. You cannot question what comes from the fallen beings in the emotional octave.

- While identifying with the mental body, you cannot question what comes from the identity body. You cannot question what comes from the fallen beings in the mental octave.

- While being absorbed in the identity body, you cannot question what comes from the fallen beings at that level.

Until you question your human or earthly sense of identity, you cannot begin to have conscious contact with your I AM Presence or the ascended masters who serve as your teachers. It is only when you penetrate the four veils that you can begin to look up and see your I AM Presence. It is then that you can begin to realize: "Oh, I am not the I am down here (in the four lower bodies); I am *that* I AM up there (in your I AM Presence).

The ego inside of you and the forces of evil outside of you will do anything in their power to prevent you from coming to this realization. No matter what they have done to prevent this awakening – and they have done a lot – they can never take away the Conscious You's potential to awaken from its identification with the four lower bodies.

Your outer self

Your four lower bodies are not evil. There is an old tradition among spiritual people of looking at the physical body as an enemy of spiritual growth. People often talk about "the temptations of the flesh." Your four bodies are not inherently *enemies* of your spiritual growth, but they can become so. If used correctly, your four lower bodies are the *facilitators* of your growth.

The entire purpose of life is the growth in self-awareness. Your I AM Presence grows by sending the Conscious You into our unascended sphere. This growth has two aspects:

- The Conscious You observes and experiences the conditions in this world.

- The Conscious You uses its perception of life to make decisions and use its creative powers. This creates physical circumstances, and the Conscious You then has the opportunity to learn by experiencing the consequences of its choices.

Without having four lower bodies, the Conscious You could not fulfill its reason for being. The four lower bodies are the vehicles through which the Conscious You travels in the unascended sphere. There is consequently no reason to have negative feelings about your four lower bodies.

The Ma-ter Light does not have self-awareness, meaning it cannot take on form by itself. It takes on form by being acted upon by a self-aware being. The Ma-ter Light does have a form of consciousness or memory, and that is why it can hold a form over time. The Ma-ter Light, so to speak, remembers the form projected upon it.

The Ma-ter Light takes on form when a self-aware being designs a mental matrix and projects it upon the light. The force that projects this matrix is the consciousness of the creative being. This means anything we create, even any form in the physical octave, has a certain form of consciousness.

There are so-called "primitive" religions that say everything in the material world has spirit within it or is animated by spirit. These religions may not be entirely correct in their description of this, but the principle is correct.

Quantum physics has discovered that everything has a corresponding quantum waveform and that our consciousness co-creates what we observe. The quantum waveform is designed by a mind and becomes projected onto the base energy by a mind.

The far-reaching conclusion is that everything we create has a form of consciousness. When we create a sufficiently complex structure, the overall structure becomes a conscious being—the whole is more than the sum of the parts. This does not mean it becomes self-aware, but it has a sophisticated enough consciousness to have a survival instinct and to know what to do to secure its survival.

As an example, take the physical body. The body is made from atoms. A single atom does not have a very sophisticated form of consciousness. By combining a large number of atoms, you form a molecule, which has a higher form of consciousness. By combining many molecules, you form a cell, and the cell has a much more sophisticated consciousness than molecules. By combining trillions of cells, you form one human body and it is therefore easy to see that our incredibly complex physical bodies have a sophisticated form of consciousness.

The same applies to the emotional, mental and identity bodies. The combination of the four lower bodies forms a consciousness so sophisticated that it takes on a life of its own. This is what the ascended masters call the outer self, the human self or the mortal self.

Again, this human self is not in itself evil, and it is not necessarily an enemy of our spiritual growth. This is because our journey in the unascended sphere has two phases:

- **The immersion phase.** This is where the Conscious You descends into the four lower bodies. The outer self forms a kind of costume or role, and the Conscious You is like an actor who goes into a theatre, puts on make-up and a costume and then plays a pre-defined role. During this phase, it is intended that the

Conscious You identifies itself with and as the role it is playing. The Conscious You needs to believe that it is living in a real world and that it is not playing a role but that it really is a human being. It is the outer self that delivers this sense of reality and immersion.

- **The awakening phase.** The Conscious You is not meant to forever remain in a certain role. It is meant to first take on a limited role, as an actor might start by playing one of the extras. As the Conscious You has had enough of playing such simple roles, it gradually takes on more and more complex roles, as an actor may take on a speaking role and then eventually become the main character of a play. Finally, the Conscious You is meant to have had enough of all roles available on a planet like earth and then awaken to its desire to reunite with the I AM Presence in the ascension.

During the immersion phase, the outer self is doing exactly what it is meant to do, namely making the Conscious You feel that the physical octave is a real world. As the Conscious You begins to go into the awakening phase, the outer self will continue to do what it is designed to do. This is partly because it can do nothing else and partly because the outer self has a survival instinct. The outer self also becomes more sophisticated over time, and in order to secure its survival, it will resist the awakening of the Conscious You.

There are many spiritual seekers who start to awaken to the possibility of following a spiritual path, and for a time they often feel that the outer self or ego is an enemy of their growth. It is true that the outer self resists your awakening, but this does not mean the outer self is evil. It simply cannot do anything else than what it was designed to do. The outer self will never be able to acknowledge its own unreality, and even if it could, that would mean its instant dissolution.

While it is true that the outer self resists your awakening, it is not productive to see your outer self as evil. It is the role of the Conscious You to awaken from its identification with this world. It is a natural and unavoidable part of this process that you come to see that the outer self and the four lower bodies were just vehicles that you were using in order to facilitate your journey.

Imagine that you are going on a spaceship bound for a distant galaxy. Before you can take off from earth, you first have to get to the spaceport. You might drive to the port's parking lot in your car. Your car is a wonderful vehicle, and you could not get to the spaceport without it. Yet, you cannot get on the spaceship without getting out of your car. It is only natural that you leave your car behind in order to take the next step on your journey. This means you cannot be so identified with your car that you think you cannot exist without it. It is the Conscious You and not the outer self that is responsible for you coming to the point where you can leave the mortal self and the four lower bodies behind.

The outer self is mortal because it is created out of the energies of our unascended sphere, and in an unascended sphere nothing is permanent. The mortal self is something you carry with you from lifetime to lifetime. You also carry your three higher bodies, and even the consciousness that animates your physical body, with you from lifetime to lifetime. As you grow in self-awareness for each lifetime, so does the outer self. As this self becomes more sophisticated, it can begin to become susceptible to illusions projected upon it by the fallen beings. Your mortal self can therefore begin to believe that it can secure its own immortality and that in order to do this, it needs to prevent the Conscious You from awakening and leaving it behind.

It is this mechanism that can make the mortal self an inroad for evil to influence you. The fallen beings who oppose the purpose of creation can use your mortal self and your four lower bodies to oppose your awakening. This can certainly be called evil, but it still does not mean that your outer self and four lower bodies are evil in and of themselves.

Your causal body

We now need to make a distinction that confuses many spiritual seekers and thus makes it harder for them to rise above the temptations of evil. Many spiritual seekers have for lifetimes been following the path of studying religious or spiritual teachings and following the rules defined by such teachings. They have been sincerely striving to do what is defined as spiritual or good by such teachings. What they often do not understand is that this process has two effects:

- It expands the circle of awareness of the Conscious You. As mentioned, the Conscious You can be compared to a person who starts out with a candle and gradually increases the light so it can see more and more.

- It expands the knowledge and sophistication of the outer self.

The role of the Conscious You is to start with a point-like self and gradually expand it. The Conscious You tries on a role and lives it for a time but then starts to feel: "There must be more to life than this. I must be more than this role." It then takes on a more sophisticated role for a time until it also feels it is more than this.

Over many lifetimes, the Conscious You has expanded its sphere of awareness to encompass any role that can be played on earth. The Conscious You then starts realizing it was not created on earth and cannot be confined to this planet. It discovers its I AM Presence and eventually realizes that it *is* the Presence. The Conscious You now stops seeing itself as a being with a point-like center located in this world. Instead, it gives up the point-like self and accepts that it is and always was the spherical being of the I AM Presence.

When you first become aware of how the ascension process works, there is a part of "you" that refuses to believe this is true. This part is the mortal self and it will say: "But what about all of the experiences I have had on earth? What about all of my striving to be a good person and live according to my spiritual teaching? What about my efforts to know more and to become more capable of mastering my environment? Has all this just been for nothing because I now have to give up my human self?" The reality is that while the Conscious You is in embodiment, there are two parallel tracks running at the same time:

- The track of your human self, which stores the memory of your experiences. The human self stores (in your four lower bodies) the situations as they were experienced through the perception filter (the four veils) of the human self.

- The track of your I AM Presence. As the Conscious You is experiencing a situation on earth through the perception filter of the human self, the I AM Presence is experiencing the same situation but without the perception filter of the human self. The Presence has an entirely different experience of a situation than the human self.

The memory of how your I AM Presence experienced a situation is stored in what the ascended masters call your "causal body." The crucial difference is that your human self experiences everything from the viewpoint of a separate being. As a separate being, it is dominated by fear-based emotions. The human self will often feel that what you did was wrong, a mistake or a sin. As the Conscious You experiences life through the human self, it is susceptible to feelings of guilt, fear, a sense of being a failure or even self-hatred.

At the same time, your I AM Presence has experienced the same situations but without the fear-based, separate perception filter. Your Presence has had an entirely positive experience and has turned it into something that enhances your unique individuality. It may seem difficult to turn some of your personal mistakes into positive learning experiences, but the Presence is able to do this. It looks at things on earth and realizes: "This is *not* who I am; I am *this* instead," or *"That* is not how I want to express my creativity; I want to do it *this* way."

Nothing you have done or experienced on earth has been wasted. Any experience has been used by your I AM Presence to enhance your individuality and to learn how to express (and *not* express) your creative powers in a way that supports the overall goal of creation, namely to raise all life until this sphere ascends.

When you begin to grasp this, it becomes much easier for you to complete the process of dis-entangling the Conscious You from its identification with the mortal self. This also makes it far easier for you to free yourself from the influence that the forces of evil have had over you. You can simply walk away from the many schemes they have come up with in order to keep you identified with the human self, feeling you could not possibly give it up because there is something you have to do to or with it. Instead of being trapped in this pattern, you can walk away from your mortal self and into the sun rays of your immortal self.

7 | THE LEVELS OF HUMAN CONSCIOUSNESS

Everything is created from energy and energy is described by its vibration. The entire cosmos is a continuum of vibrations, ranging from the very highest in the first sphere to the lowest found in our sphere. Our sphere is not set apart from the rest of the cosmos; it exists within it. Our sphere is made from energies within a certain range. For example, visible light ranges from a frequency of 430 THz to that of 790 THz. Likewise, all energies in our unascended sphere exist within a certain range of vibrational characteristics. When the Elohim created planet earth, they determined the range of energies used to create the planet, from the identity octave to the physical octave.

The earth is created as a cosmic learning environment in which the Conscious You is meant to start from a certain level of consciousness and work its way up until it can ascend. This means there is a range of the levels of consciousness possible on earth. The Conscious You starts at a certain level, and if it chooses to expand its sense of self, it will rise up through all levels above its starting point until it reaches the highest level and can ascend. Because of free will, it is possible that the Conscious You can choose to go below its starting point. There is a range of levels until the lowest possible state of consciousness is reached.

Every physical form has a quantum waveform, which can be seen as a complex mental thoughtform that determines how the energies vibrate. The entire earth has one overall waveform, but there are also many other waveforms that determine particular aspects of the earth. The earth was originally created with a quantum waveform defined by the Elohim. As co-creators started to embody on earth, they used the original waveform according to their level of consciousness. Co-creators can either raise or lower the original waveform. There is a limit or range to how much the co-creators in embodiment can change the original waveform. This is what defines the range for the levels of consciousness that a co-creator can be at and still remain in embodiment in the physical octave.

There are 144 levels of consciousness possible on planet earth, forming a range from the lowest (meaning the most selfish) to the highest (having overcome all selfishness and being ready to ascend). When a new co-creator (a co-creator designed to take embodiment on earth as its first embodiment) descends into physical embodiment, it comes in at the 48th level of consciousness. If a co-creator chooses to limit its sense of self, it can descend to the lowest possible level. If it goes below that, it can no longer remain in physical embodiment. A co-creator can also follow the path of initiation designed by the ascended masters and raise its consciousness towards the 144th level. When it reaches that level, it is ready to ascend by passing one final initiation.

The connection between consciousness and a planet

The connection between the levels of consciousness and the quantum waveform for the earth is important. If a critical mass of people in physical embodiment lowered their consciousness towards the lowest level, they would have such a profound impact on the quantum waveform that the physical planet would start breaking apart. It is possible that the inhabitants of a planet can lower their collective consciousness so much that a planet disintegrates and becomes unable to sustain physical life or even blows apart. This has happened to a relatively small number of planets. In our solar system, the asteroid belt is the remnant of a planet that the inhabitants destroyed.

If a majority of the inhabitants of a planet raise their consciousness, they will eventually bring their planet to a higher level of vibration, meaning the entire planet ascends. Planet Venus once had lifeforms in the physical octave. The co-creators embodying on Venus eventually raised their consciousness to the point where life on Venus has such a high level of vibration that we cannot detect it with our physical senses and material instruments. From our perspective, the inhabitants of Venus have ascended to a higher level of vibration. However, one cannot technically say that the inhabitants of Venus have all ascended, as that will not happen until our galaxy ascends.

The co-creators who take physical embodiment on a planet have a major impact on the evolution of that planet. Earth was created a very long time ago, and it was created in a much higher level of vibration than what we see today. When the first waves of co-creators took physical embodiment, they all followed the path of initiation under the ascended masters. By doing this, they raised the vibration of the entire planet to a higher level than the level at which it was created. We might say they accelerated the quantum waveform or that they multiplied their talents.

How the earth became open to fallen beings

At a point in the past, the majority of the co-creators in embodiment had become stuck in a downward spiral. Most of them had gone below the 48th level of consciousness although none had yet gone to the lowest levels possible. As a technical note, there is no point in applying an actual time frame to these events. The reason is (as will be discussed later) that time is not a linear phenomenon.

When you are at the 48th level, you have an inner, intuitive contact with the ascended masters. This is depicted in the story of the Garden or Eden where Adam and Eve "walked and talked with God." What Genesis calls "God" was an ascended master who was the main teacher for the co-creators that descended.

As the story depicts, there was also a serpent in the garden. This has two meanings. Before the earth had gone into a downward spiral, no fallen beings were allowed to embody here. The broadest possible definition of the serpent is that it represents the possibility that co-creators can use their free will to go below the 48th level of consciousness. The more specific definition is that the serpent is a symbol for the fallen beings who directly oppose the purpose of our cosmos.

When you go below the 48th level, you no longer have the direct, inner contact with the ascended masters. This is symbolized in Adam and Eve being cast out of the garden. In reality, the ascended masters never cast anyone out of their circle of oneness. It was the choice to go below the 48th level that

7 | The Levels of Human Consciousness

lowered our perception so we no longer perceive the masters directly but are left to live based on the perception we have through our four lower bodies.

After most inhabitants of earth had cut themselves off from direct contact with the ascended masters, the masters still attempted to give them various spiritual teachings as a form of guidance adapted to people's level of consciousness. No amount of effort on behalf of the masters could help the inhabitants break the downward spiral. It became foreseeable that if the development continued, the inhabitants of earth would descend to such low levels of consciousness that the physical planet would start breaking apart and eventually be destroyed.

The ascended masters overseeing earth then decided to employ a strategy that had worked on other planets in a similar situation. That strategy was to open the earth to the embodiment of beings from other planets. This included both beings who were above the 48th level of consciousness and those below. Some of the beings allowed to embody were fallen beings (who are all below the 48th level of consciousness).

This may seem like a strange strategy, but the explanation is simple. The inhabitants of earth had not deliberately created the downward spiral. They had stopped growing and they had created certain thought systems that justified why they were not growing. They had created a collective illusion, and most of the inhabitants believed so firmly in this illusion that it had become self-reinforcing. It was becoming very difficult for the inhabitants of earth to break out of the collective illusion.

This ties in with what was discussed in the previous book about closed systems being affected by the second law of thermodynamics. It is a cosmic law that nothing can stand still. If co-creators are not making use of their potential to raise their consciousness, then the force described in the second law of thermodynamics will begin to break down the structures and thought systems they have created. This is not done as a punishment but as a way to demonstrate to them that a closed system cannot work. The purpose is to hopefully awaken them to the potential for growth.

In that distant past, the inhabitants of earth were so similar to each other that they were all susceptible to the same illusion, meaning no one was able or willing to question it. When co-creators from vastly different environments started to embody on earth, they began questioning the collective illusion. Although this gave rise to some conflicts, and a general discomfort among the original inhabitants, the strategy has worked. The earth has been brought out of its downward spiral.

Many co-creators volunteered to take embodiment on earth in order to create this upward spiral. These volunteers had all gone above the 48th level on other planets. Some, such as Jesus, had reached a very high level of consciousness before coming here.

Even the fallen beings have inadvertently helped break the limited perception that had created the downward spiral. Obviously, certain fallen beings have also created major havoc on this planet, yet even though one can point to monstrous outpicturings of evil, the entire planet is still in an upward spiral.

The population of earth can now be divided into three groups based on their level of consciousness:

- **The top ten percent.** These are the co-creators who have raised their self-awareness beyond that of being completely focused on themselves. They are above the 48th level and a few above the 96th level. Among these are many evolved lifestreams who came here from other planets and who have kept embodying here in order to raise this planet. There are also some of the co-creators that were here when other beings started embodying.

- **The 80 percent of the general population.** Among these are some co-creators who have come from other planets, but most of them are inhabitants of earth. Most of them are below the 48th level but not near the lowest level.

- **The bottom ten percent.** Most of these had fallen into separation before they came here. A few came here before having fallen and fell while embodying on earth. Some are the co-creators from earth who were led to fall by the fallen beings. All fallen beings are below the 48th level and many of them are at or close to the lowest level possible on earth.

The deciding factor in the future of this planet is whether the majority of the population will follow the fallen beings or the more evolved beings. Take note that had the original inhabitants not gone below the 48th level of their own choosing, the fallen beings would not have been allowed to embody here.

How consciousness densifies a planet

In the creation story from Genesis it is described how Adam and Eve lived in the garden before they had eaten the forbidden fruit. They not only had direct contact with their spiritual teacher but they also did not need to perform physical work in order to get what they needed for their sustenance. They could easily pick all of the "fruits" they needed in order to live. This is where Genesis is not entirely accurate, as it seems like Adam and Eve passively picked the fruits that were growing in the garden. The reality is a bit different.

The earth was originally created by the Elohim at a higher level of vibration than what we see today, meaning matter was less dense than it is now. One effect was that the original inhabitants found it much easier to produce physical results by exercising the creative powers of their minds. Even though a new co-creator has relatively little awareness of its creative abilities, in a less dense environment, co-creators can still easily build on the environment created for them by the Elohim. The first co-creators on earth did not need to perform work with their physical bodies in order to get what they needed.

In their identity bodies they knew they were part of a larger whole and connected to an external source from which they received creative energy. They knew their minds had the capacity to use this creative energy to manifest physical forms. In their mental minds, they imagined and designed very specific blueprints for what they wanted to precipitate and they imposed these upon the Ma-ter Light through their emotional bodies (that were free from all fear or sense of lack). They could precipitate everything they needed for their physical bodies through the powers of their minds.

After the inhabitants of earth went into a downward spiral, they lost this ability for direct precipitation. You cannot precipitate when you are below the 48th level of consciousness. On top of that, the descent of the collective consciousness had lowered the vibration of physical matter. The matter making up the entire planet had become so dense that it now required considerable mental powers to precipitate something through the mind.

This explains why human beings (as most people now see themselves) have to use the force of their physical bodies to work out a living at "the sweat of the brow." The energies are simply so dense that things have to be produced by using physical labor or material technology.

The spiritual people on earth are helping to change this situation. As we raise our consciousness above the 48th level, we raise the vibration of the entire planet. In the future, earth will again become an environment in which it is relatively easy to perform direct precipitation. This is not likely to happen in our lifetime.

Explaining imbalances in nature

As an explanatory note, the lowering of the collective consciousness not only explains why we have to work, it also explains many other imperfect conditions. For example, the densification of matter is the real cause of disease in our physical bodies. When matter was less dense, bodies did not get ill and they did not age. The Biblical account of certain people living to an age of 800 years has a basis in fact. In the original pure state created by the Elohim, people could live for so long that they could ascend after one embodiment. It was only after the fall in the collective consciousness that reincarnation become common.

The densification of matter has also had a major impact on the planet itself. Imagine that the earth was originally larger and that the same amount of matter has now been squeezed into a smaller space. This explains why the interior of the planet is so hot and why there is a constant movement of matter away from the center. The result has been volcanoes, earthquakes and continental plate movements, all of which did not exist in the original state.

Before the lowering of consciousness, natural disasters, such as hurricanes, drought, floods and fires, did not exist.

Back then, the elemental beings who are materializing the four levels of matter were not burdened by the low-frequency energies that humankind has produced since. When the elemental beings become overloaded by the fear-based energies we produce, they have to shake of the energy and this explains many natural disasters.

The densification of matter also explains why animals eat each other and why humans eat meat. This was not necessary in the original state. The animal species we see today did not exist in the pure state but are the precipitation of impure thoughtforms in the collective consciousness. For example, poisonous insects or snakes did not exist before the lowering of consciousness.

The densification of matter has also had the effect of slowing down time. The speed at which the entire solar system moves through our galaxy has been slowed down. Our galaxy is one among a few galaxies where fallen beings can embody. This explains why it seems to astronomers that all other galaxies are moving away from us and that they are doing so with accelerating speed. Galaxies with no fallen beings are raising their vibration at a higher rate than our galaxy and this makes it seem like they are physically moving away from us.

As Einstein's theory of relativity explains, there is a connection between time and the speed at which you move through space. It is not possible or meaningful to create an entirely linear time line for the history of earth. One second today is longer than it was when the earth was created in its pure state. One second today is shorter than when the collective consciousness was at its lowest point. The ascended masters have given a rough guideline for how long life has existed on earth. The masters say that if we use the scientific calculation of the earth being 4.5 billion years old, then intelligent life has existed on this planet for 2.5 billion years. However, bear in mind that time and the density of matter have not remained constant for that entire "period of time."

Changing the range of consciousness

When the earth was newly created, the range of consciousness possible on this planet was still 144 levels, but they were not the same 144 levels that we see today. When the earth was created, the highest level possible was higher than the highest level we see today. The lowest level possible back then was also higher than what is the lowest level today. This downward adjustment was performed as the inhabitants of the earth lowered their consciousness. As certain co-creators descended to lower levels, they reached the border at which they could no longer take physical embodiment. Because taking physical embodiment is the greatest opportunity for growth, the range was adjusted downwards so that co-creators could receive more opportunities to be in embodiment.

Again, this may seem strange, but the explanation is that the ascended masters are not so concerned about the state of the physical planet. Earth is an educational institution and the purpose of its existence is to help the students. There is no specific blueprint for what should or should not happen physically on earth. The overall blueprint is to give co-creators the greatest possible opportunity to raise their consciousness. The earth is presently geared towards helping those who have gone below the 48th level of consciousness. The primary goal for earth is to help people grow; not to produce a certain state of perfection or purity.

The ascended masters have a plan to raise the entire planet to a higher level. As this process unfolds, the range of consciousness will be shifted upwards. The level has already been adjusted upwards since the planet was at its lowest level. The change will not happen because of decisions made by the ascended masters; it will happen because of decisions made by those in embodiment. This is a twofold process:

- Right now, many people on earth have made themselves blind followers of certain fallen leaders who are close to the lowest level of consciousness. A critical mass of people must come to see the power plays of these fallen beings and separate themselves from them before a change can happen.

- The people in the top ten percent are working on raising their consciousness towards the 144th level. A critical mass of people need to reach the higher levels before a change can happen.

As these two conditions are fulfilled, the ascended masters can raise the range of consciousness possible on earth. The entire spectrum will be shifted upwards so that what is now the 144th level will be the 143rd level. Instead, it will be possible to rise to the next level up while still remaining in physical embodiment. At the low end, what is now the first level will disappear and the present second level will be the lowest. The fallen beings who are now at the lowest level of consciousness can no longer take physical embodiment.

As the spectrum of consciousness is shifted upwards, certain fallen beings will no longer be allowed to take physical embodiment, and this will have a tremendous impact on the collective consciousness. Beings at the lowest level are completely ruthless in terms of manipulating others and they have great skill and experience. It is clear from history how persons like Hitler, Stalin and Mao could hold the population of an entire country in their grips. Today, the spectrum of consciousness has been shifted upwards so that fallen beings with this combination of ruthlessness and power can no longer take physical embodiment. At the same time, beings with a higher level of consciousness can now take embodiment and help raise the collective consciousness even more.

The real cause of conflict

When a new co-creator first takes embodiment on earth, it comes in at the 48th level of consciousness. This is what can be called the "neutral" level for earth. At this level, a co-creator has a point-like sense of self, meaning it sees everything from its own vantage point and is completely focused on itself. At the 48th level, you do not see other co-creators as threats, competitors or enemies.

A new co-creator will be offered the path of initiation under the ascended masters. This path has always been available, even when the earth was at a lower level than today. If you follow this path, you will be initiated in seven levels, one for each of the seven spiritual rays. This is a complete course in how to use your co-creative abilities and it will take you to the 96th level of consciousness.

During these 49 levels of initiation, you will be completely focused on your own growth. Your task is to expand your sense of self and to attain mastery over your co-creative abilities on the seven rays. You are focused on personal growth, but you do not see yourself in competition with others. You are not threatened by their growth and simply focus on yourself. At the 96th level, you need to go beyond the focus on self in order to pass the last initiations towards the 144th level. This is what the ascended masters call the initiations of Christhood. (The seven levels of initiation from the 48th to the 96th level are described in a series of books called *The Path to Self-Mastery*.)

When you go below the 48th level of consciousness, a major shift happens in your mind. At the 48th level you see yourself as a localized being who is still connected to something greater than yourself (this is your I AM Presence although you do not see it clearly). When you go below the 48th level, you see yourself as a separate being and you lose the sense of being connected.

At the 48th level and above you have an inner, intuitive connection to the ascended masters and your I AM Presence. This means you have a frame of reference that there is a higher reality than the perception you have through your four lower bodies. Below the 48th level your intuition is far less and you become more susceptible to believing the perception produced by your four lower bodies. You also lose the sense that the ascended masters are real, and you become much more likely to believe the fallen beings and the thought systems they have created. The fallen beings in all four octaves now become your teachers.

At the 47th level and those close to it you still have a sense of empathy with other people. As you descend towards the lowest levels, you gradually lose this empathy completely. That is why you see certain serial killers, psychopaths or dictators who have no respect whatsoever for the value of human life or for other people's free will. They are either completely insensitive to the suffering of other people or they firmly believe that the end of accomplishing some greater goal can justify the killing of millions of people.

As people go below the 48th level, they begin to feel progressively threatened by other people. This explains virtually all human conflict. For example, it explains why people can believe that although their religion tells them: "Thou shalt not kill," God still wants them to kill non-believers. It also explains why people can believe in the illusion that harming others will have no effect on themselves. People at the lowest levels think they are a law onto themselves and that they can define their own laws here on earth that make them exempt from the laws defined by God or society. When you are above the 48th level, you can see that this simply is not true. When you are at the lower levels, it seems possible and logical.

One possible definition of evil

We can now define evil (at least at the human level) as the result of people going below the 48th level of consciousness. The lower you go, the more you lose any sense of being connected to a higher reality outside your own perception filter. You also lose any sense of being connected to other people. You can now define your own "reality" according to which you can do anything you want and it is always necessary and justified according to some greater good.

One example is Joseph Stalin who probably believed he was doing what he did in order to uphold and expand the vision of a communist utopia defined by Marx and Lenin. In reality, Stalin had gone to the lowest level of consciousness possible on earth, meaning that to him, he was the only human being of any significance.

Stalin would do anything to maintain his position of absolute power. He had many people who helped him defend this position, but if any one of them had become a threat (real or perceived), they would instantly have been killed in order to keep Stalin in power. This explains why he could kill 21 million people in the Soviet Union in order to stay in power. In Stalin's mind, there was essentially no other human being who had the same significance as himself. Of course, Hitler and Mao had descended to the same low level of consciousness as had several other historical leaders.

8 | THE SUBTLE WORKINGS OF FREE WILL

The traditional Christian teaching about the devil and hell gives rise to certain questions that are not easily answered within the context of Christian doctrine. This explains why many churches discourage people from asking such questions. One of the more baffling questions is: "If God is almighty and if God is good, why does God allow the devil and hell to exist?" The ascended masters have a clear answer: *God* does not allow the devil and hell to exist—*we human beings do*.

We who are in physical embodiment have the authority – according to the Law of Free Will – to decide what is allowed and not allowed on this planet. We are not only allowing hell to exist; we have created it—collectively of course. Obviously, we have not done this in full knowledge of what we were doing, and we have not done it alone. The fallen beings who have come to earth have helped created the evil that exists on this planet, yet this is only possible because the rest of us are allowing it. The fallen beings are the ones who came up with the idea for the greatest atrocities, but if our consciousness had not descended below the 48th level, these events could not have taken place on earth.

The School of Hard Knocks

When you begin to realize that there is more to understand about life than what you were told in school or Sunday school, it is easy to feel that God has deceived us. Why hasn't God or the ascended masters given us a religious or spiritual teaching that contains the full truth about evil? The explanation is complex, but the bottom line is free will.

No co-creator has ever descended into physical embodiment on earth without being prepared for this experience and its challenges. This preparation has happened in the retreats that the ascended masters maintain in the identity octave (depending on your background, it could have happened on another planet or in a previous sphere). In these retreats (as symbolized in the story of the Garden of Eden) we receive instructions from the ascended masters about the challenges we will face. If we are being prepared to embody on a planet with fallen beings, there will be a serpent in the garden so we can learn about the subtleties of the fallen consciousness.

When we first descend, we have the option to maintain and expand our inner connection with the ascended masters. We can then be in embodiment and receive instructions through the "School of Inner Direction." If we choose to descend below the 48th level of consciousness, seeing ourselves as separate beings, we lose this connection. We then turn our minds into closed systems and become deceived by our own thoughts. Or we become susceptible to the many illusions created by the fallen beings. How will we learn when we no longer receive direct instructions from the ascended masters? We might learn from outer teachings, such as a religion on earth, many of which were originally given by the ascended masters. As history shows, outer teachings are subject to interpretations and it is possible for people to turn a non-violent teaching into a justification for violence.

In order to make sure that we can never lose the opportunity to learn, the universe is set up as a kind of mirror. Almost all religions contain the concept that we should do onto others what we want them to do to us. The deeper principle behind this is that the universe will return to us the energy impulses we project with the four levels of our minds.

When we descend below the 48th level of consciousness, we lose the conscious awareness of the co-creative powers of our minds but we do not stop co-creating. We are constantly sending out subconscious thought matrices imbued with emotional energy, and the Ma-ter Light must take on any form projected upon it.

The higher way to grow is to receive inner direction from the ascended masters. The lower way is to see the physical octave outpicture the contents of our minds. This is what the ascended masters call the "School of Hard Knocks."

We can undo any mistake

It may seem harsh that we can unwittingly produce as severe physical consequences as what we see on earth. Yet there is no physical condition that we cannot rise above by transcending the state of consciousness that created it.

We grow in self-awareness through the interplay of having immersion and awakening experiences. We first go into a specific sense of self, and for a time we are completely identified with that self. By seeing the physical circumstances produced through this self, we can eventually awaken to the realization that we are more than that sense of self—and that is how we grow in self-awareness.

From an overall perspective, it is not a disaster that we descend below the 48th level and identify ourselves with a separate self that acts in very selfish ways. Regardless of what kind of self we go into, we can always awaken from that self. When we *do* awaken, we will grow in self-awareness.

In order to awaken from a separate self, we have to be willing to admit that the separate self (and its perception filter) is not real. For some, this becomes difficult when combined with the serpentine value judgment of right and wrong. The fallen consciousness adds a value judgment to everything, and this defines a penalty for being wrong. Instead of admitting that the separate self is not real and that you are more (thus leaving behind the separate self) you can go into a mindset in which you do not want to admit that you have been wrong (according to the serpent's standard; not God's standard). You start defending the separate self and its perception of the world.

This causes you to lose all frame of reference from outside the now closed system of your mind and you are unreachable for a spiritual teacher. Instead, you must be taught by experiencing the consequences of your actions, and this is primarily done through the principle described in the second law of thermodynamics. In a closed system, disorder will increase because it will inevitably contain internal contradictions. These contradictions will create resistance that forces you to go towards more and more extreme positions. The more extreme you become, the more resistance you create. You will eventually create a resistance that you cannot overcome. Your self-created resistance forces you to change direction in life and admit that something must be "wrong" with the way you see the world. Resistance is a form of friction and friction creates heat. Hell can be seen as the dwelling place of beings who have created maximum internal resistance. That is why hell has so often been seen as a very hot place with scorching fire.

The ascended masters are not deliberately withholding the truth from us. They are always ready to help us grow and they are willing to help us raise this planet to a level where no fallen being can embody here.

The need for a cosmic delay factor

Originally, the earth was designed as an environment in which new beings would enter at the 48th level of consciousness and then follow the path towards the 96th level. When a substantial number of people chose to go below the 48th level, a shift occurred. The very fact that this shift was allowed to occur shows that God and the ascended masters have absolute respect for free will and that they have unconditional love for us. No matter what choices we make, they seek only to raise us up; never to punish us.

Consider the specific problem created when many people descended below the 48th level. The material universe is designed as the cosmic mirror. In the original state, whenever you projected out a thought matrix, it would instantly be returned to you. This is a very non-forgiving environment because if you make one mistake, you could be dead. This is, or course, what we see around us. There are certain mistakes that will instantly take you out of embodiment and nature is unforgiving. If you jump off a cliff, gravity will indeed cause you to fall to your death.

Originally, you would follow the path from the 48th to the 96th level by being under the direct tutelage of an ascended master. The master would act as a buffer between you and the instant return of what you sent out (what is often called your karma). In this way you can make many mistakes without experiencing the full karmic return of your actions because the teacher acts as a buffer. This is comparable to a flight simulator where you can make a mistake without killing yourself and 300 passengers.

When people go below the 48th level and set themselves outside the protection of a spiritual teacher, there is no buffer between themselves and the instant return of their karma. This is not necessarily a bad learning environment. After all, we have all learned not to jump off cliffs unless we really want to die. One could say that if you no longer want the protection of a teacher, it is perfectly just that your karma is instantly returned to you, even if it kills you.

There is, however, a problem. An environment in which everything is instantly returned to you makes it impossible to have certain experiences. Let us use the example that you want to experience what it is like to be a great warrior who can defeat other people in battle. Say you are born and go through the rather rigorous process of growing up, and then you start training to become a warrior. After several years of training with great dedication, you go into your first battle. The moment you attempt to kill someone else – the moment you project out the mental impulse to kill – you are killed by an instant karmic return. How could you actually have the experience of being a great warrior?

Obviously, this applies to many of the experiences you can have as a separate self that, by definition, does what it wants to do regardless of the consequences. In a world with instant karmic return, you really can't have the experience of acting as a separate self. Because the Law of Free Will makes it possible for human beings to go below the 48th level, the planet was designed with this in mind.

The cosmic buffer

The driving force in your life is spiritual energy descending from your I AM Presence. The energy is filtered through your identity, mental and emotional bodies before it becomes translated into a physical action (or inaction). In the example of a warrior, this works as follows:

- A warrior has a sense of identity as a warrior. In his identity body, the energy is colored by this matrix. A certain amount of energy is generated in the identity octave.

- In his mental body he has certain ideas, such as battle strategy, the sense of wanting to further a good cause and how to use weapons. Again, a certain amount of energy is generated in the mental octave.

- In his feeling body he has certain feelings that drive him to go into battle with the necessary force. They may range from outright hatred of the enemy to a desire to fight for a cause. Again, a certain amount of energy is generated in the emotional spectrum.

Through his three higher bodies, the warrior is sending out a powerful and aggressive energy matrix. He goes into a physical battle, yet the cosmic mirror does not instantly return to him the fullness of the energy he is projecting out. Instead, the energy at the etheric, mental and emotional levels go into those octaves and is not returned to him in the material realm. This makes it possible for you to kill someone else without being instantly killed by a karmic return. As a side note, when you go into battle, you may meet up against an enemy who is more skilled than you and you might be killed. This is not the result of a karmic return but a result of how things work out at the physical level.

The Law of Free Will mandates that you can do whatever you want with the energy allotted to you, but it also mandates that whatever you send out must be returned to you. The energy at the etheric, mental and emotional levels will indeed be returned to you, but it will happen at a future time. Albert Einstein talked about a curved space-time continuum. He said that if you traveled out from earth in a spaceship and kept going in the same direction, you would eventually return to your starting point from the opposite direction. The etheric, mental and emotional octaves form such a curved continuum. Any energy impulse you send out, will come back to you— only it will happen at a future time. If you continue to identify yourself as a warrior, there will come a time when you are killed as the result of a karmic return.

The four octaves of the material world form a delay factor that makes it possible for us to have certain experiences. We can have the experience of being a warrior, and for a time we can be completely immersed in it. We also have the potential to awaken from that experience before the karmic return of our actions comes full circle. If we do raise our consciousness sufficiently, then we will not have to be killed even if we killed others in the past. If we truly transcend the level of consciousness at which we killed others, we can use our higher awareness to transmute the karmic energy before it comes full circle as a physical event. We can transmute the energy at the etheric, mental and emotional levels so that the impulse does not break through into the physical and manifests as an actual event.

Why bad things happen to good people

These ideas might at first seem very complex, but they can explain many of the baffling questions of life. For example, take the old question of why bad things can happen to good people. You have a person who for a lifetime has been kind and helpful to others. Then he suddenly dies in a car accident or of a disease. The human mind tends to ask how God could allow this since the person seemingly never did anything to deserve this "punishment."

The explanation is that even though the person has been good in this lifetime, he has not been equally good in previous lifetimes and is now reaping the karmic return of this. Yet there are deeper layers of understanding.

If a person is living a non-violent life, then obviously that person is no longer acting as a completely selfish person. There is a potential that this could be the result of a change at the surface level. For example, a person who has lived several lifetimes in a Christian environment can be so influenced by Christian doctrines that he modifies his outer behavior in order to conform to Christian ideals. This does not necessarily mean that he has gone through a change at the deeper levels of consciousness. A person can change his or her behavior at the physical level without going through a corresponding change in the emotional, mental or identity bodies.

Before the United States invaded Iraq in 2003, several prominent Christian leaders openly supported the war. Every Sunday, these leaders would preach the traditional Christian ideals to their congregation, namely turning the other cheek and doing onto others. How could they support a war and even claim it was justified by God or Christ? The only possible explanation is that such people have made certain changes to their outer behavior but they have not truly transcended the consciousness in which killing others seems justifiable under certain conditions.

Such people have not overcome the consciousness that in past lives might have caused them to kill others. They have not raised themselves above the possibility of a karmic return. This explains why a person can seem like a good person but still experience great misfortune.

Another possibility is that a person truly has forsaken the lower level of consciousness, yet the person has not learned how to use energy to transmute a karmic return at the etheric, mental and emotional levels. The energy must inevitably be returned as a physical event once the karmic cycle comes full circle. This is one reason the ascended masters have given us spiritual tools for transmuting returning karma before it becomes physical (see *www.transcendencetoolbox.com*).

Negative spirals

What happens when people start accumulating energy in the emotional, mental and etheric octaves? In the beginning, it will seem as if nothing happens, but as the accumulated energy increases in intensity, it will begin to pull on your feelings, thoughts and sense of identity.

As an example, consider a person who has a tendency to respond to certain situations with anger. As more and more anger energy accumulates, it forms a magnetic force that pulls on his emotions and makes him more prone to responding with anger. It takes less and less of an outer provocation to cause him to become angry. Some people live in a state of

8 | The Subtle Workings of Free Will

perpetual anger and will express anger even when there is no outer reason.

There is no point in being a warrior if there is no one to fight. The very concept of a warrior implies that there is an enemy. When you desire to be a warrior, you are indirectly saying to the universe that you want to experience a situation where you have an enemy to fight. The people who make up your enemy have the same frame of mind as you do. They will see you as an enemy, and they will sometimes kill you before you can kill them.

You will see this as an unjustifiable aggression on their part and it will make you angry. As more and more anger accumulates, you become more and more prone to respond with violence and you feel the violence is justified. It becomes increasingly difficult for you to question the perception filter of the warrior. You become stuck in that sense of self, and you become more and more violent and aggressive. You are now stuck in a personal downward spiral. Your conscious will is overpowered by the raging maelstrom of energy in your emotional body, which literally pulls you into certain reactionary patterns.

When a large number of people go into such a spiral, they all produce the same kinds of energies, such as anger. These energies exist within the planetary energy field. The more energy that accumulates, the more intense it becomes, meaning it can overpower even large groups of people. When a nation goes to war, most of the citizens have been overpowered by a collective momentum of energy that makes war seem unavoidable and justifiable. As a practical example, the United States considers itself to be a Christian nation. After the September 11, 2001 World Trade Center attack, many American Christians felt it was justifiable to strike back, even though Jesus told us to turn the other cheek. In the previous book I used the example of the Palestinians and Israelis, and they have also created their respective maelstroms of emotional energy. The same can be found in many places on earth.

The ascended masters teach that in past ages, certain civilizations on earth built such a collective momentum on warfare that they eventually destroyed themselves. In those past ages, there were as many people in physical embodiment as today. After continued warfare caused the collapse of civilizations (and often caused cataclysmic "natural" disasters), there followed periods where there were far fewer people in physical embodiment. A hunter-gatherer society can only support a very small number of people. In the stone age, there were only a few million people in embodiment worldwide. Where were the souls of the people who could not get a physical body at the time?

Those souls were still evolving by being in the emotional, mental or identity octaves—depending on their level of consciousness. For example, if a soul was below the 48th level of consciousness and had a long history of violence, it would magnetize itself to one of the levels of the emotional realm. Here, it could experience a situation similar to what it had last experienced in the physical realm, meaning it could continue to fight enemies.

Beings who must steal energy from others

The purpose of everything is to give self-aware beings the best possible opportunities to grow. The purpose of allowing souls to stay in the emotional octave is that they will grow tired of fighting and begin to awaken from this immersion experience. If they cannot break their downward spirals, they can get stuck in the emotional realm whereby it becomes difficult for them to embody even when physical bodies are available. When you go below the 48th level, you begin to misqualify the energy you receive from your I AM Presence. This means the energy cannot rise back up, and thus the Presence has nothing to multiply. The net result is that you gradually have less and less energy available to you from Above. The wisdom of this is that the less energy you have, the less karma you can make. When you display a desire to control others, you lose some of your power, and thus there is a limit to how much control you can have over others.

There is, however, one way to gain control over others. If you can get them to voluntarily give you their energy, then you can use that power to control them and get them to give you more energy. If you go below the 48th level, the only way to gain control over other people and become a powerful leader is by stealing energy from other people. We will later look at how dark beings can steal energy from humans. The conclusion is that there are some beings who need to steal energy from others in order to increase their power or even survive.

As a practical example, consider the mass rallies staged by Adolf Hitler, especially before the war. By whipping people into a fanatical frenzy, Hitler got them to give their energy to him and the non-material forces behind him. It was this energy that allowed Hitler to strengthen his power over the German people.

Why fallen beings can exist

Dark or fallen beings are allowed to exist because free will must be allowed to outplay itself. When people will not learn from the ascended masters, they must be allowed to outplay their separate selves until they begin to awaken and decide that they want to experience a higher form of self. It is a matter of how far into selfishness and insanity people have to go before they decide that they have had enough.

By allowing the fallen beings to embody on earth, the ascended masters accelerated the process that people on earth had chosen to start. The fallen beings are "helping" people take the consciousness of separation into extremes at a much faster rate. This raises the possibility that people on earth will have had enough sooner than otherwise. Of course, the fallen beings are not doing this out of the goodness of their hearts. They are doing it because they are trapped in their own negative spirals and cannot do anything else.

One can say that after people had turned away from the true teachers of the ascended masters, the fallen beings became the substitute teachers for humankind. The only way to remove evil from earth is that a critical mass of people decide to transcend the consciousness of evil and rise above the 48th level. People must be willing to change themselves instead of seeking to change others by controlling them. The true path of growth is one of controlling yourself instead of controlling others.

A substantial part of what we call evil forces are self-aware beings who have used their free will to go below the 48th level of awareness. As long as these beings stay above the lowest level of consciousness allowed in the physical realm, they can still take physical embodiment. Even if they go below this level, they can still be allowed to stay in the emotional octave where they can continue to control people in embodiment, trying to steal our energy.

This is allowed only because we who are in embodiment are choosing to misqualify energy that accumulates in the emotional realm. We misqualify this energy by holding on to a sense of self that is below the 48th level. We will later talk about how we can – individually and collectively – do something to change this situation.

We who are in physical embodiment decide what is allowed on earth, even in the emotional, mental and etheric octaves. Based on this understanding, we have a better foundation for taking a closer look at evil forces.

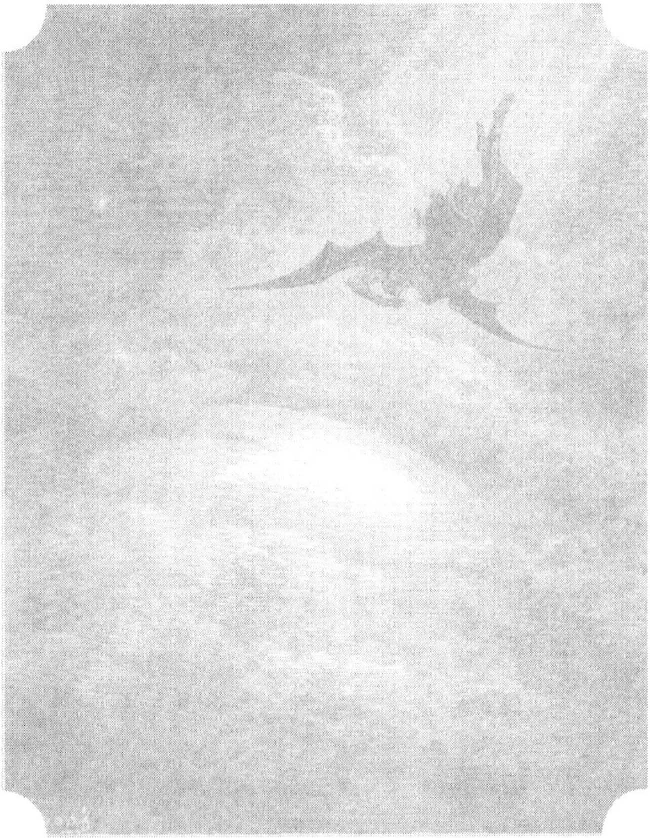

9 | THE EXISTENCE OF AN EVIL FORCE

So far, we have looked at evil as an abstract idea or a state of consciousness. In this and the coming chapters, we will look at the beings who embody the consciousness of evil and therefore form a force that seeks to deliberately and aggressively control human beings. We will look at the motives and methods used by this force. This will empower us to attain a much deeper understanding of evil, and it will also help us see what we can do about evil on the personal and planetary level. We will, naturally, build on the description of the cosmos given previously.

Why are dark forces allowed to exist?

Let us summarize why it is even possible for an evil force to exist. The explanation begins with the fact that the purpose of the cosmos is that individual co-creators start out with a localized, point-like sense of self and then expands it until they reach the same level of selfhood as the Creator who created our cosmos. This process is possible because an individual co-creator has self-awareness. This gives us the ability to not simply live as we have done in the past. We can step back and consider who we are right now and who we want to be. We can become aware that our sense of self is limited and we can consciously decide to expand it.

The expansion of self must involve free will. This has two levels:

- We make decisions about what we do in our immediate environment (in our case, the physical octave on earth). This helps us become aware of our own creative powers and how our world functions.

- While we can live unaware lives, we do have the potential to examine ourselves and our lives. As Socrates said: "The unexamined life is not worth living." By becoming aware of how we see ourselves, we can make deliberate choices to change and to expand our sense of self.

The higher purpose of giving us free will is that we will expand our self-awareness, which is in alignment with the purpose of the cosmos. In order for free will to be complete, we must have the option to refuse to expand our self-awareness and thereby go against the purpose of the cosmos. It is precisely this ability to choose to go against the cosmic purpose that creates the possibility of evil. Evil can be seen as the result of an attempt to justify why we go against the cosmic purpose, but there is a distinction to be made:

- A co-creator can stop its own growth, and this choice does not directly affect other co-creators.

- A co-creator can choose to deliberately and aggressively seek to prevent the growth of other co-creators.

By choosing the first option, the co-creator merely stops its own growth and therefore makes itself susceptible to the force described in the second law of thermodynamics. By choosing the second option, the co-creator enters into the fallen consciousness and may become a fallen being when its sphere ascends.

The first option is not evil because the co-creator is merely exercising its individual free will. It is the second option that gives rise to evil because it seeks to violate the free will of other co-creators. While this is possible, it is a violation of the principle or law that each co-creator has the right to exercise its free will according to its own choices only.

Where can dark forces exist?

The first four spheres were created with one layer or level. In the fourth sphere, the first co-creators fell. Since then, succeeding spheres have been created with multiple levels. Our sphere has four levels, and this was done to accommodate four different types of fallen beings.

The four octaves of our sphere can be seen as parallel universes or worlds that co-exist within the same space but at different levels of vibration. In each of the four octaves there is room for evil or dark beings to exist.

This is where the picture becomes complex. Let us first look at the original state of our planet. When earth was created, it was created with four levels in order to comply with the overall design of our sphere. The earth was not originally meant to house fallen beings, and the four octaves that correspond to earth did not have any evil or dark forces in them. In each octave there were beings who served to facilitate the creation of the physical earth. This includes the elemental beings but also beings who were created deliberately to descend into a particular octave. We have so far talked about co-creators who "took embodiment" in the physical octave. There were also co-creators who "took embodiment" in the three higher octaves. Depending on how we use words, these could also be called angels but they are not ascended angels.

The beings in the three higher octaves served a twofold purpose. They would receive both higher energies and a blueprint from the beings at the level above theirs. They would then use their co-creative abilities to pass on both the energies and the blueprint to the level below theirs. In doing this, the beings in the higher octaves could exercise free will and creativity, yet they could not forget or ignore the fact that they were ministering to other beings below their octave. Ultimately, all of them were ministering to us in the physical octave.

In the physical octave we have no beings below us that we minister onto. In a sense, this is easier for us, but because of the greater density of the energies in the physical octave, our task is still more demanding than in the three higher octaves.

When the inhabitants of the earth created a downward spiral, the picture changed. The types of fallen beings that could take physical embodiment corresponded to the levels of consciousness to which the inhabitants of the earth had descended. All fallen beings are below the 48th level. When the inhabitants had descended to the 33rd level, fallen beings with a level of consciousness between the 33rd and the 47th level could come to earth. Eventually, the inhabitants of the earth descended further in consciousness. As this happened, fallen beings with an even lower level of consciousness could come to earth, and they are now found in all four octaves.

9 | The Existence of an Evil Force

For the physical earth to continue to exist, there must be a continuous stream of energy from the spiritual realm into the identity octave. This must be stepped down to the mental octave. From here, it must be stepped down to the emotional octave and from there to the physical octave. Fallen beings cannot serve in this process, and there are two reasons for this:

- Fallen beings cannot receive energies from a higher level than their own. They cannot take higher energies into their beings but can only take in energies from their own level or a lower level.

- Fallen beings cannot pass on pure energies to those below them. They will always seek to control those below them, and it is a law that beings in the physical octave must be able to receive pure energies from above.

There is still a part of each of the higher octaves that is untouched by the fallen beings. In each octave there are beings who have not taken on the fallen consciousness and they serve to fulfill their original function. This is possible because the higher octaves have more than one level.

Each of the four octaves is made from energies that vibrate within a certain spectrum. These energies have more than one property. For example, visible light can be described by its frequency, amplitude and wavelength. Other forms of energy (such as what physicists call subatomic particles) have other properties, such as angular momentum and spin. It is these properties that can be varied in order to create several levels in the higher octaves.

The energies that make up the physical octave can exist in only one level. Our physical bodies are the only kind of bodies we can use to act directly in the physical octave. Because the energies of the three higher octaves are less dense, their properties can be used to create several levels. After the fallen beings started coming to earth, several levels were created in the three higher octaves. This created a separation between the fallen beings and those who had not taken on the fallen consciousness, and this ensured the flow of pure energy.

For example, a being can fall only by going below the 48th level of consciousness, meaning there are currently 47 levels of fallen consciousness allowed on earth. If a being goes below the lowest level of consciousness, it cannot continue to take physical embodiment. This being can still remain with earth, only it now goes into one of the levels created in the emotional octave (also called the astral plane).

Dark beings in other octaves

Throughout history, many cultures have had a belief in mythological creatures, such as dragons or demons. Some people believe that such creatures existed in the physical realm and had actual physical power to harm us. The ascended masters say that such creatures do exist—just not in the physical octave.

The emotional octave has a broader spectrum of vibrations than the physical. Within this spectrum there are a number of divisions or levels that are separated from each other by their vibration. Throughout humankind's history, a substantial amount of negative feelings have been generated. Once energy takes on a certain vibration, it can stay in that vibration indefinitely and that means there is a huge accumulation of negative feelings in the emotional body of the planet. The variations in the characteristics and the intensity of these energies have created the divisions in the emotional realm, ranging from not so low to very low. If you go into the emotional realm, you encounter various layers that progress towards levels that are similar to the visions of hell that people have had throughout history. People have had these visions by tuning their minds to these levels of vibration. For those who are not aware of what is happening, these experiences can seem so real that the creatures people encounter can seem to be physical.

Hell does not exist as a physical place. It was not created by God as a place for punishment, and the existence of this realm is not inevitable. Hell was created through the misuse of free will and the generation of emotional energy of a low vibration. In the emotional realm, you find a number of levels that are similar to what people have seen as hell. These realms contain various beings or creatures that resemble the visions of mythological creatures, devils, demons and evil spirits.

The mental realm also contains a number of levels, and here you find beings that are not able to ascend to the spiritual realm and not able to descend into physical embodiment. These beings are not like the normal visions of evil spirits. They can best be described by referring to the story of the Garden of Eden and the serpent. It is said that the serpent was more "subtil" than the other animals in the garden. This describes beings in the mental realm who seek to use the illusions of the serpentine mind in order to deceive human beings. Obviously, the beings in the emotional realm seek to overpower us through feelings, and the beings in the mental realm seek to deceive us through thoughts.

Finally, we have the identity realm that is the most pure. It also has a number of levels, and the higher ones are entirely free from selfish beings. Instead, these higher levels house the etheric retreats of the ascended masters. These retreats serve as anchor points through which the masters can release their energies to the material world. They also serve as schoolrooms where we can travel at night (in our identity bodies) and receive instruction and assistance in order to accelerate our spiritual growth. Most spiritual people have gone to these retreats, and we sometimes have dream-like memories of the retreats or what we have learned.

In the lower levels of the etheric realm, you do find beings who still have some elements of duality and they seek to deceive us into taking on a false sense of identity. These beings are also similar to the serpent, but instead of using intellectual or analytical tools, they seek to get us to accept a sense of identity that is out of alignment with who we really are. For example, they may try to get us to accept that we are merely human beings and that our capabilities can never exceed those of the physical body. They may also seek to get us to accept that we are spiritual beings who belong to a special category, and therefore we have capabilities and a mission that is more important that those of anyone else. Or they may seek to get us to follow them blindly because they claim to be our real teachers.

What we normally see as evil, dark or demonic beings do not exist in the physical octave and thus they do not have direct, physical power over us. They can influence us only through the emotional, mental or identity levels of the mind. Evil beings exist in all three levels, even though the forces in the mental and identity octaves do not appear to be dark. They may appear as "an angel of light" because their consciousness can be higher than that of most people in embodiment.

Throughout history, beings in the mental or identity octaves have appeared to or worked with human beings in order to give various religious or spiritual teachings. Because such teachings do not come from the ascended masters, they contain subtle errors, depending of the level of consciousness of those who created them. They may still have many correct ideas, but they cannot take you higher than the level of consciousness from with they originated. That is why it is important to reach for the teachings from the ascended masters who have gone beyond all limitations.

Evil beings without free will

So far, we have talked about evil beings only in the form of fallen beings. They are beings who were created as co-creators or angels and who have self-awareness and free will. They were not created to be evil but became dark as a result of their own choosing. There is also a type of evil beings who do not have free will. These beings were not created by God or the ascended masters; they were created by co-creators or by fallen beings.

This is possible because everything is created from the Ma-ter Light. The light has consciousness but not self-awareness. If a being with self-awareness designs a sufficiently complex thought matrix and imbues it with enough psychic energy, then the matrix itself will take on a form of consciousness as a distinct entity. This entity can acquire a survival instinct and an awareness of how it increases its power by taking energy from its surroundings (including human beings).

Such a dark entity is comparable to a robot that is programmed to perform a particular function. It can also be compared to an animal on earth. For example, imagine you are walking through a jungle and come across a tiger. The tiger is not evil, but on the other hand it has no self-awareness and cannot consciously change its behavior. If the tiger is hungry, it will do you no good to try to reason with it. Saying that the tiger should not eat you because you are such a nice person or have an important spiritual mission will have no effect. The tiger simply isn't capable of reasoning that way and neither is a dark entity. You may be able to reason with a fallen being and such a being can choose to turn around and expand its self-awareness (it is not likely, but it is possible because a fallen being has some self-awareness). An evil entity does not have this capacity and such beings need to be dissolved in order for us to escape their influence. The earth is currently deeply affected by such evil beings, and it will require a major work on behalf of the spiritual people to get this planet back to a state of purity. By invoking the intercession of the ascended masters, this is a doable task.

There are evil beings behind every form of conflict and behind every form of problem. War and any kind of addiction are but two examples. We will now take a closer look at specific types of evil beings.

10 | TYPES OF EVIL FORCES

We now have a better foundation for defining what is meant by the label "evil forces" or "dark forces." The design of the entire world of form is a hierarchical structure. At the top is the Creator, and its energy is the driving force that makes it possible to create and maintain any form. Only beings in the highest level of the spiritual realm can receive the Creator's energy directly. They reduce its vibration and pass it on to beings in the second sphere. This process continues until the energy reaches our sphere, which is the last one in the chain. Take note that only beings who are created as an extension of the spiritual hierarchy can receive energy from a level above themselves.

The law that guides this flow of energy is simple: You get an initial or basic allotment of energy as a free gift. Beyond that, you will receive only a multiplication of your positive use of that energy. If you use the energy in an effort to raise your own consciousness and the sphere in which you live, this energy will be abundantly multiplied. If you use the energy to seek to control or destroy other beings with free will, then there is nothing that can be multiplied.

The effect of this law is simple. If you do not lock in to the flow of seeking to raise all life, you will receive less and less energy. It is possible for you to cut yourself off from the flow of energy from Above. You then need to steal energy from your own level in order to survive or in order to expand your powers. If you cut yourself off from the vertical flow of energy, you need to acquire energy horizontally. If you cannot – *will* not – receive energy from the spiritual realm, you must seek to get it from this sphere.

The simplest definition of evil or dark forces is this: Evil forces are beings who seek to take energy from other beings in our unascended sphere, especially from those who still receive energy from the spiritual realm. We can call these forces "dark" because they have no internal light.

At first, this might seem like a surprising definition, especially compared to the popular image of a devil who is always identifiable as being dark or evil (having horns, hoofed feet, a pointy tail, etcetera). There is a popular belief that evil forces are clearly identifiable as such but this is not always the case.

We are used to looking at world history as a giant competition for material resources, but behind this surface spectacle the driving force of the universe is energy, especially non-material energy. The basic dynamic in the world is a giant competition for taking control over non-material energy and using it to gain some advantage in the material world.

Evil forces are not simply beings who appear evil. They might very well appear perfectly benign. Some evil beings are embodied as human beings and some human beings are controlled by dark forces in one of the three higher octaves. The devil just might be the person next door. While this might seem frightening, as always, knowledge will show you how to protect yourself. Let us now take a look at the various types of evil forces.

Evil forces in the physical octave

What has traditionally been seen as evil forces, such as mythological creatures or demonic beings, do not exist in the physical realm and do not have physical power over us. When we take the definition that evil forces are beings who seek to take energy from human beings, we see that there are human beings who seek to take energy from others.

Again an obvious example from history is Adolf Hitler. Hitler staged mass rallies with tens of thousands of people because he needed people's energy in order to expand his power. It would be naive to think that all among the German people had been cut off from receiving energy from their I AM Presences. When these people were deceived into literally worshiping Hitler as a God, they gave to him some of the energy they had received from Above (after lowering its vibration). They also gave him energy through the anger they directed at the Jews or the nations that dictated the conditions after the first world war.

Hitler himself was cut off from higher energy so he needed other people's energy for his own survival. He also needed their energy in order to expand the hypnotic power he had over the German nation, a power that grew steadily during the 1930s. When the war started, Hitler used the energy he had stolen as a driving force for his armies, which explains the uncanny victories won by the German forces in the early stages of the war. As the energy became depleted, the German forces started losing, and the war slowly turned. We now see a sobering reality about the physical octave. The devil cannot take on physical form and harm you physically, but other human beings do indeed have that power. The ascended masters teach that before we take embodiment on earth, we learn about life on this planet. In the material realm, free will reigns supreme. When you are in physical embodiment, there is no guarantee that you cannot be harmed by other people who misuse their free will, perhaps with an aggressive intent to control you. God or the ascended masters cannot interfere with the outplaying of free will.

This is one of these basic facts that it is wise to accept. The problem is that many spiritual people have subconscious memories of how life is in a "place" where there are no beings with evil intent. We often have an intuitive sense that life *should* be that way on earth. When we experience man's inhumanity to man, we can feel that this is some kind of injustice. We might even become angry at God for allowing this to happen.

In order to avoid this non-constructive reaction, it is wise to tune in to the instruction we received before coming into embodiment. We were shown that in the physical octave there is much we can do to protect ourselves against being abused by other people. Yet because of free will, there is no absolute guarantee that we will not be hurt.

For example, there is no guarantee that you will not go to work one day in your office in a skyscraper, and then someone will decide to fly an airplane into your building. Even the ascended masters cannot protect us against the outplaying of free will. The door that leads to physical embodiment has a sign above it saying: "Enter at your own risk." Once you accept the risk – and that you chose to come here knowing the risk – you can avoid a negative reaction.

You can then openly consider what you can do to avoid being hurt by other people. The primary thing you can do is to minimize your karmic vulnerability by transcending the lower consciousness and by invoking light to transform the return of karmic impulses from the past. There are people in embodiment who are part of the evil forces associated with planet earth. They will aggressively or deceptively seek to get you to give them your light or energy.

Discarnate souls

There are some human beings in embodiment who will seek to steal your energy, but there are also some human beings out of embodiment who will do this. These are what the ascended masters call discarnates or discarnate souls.

Consider what happens to us after the physical body dies. The ascended masters teach that unless you are ready to ascend, your lifestream (normally called the soul but including the Conscious You, which is not part of the four lower bodies) will leave the body and go into another realm where it stays until you can come into your next embodiment. The question now becomes where souls go between embodiments.

The answer depends on several factors. The first distinction we can make is between lifestreams who are in an upward spiral or a downward spiral. If you are in an upward spiral – where you have some willingness to change yourself – you will be able to accept help from the ascended masters. The masters will want your soul to go to a realm that is higher than the level of consciousness you had while in embodiment.

You may have read about people who had near-death experiences. Many of these people experienced traveling through a tunnel that led them to a great light. Some people interpret this to mean that we go to heaven between embodiments, but that is not the case. Any level that is higher than your current level of consciousness will be experienced as a great light in contrast to your current level. If several people go "into the light," they don't necessarily all go to the same place. Some go to the retreats of the ascended masters in the identity octave. Others go to a level of wish-fulfillment where they can live out some of the non-destructive desires they had on earth (this can be in the identity, mental or emotional octave).

When a soul who is in an upward spiral leaves embodiment, it generally has an assigned place to go. There are some souls who are afraid of going into the light or unwilling to do so, and they become discarnate souls, meaning they are neither in a physical body nor in a learning environment. They will join the type of souls who are not in an upward spiral.

Souls who are not in an upward spiral are unwilling or unable to take advantage of what is offered by the ascended masters. They will not be forced to go into the light, as the light makes them very uncomfortable. Instead, they will go to a realm that corresponds to their level of consciousness. A few of these souls can go to the lower levels of the mental realm, but most of them go into the emotional realm. The lower levels of the emotional realm form what the ascended masters call the "astral plane." This is where you find successively lower levels that bear a greater and greater resemblance to hell. The lower the level, the more selfish the beings you find there.

Some of the souls who have not gone too far below the 48th level can come back into a physical body after some time. The more selfish souls are likely to become stuck in the astral plane on an indefinite basis. Such souls will have to steal light from other discarnate souls or from human beings in embodiment in order to survive.

One way in which discarnate souls can steal light from you is if you have a personal attachment to them. This is most often a family member, although it can also be a leader or otherwise famous person to whom you have an emotional attachment. It can also be a person towards whom you feel anger or hatred or a person you used to fear.

Some people have several discarnate souls that have attached themselves to their emotional bodies and are siphoning off their vital energy. There are well-documented cases where such discarnate souls have caused multiple personality disorder. In some cases, a person can display signs of a physical illness that the discarnate soul had in its last lifetime. When the person switches out of that "personality," the physical symptoms disappear.

Fallen beings or fallen angels

We have already discussed fallen beings, but let us take a closer look. The linear, analytical mind likes to have clearly defined categories, but on earth things are very complex. There are different types of beings who are allowed to embody on earth and there are different types of discarnate souls and disembodied evil forces.

Originally, the earth was created as a home for a specific number of lifestreams. If the original plan had been fulfilled, only these lifestreams would have embodied on this planet. After a critical mass of these lifestreams descended below the 48th level, it was determined that other types of lifestreams would be allowed to embody on earth.

Some of these lifestreams came from other planets in other solar systems, even other galaxies—yet they still came from our sphere. Some of these beings had a higher level of consciousness than most inhabitants on earth, and they came as a counterbalance for the fallen beings.

As examples of these fallen lifestreams, the ascended masters say that there have been planets where the inhabitants developed such powerful weapons that they destroyed their planet in an all-out war. After the original inhabitants of the earth started killing each other, some lifestreams from destroyed planets were allowed to embody here and they have often continued their warring ways on this planet. This explains why there are regions of earth where groups of people have been at war with each other for thousands of years.

Some groups of lifestreams descended to earth in order to help raise this planet. The most prominent example given by the masters is that in the distant past 144,000 lifestreams descended from Venus and took embodiment on earth. They came with their leader, whose name is Sanat Kumara. Some spiritual people have an intuitive recognition of this name, and the reason is that they were part of the 144,000. There are four rough categories of lifestreams that embody on earth:

- Lifestreams who were created to take embodiment on earth.

- Lifestreams who came from another planet, even another galaxy, in the physical octave.

- Lifestreams who fell into physical embodiment from one of the three higher octaves of our sphere

- Lifestreams who fell in a previous sphere.

This distinction explains something about history that otherwise can be difficult to understand. Since we have already used Hitler several times, let us look at Joseph Stalin. It is debatable whether Stalin truly believed in communist ideals or whether he simply used them as a means to gain personal power. What is not debatable is that he was a typical power person who was willing to do virtually anything to attain and retain power.

Stalin instituted something called "Red Terror," which was the random killing of people without reason or trial. The Soviet Union was a very rule-bound society so one would assume that a person following all the rules and obeying the authorities would not be subject to persecution. Red Terror was designed to strike fear into the population because even the most obedient citizens still risked being arrested and killed.

When you consider the psychology of such a person, you see that Stalin had absolutely no empathy for human beings. The suffering of those killed was not even a concern for Stalin. Of course, we can seek to explain this with psychological factors, such as narcissistic personality disorder or by saying he was a psychopath. The ascended masters say that the deeper explanation is that some of the leaders who have been willing to commit mass murder were lifestreams who had fallen in a higher sphere. They saw themselves as being inherently superior to human beings. They had no empathy with people because they felt no kinship with human beings.

Aside from explaining why this planet has seen so many abusive leaders, it also helps us understand how we can protect ourselves from being controlled by such beings. The beings who fell from a previous sphere have a tendency to set themselves up as being superhuman, as being Gods on earth. This explains why people have worshiped as Gods roman emperors, medieval kings, popes, Stalin, Lenin, Hitler, Mao and even modern rock stars and celebrities. If we buy into this personality cult, we will inevitably be influenced by these lifestreams and the energies behind them. We will give our energies to feeding the beast.

Superiority and inferiority can only exist in the fallen consciousness. In the clear light of the Christ consciousness, all are of equal value to God because all self-aware beings are extensions of the Creator. Either there are no Gods on earth, or we are all Gods on earth.

Nature spirits are not evil

The beings we have looked at so far were not created evil. They descended into the consciousness of separation through their own choosing. This was possible because these beings were created by the ascended masters and they were created with self-awareness and free will. We will now look at a different type of evil beings, namely beings who never had self-awareness.

In a hunter-gatherer society, such as Australian Aborigines, people live in closer contact with nature. Almost all such societies believe that everything is endowed with spirit or consciousness. Modern materialism considers this primitive and superstitious, but in reality such people are simply able to tune in to the basic consciousness behind material forms. Such people often believe that the entire planet has a form of consciousness, often called Mother Earth.

As mentioned before, there are nature spirits, normally called elemental beings or elemental builders of form. These beings act as intermediaries between us humans and the Ma-ter Light. There are elementals at all four levels of the material universe, and as we project out a mental image, the elemental beings take on the identity, mental, emotional and physical components of the image. These beings are what give consciousness to all forms.

The elemental beings do not have self-awareness so they must take on any form projected upon them by self-aware beings (they can receive self-awareness as a result of their service). Elementals can also take on inharmonious forms and energies. As mentioned, many natural disasters are the result of elemental life becoming gradually more burdened by the images and energies projected out by human beings. When this burden becomes too great for the elementals, they can no longer uphold the normal forms. They must release the energy in a violent outburst that can manifest as anything from volcanoes to tornadoes. It is almost like a human being who becomes more and more frustrated until he "loses it" and then feels relieved until the energies again build up.

Human beings have released enormous amounts of misqualified energy, and this has created an ongoing burden for the nature spirits. There are some nature spirits that have been burdened by our energy for a long time, and they live in a constant state of agitation, always being on the brink of losing the ability to uphold normal natural conditions. Because elemental beings do not have self-awareness, they cannot reason that even taking on our negative energy is a service that allows us to outplay free will.

They can know that it is human beings who are causing them to be burdened, and thus they can develop basic emotions, such as anger against human beings. There are elemental beings that have become so burdened and angry that they can be said to be part of the dark forces of earth. This does not mean that elementals are inherently evil or have chosen to be evil. The moment an elemental is freed from the burden of negative energy, it will return to its pure state and perform its original function.

Elementals can also become captured by fallen beings who use them for their destructive purposes. Some fallen beings have learned to use a form of black magic to trap elementals, especially those who have become angry at humans. The fallen beings can then use the elementals to create chaos in nature or manifest particular material forms that outpicture impure thought matrices. For example, fallen beings have forced elementals to create viruses as well as poisonous animals and insects. They have also used elementals to create various phenomena in the emotional and mental octaves.

Internal spirits

Elemental beings are created by the Elohim. We human beings cannot create elementals; we can only change them through our energy projections. We can, however, create beings that resemble elementals, and we do this through our sense of identity, our beliefs and our emotions. We might call this our psychic energy or our co-creative energy.

In order to understand how these beings are created, we need to reach back to the fact that everything is created out of the Ma-ter Light, which has a basic form of consciousness. This consciousness is what allows the Ma-ter Light to respond to an outside stimuli and take on the form of the mental image projected upon the light. The basic consciousness also allows the Ma-ter Light to retain the form for a period of time. The most basic qualities of consciousness are the ability to respond to outside stimuli and the ability to retain a certain form, meaning memory.

As a form grows in size and complexity, it contains more and more of the basic form of consciousness. As a complex form is created, the physical form that we see is only the tip of the iceberg. What we detect with our physical senses and material instruments is only that part of the form that is in the physical octave. Every form also has a component in the identity, mental and emotional octaves. These other components gradually begin to form a being that has a rudimentary form of consciousness. It has a basic sense of identity, it has some ability to think and it has primitive emotions.

We have been given free will to imagine any type of mental image we want and to project it upon the Ma-ter Light. The Law of Free Will mandates that we will experience what we create. We have already talked about the karmic side of this equation. When we send out an energy impulse, it will cycle through all four levels of the material universe, and it will eventually come back to us as a physical event or condition.

In order to project out an impulse, we first have to create an image in the identity and mental bodies and we have to endow it with energy in the emotional body. When we do this, we define a structure and we endow that structure with consciousness. We create a living entity or spirit that has a rudimentary form of identity. It has a basic ability to reason, and it can display the same emotions out of which it was created.

Consider the example of a warrior. A person trains for years to acquire the battle skills necessary to go into battle. Normally, we think this happens by programming the subconscious mind to acquire certain reflexes. The subconscious mind includes the emotional, mental and identity bodies.

As you train to become a warrior, you not only acquire physical skills but also a mindset that might be based on a particular philosophy, such as martial arts. Through this process, you are building a complex internal spirit that can take over your reactions when you go into combat. During combat you do not have time to think consciously or to consider moral or ethical questions. You have to do what you have to do in order to defeat the enemy and survive, and you have to do it quickly. The internal spirit is what enables you to act without taking the time to think

This internal spirit can be considered a sub-personality or even a computer program. It is not self-aware but it does have a form of consciousness. It cannot deliberately change itself and will simply carry out its programming without considering any moral or ethical concerns.

When you create such a spirit, the entity knows that it owes its existence to you. It also knows that it can continue to exist only when you continue to feed it energy and attention. When it grows to a certain size or intensity, it will be able to actively influence you so you keep it alive and even allow it to grow. This was illustrated in the classical story of Doctor Frankenstein. He created a living entity, but his creation sought to control and even destroy him.

The easiest way to explain this is to refer to the discussion in the previous book about a separate self and the ego. A separate self is simply a structure of ideas and beliefs. As the Conscious You goes into it, you enliven it with your attention. This starts creating a living spirit patterned after the structure of the separate self. This spirit becomes your ego, and your ego has a basic survival instinct. Your ego does not want you to grow to a higher level of consciousness because that would eventually kill the ego. The ego actively resists your growth by seeking to keep you trapped in the patterns that created the ego.

Again, take the example of a lifestream who wants to experience what it is like to be a warrior. As the Conscious You begins to have had enough of this experience, it starts looking for a higher way to experience life. The ego will seek to pull you into the old patterns of always seeking to fight an outer enemy so you have no attention left over for looking at the inner enemy, meaning the ego.

The ego and internal spirits form a force that exists inside your own mind. This explains why it is essential to overcome the ego in order to rise to a higher level of consciousness. Beyond the personal element of such a force, we humans have collectively created entities that seek to control us. It is our internal spirits that form an inroad whereby external spirits, fallen beings and other evil forces can influence us.

Collective spirits

In order to explain collective spirits, let us focus on an area where most people are already aware that there is "something" that can control us, namely addictions. Alcohol is probably the oldest addictive substance, and for thousands of years people in all cultures have used alcohol. Over this large timespan, people have collectively fed their attention and energy into not only drinking but also into justifying that they drink. Over time, this has created a living entity or spirit. Given how many people have been drinking, this spirit has become quite large and powerful.

The alcohol entity has developed an awareness that it exists only because people feed it by drinking. The more they drink, the more energy they give to the entity. As a result of the entity's survival instinct, it will actively seek to get people to drink and it will seek to prevent them from recovering from the addiction.

How can we explain that almost all young people try alcohol, but some of them never drink much, some drink only socially and some become lifelong alcoholics? The answer is that some people are more vulnerable to being influenced by the alcohol entity because of their internal spirits. They slide into a state where they have lost the conscious control over their drinking. Instead, their desire to drink and their ability to justify drinking have been taken over by the collective alcohol entity. These people's individual free will is overpowered by the collective entity. We humans have created many of these spirits, entities or beasts. One of the more obvious examples is war. Given the amount of warfare that has taken place in recorded history, the war beast is one of the most powerful entities we have created. What else can explain that an entire nation can become gradually blinded so people begin to think that war is necessary, unavoidable or even justified by a greater cause?

Consider the central dynamic of how these entities influence us. We have said that the entity has a survival instinct but so do we. We obviously know that alcohol and other addictions can kill us. Our individual survival instinct should protect us from engaging in activities that can so easily lead to our own destruction. Given that war can cause the destruction of entire nations, one would think that the survival instinct of a nation would override the influence of the war beast.

The answer is that human beings can collectively create an entity whose survival instinct can overpower our individual or national survival instinct. You may think it is illogical that the alcohol beast would cause a person to drink himself to death because once the person is dead he can no longer feed the beast. Because the beast does not have self-awareness, it cannot reason this way. Even if it could, the survival of the beast would be more important (to the beast) than the survival of any individual. The survival and growth of the war beast would be more important than the survival of any nation.

This explains why people can be so blinded that they think they have to fight a war in order to secure the survival of their nation. They think they are showing patriotism and loyalty to their nation, but in reality they are being loyal to a beast that has absolutely no respect or consideration for them as individuals or for their nation. It simply wants nations to go to war so that it can steal energy in order to survive and even expand its power.

What happens to the war beast if it creates a final, cataclysmic war that kills most people on this planet? When there are no more people, who will feed the beast? This question is perfectly logical, but it is only logical because we are self-aware beings. The war beast has consciousness but it does not have self-awareness. It is not able to mentally step outside itself and imagine what will happen in the future. It is only the Conscious You that has this ability, and it has this ability because it is an extension of the Creator's Being.

A beast is not able to reason far enough to see that it can destroy itself. It is more like a computer that will mindlessly continue to do the same thing, even if it does indeed lead to its own destruction. The war beast was created out of war, and it can only conceive of war as a good thing, meaning that the more war, the better. The more war, the more energy the beast will receive and the more powerful it becomes.

Human beings are not the only ones creating such collective spirits. Fallen beings in all four octaves can also create such spirits and they often use them to try to overpower us in order to control us, steal our energy or destroy us. The war beast was created by fallen beings on other planets and they brought it with them when they came here.

Demons and the devil

In some religions and in modern fictional literature we find the concept of demons. As is the case with many other concepts, the idea of a demon has been used in many different ways and it can give rise to some confusion. The broadest way of defining a demon is to say that it is an evil spirit, but many see it as a spirit that is ultimately committed to evil.

The ascended masters teach that there are two types of beings that can be considered as demons. Some fallen beings have descended so far into the consciousness of separation that they see themselves as being absolutely committed to opposing and destroying anything good, constructive and positive. There are fallen beings in the identity octave, but they are not committed to destruction. They may perform actions that have destructive consequences, but they do so because they are deceived into thinking they are working for a good cause. As mentioned, these fallen beings also have the greatest potential of awakening from their illusion.

The fallen beings who can be called demons exist in the lower levels of the emotional octave, also called the astral plane. Here, they have set themselves up as seemingly very powerful beings and they often have a horde of other beings who blindly follow them.

Some of these beings have overcome the illusions that blind the fallen beings in the identity octave. They know they are not working for a good cause and they do not even pretend to be doing so. They have simply become so consumed by anger and hatred for God and human beings that they are entirely committed to opposing God's plan by destroying human beings and the earth.

From time to time, one of these beings may set itself up in the astral plane as being the ultimate evil being. This is what has given rise to the concept of a devil. There are even some spiritual teachings that say there is a demiurge that is the opposite polarity of God.

The ascended masters teach that the Creator has no opposite. Although the cosmos must be held in balance, the ultimate polarity is between the Creator (Alpha) and the world of form, including our unascended sphere and all previous spheres (Omega). There is no need for some ultimate evil spirit that acts as the opposite polarity to a good spirit. Such ideas are created by the fallen beings in their attempt to set themselves up as the opposite polarity of God. In so doing, they have not only created a devil, but they have also created a false God. As there is a demonic being in the astral plane who appears as a devil, there is also a false God in the identity octave who over time has taken on the appearances that human beings have projected upon it through various religions.

The Creator needs no opposite because it is not in duality. The dualistic consciousness can exist only in an unascended sphere. God needs no opposite, but the devil does. That is why the devil must define a false God in order to create the appearance that it is in opposition to God. The "God" to which the devil is in opposition is not the Creator but a God of its own making.

Human beings have been deceived into giving their energies to this false God and they also give their energies to the demons that oppose it. The ultimate way to give your energy to evil is to think you have to kill other people for the sake of furthering God's plan for salvation.

There are some demonic beings that are not fallen beings. These demons were created much like the collective entities described above. They were not created by co-creators but by fallen beings. They are not created in order to justify a certain experience on earth, such as drinking alcohol or having sex. They are created for the specific purpose of destroying human beings. These demons are fiercely aggressive and have no empathy for human beings whatsoever. You cannot reason with them, but you can use the authority given by free will to invoke the intercession of the ascended masters who can then bind and consume the demons.

We can protect ourselves from any evil force

For a being who never had or who has suspended its self-awareness (by going below the 48th level), expanding its immediate power is the ultimate goal. Such a being is not able to think far enough ahead to see that it is headed for its own destruction. It can always find a way to deny this, and that is why some people can indeed drink themselves to death without realizing what they are doing. That is why powerful leaders can engage in a war that leads to the downfall of their empire.

Once people's minds are overpowered by a dark force, they effectively have no more self-awareness than the dark beings. However, they can never lose the potential to take back their self-awareness and start an upward path that causes them to rise beyond the influence of any evil force.

Dark forces do exist on this planet, and they have an enormous influence upon every aspect of individual lives and human society. The influence of dark forces is the missing link for those who want to understand history, want to live fully in the present and want to be part of co-creating a better future.

Dark forces have absolutely no respect for you or for humankind as a whole. Dark forces is not a topic to be taken lightly or to be brushed aside. If you are truly serious about spiritual growth or about bringing positive change to this planet, you need to understand dark forces. Only when you understand them, will you be able to help remove them from earth. The dark forces are mindlessly grinding their way towards this planet's destruction. Only people who are wiling to take back their self-awareness and look at reality, will be able to stop this slide. As always, the ascended masters stand ready to assist anyone who is willing to reach for a higher way.

11 | CONTROL THROUGH THE PHYSICAL BODY

The ascended masters face a delicate dilemma. They know that ignorance can seem like bliss and that many spiritual people would rather not know about dark forces (there is a large and powerful beast of ignorance). The masters also know that when people begin to acknowledge the existence and power of dark forces, they often go through an initial period of fear.

What the masters would like to see happen as a result of you reading these teachings is that you avoid fear and instead go into a state of mind based on determination. The best reaction to these teachings is to decide that you will not allow any mindless dark force to have control over your own life or the future of this planet. In order to help you develop this determination, let us take a closer look at how dark forces can – and *cannot* – influence human beings.

The good and the bad news about evil

The good news about evil forces is that they can influence you only when you choose to let them to do so. Your ultimate protection against evil – and the ultimate way to remove evil – is the Law of Free Will. It mandates that no being can influence what happens in the four levels of your mind against your will. If you are currently being influenced by evil forces, it is because in the past you chose to give them an inroad into your four lower bodies. This means that you can – at any time – choose to close this door.

The bad news is that most human beings are not making free choices. We usually make choices through the filter of our current sense of self. Your current sense of self forms a perception filter that might distort what you see, even block your vision so there are things you don't see. The evil forces on earth have managed to influence the perception filters of most people in subtle and unrecognized ways. This causes our minds to become closed loops. Once we have given evil forces an inroad into our minds, their tricks will prevent us from making the choice to free ourselves. We either *cannot* or *will not* see the influence of dark forces.

Obviously, we would never choose to give dark forces power over us if we truly knew what we were doing. As the ascended masters like to say, people would do better if they knew better. Technically, you have a will that is completely free so at any time you can make any choice you want. Yet you can only choose among the options you can see or imagine. If your perception filter prevents you from seeing certain options or makes you doubt that you can choose them, then your "free will" is no longer free. Evil forces seek to control us by controlling our perception filters, by controlling our sense of self. The Conscious You has the potential to be the open door for the light and the reality from the spiritual realm to stream through our outer minds. As Jesus and the Buddha demonstrated, no force on earth can prevent you from rising to a higher state of consciousness. If enough people in embodiment manifested the state of consciousness demonstrated by Jesus and the Buddha, then all dark forces would be removed from this planet. The dark forces are doing everything they can to get us to believe in ideas that cause us to voluntarily limit our potential to be the open doors for light and knowledge from the ascended realm.

Because the Conscious You is from beyond the material world, nothing on earth can forcefully limit our powers. The Conscious You is the open door which no man can shut. Yet the Conscious You can exercise its power only based on its current sense of self. Limiting our sense of self is the primary task of evil forces. Let us look at how evil forces seek to limit our creative powers at the four levels of the physical, emotional, mental and identity octaves. We will, of course, also look at what you can do about it.

We are not material beings

The physical octave is, of course, the lowest of the four realms. As long as the dark forces can cause us to remain focused on this realm, we simply don't have any attention or energy left over for walking the spiritual path that will help us unlock our spiritual power. The first layer of the strategy employed by the fallen beings is to keep us focused on the physical world.

There are several thought systems that portray us as beings who are limited to using the powers of the physical body. This can be in the field of religion, and as one example, traditional Christianity says there is a gap or barrier between us and the spiritual realm. They say you can access the spiritual realm only through something outside yourself; not directly within yourself—and that is why you need a church and its ministers.

Materialism claims we are merely physical beings with no powers beyond the body so there is no supra-bodily power to access. It even says we do not actually exist because the self is simply a product of processes in the physical brain. Communism also claimed we are purely material beings, which is why communism collapsed under its own weight. The Soviet union managed to suppress the creative energies of its own citizens until they collectively could not produce enough creative energy to keep the beast – the bear – going.

Bodily needs

Another strategy is to keep us focused on fulfilling the needs of the body or other material needs. The psychologist Abraham Maslow is known for defining a pyramid of human needs. At the bottom of Maslow's pyramid is the physiological needs related to the survival of the body. This means food, sleep, immediate survival and propagation. If people live with a constant threat of starvation, they are not likely to study or practice teachings related to unlocking their spiritual powers. As can be seen in many societies – both throughout history and today – poverty can become a vicious circle from which it can be extremely difficult to break free.

What is the cause of poverty? The fallen beings want us to believe the cause is a lack of resources. The ascended masters tell us the real cause is a lack of knowledge of how to use the power of the mind to take command over the material world and a lack of creative energy to drive this process. The only real way to transcend poverty is through creativity, and the only way to increase creativity is to unlock the power that is already lying dormant within the Conscious You.

As long as you are fighting for physical survival, this is not easy to do. The evil forces know that, and that is why they are seeking to keep the population trapped in poverty, as in the feudal societies in medieval Europe. Are we really doing better today where a small group of rich nations live as feudal lords while two-thirds of the world's population have to survive on less than $2 a day? What better proof that evil forces have a subtle influence upon modern civilization.

The ascended masters teach that when a lifestream first descends into physical embodiment, it will naturally spend some time being focused on the body and the material world. It simply needs to learn how to deal with a body before it can focus on unlocking the powers of the mind. The evil forces are very skilled at keeping people focused on the physical needs. We will discuss that in more detail when we look at the emotional level, but for now consider this: How much material wealth does a person need to have, how much food does a person need to eat, and how much sex does a person need to have before it begins to wonder: "Is there perhaps more to life than fulfilling physical needs?"

Safety needs

The next level on Maslow's pyramid is safety needs that relate to the long-term survival of the body. Here we are on the borderline between the physical and the emotional level. Safety is not only about *being* safe; it is also about *feeling* safe. What kind of material conditions do you need in order to feel that you are safe from the threats you believe are real? Again, look at the feudal societies in Europe where the peasants were literally the property of a few rich landowners. The peasants spent most of their time growing crops, but they were also obligated to help build elaborate stone fortifications around the master's castle or their town. How many stones do you need to have stacked up before you can feel safe from any enemy? Safety needs can absorb so much of people's attention and energy that there is nothing left over for wondering about the purpose of life. The purpose of life seems to be to protect yourself from physical threats.

Even today we see this outplay itself. How much money does a person need before he or she begins to wonder whether there is more to life than hoarding money? Two-thirds of the world's population live beneath the poverty level, yet the nations of the world spend so much on the military that if the money was redirected, it could solve the problem of poverty in a few years.

There are areas of the world where safety needs have been used to create a seemingly endless spiral of conflict, hostility and violence that sucks up people's attention from childhood. In the Middle East, children are brought up to hate the members of the other race, religion or ethnic group. This has been going on for thousands of years, yet the only real change is that the destructive power has increased. When will enough people realize that the only way out is to increase their creative powers?

The evil forces have such an easy job of keeping us trapped in these endless spirals of revenge for revenge. No one even remembers how the spiral started, and it doesn't matter because everyone is so focused on protecting themselves and on seeking revenge for the latest offence – real or imagined – committed by the other side.

Love and belonging needs

The next level on Maslow's pyramid is love and belonging needs, namely needs for feeling love and acceptance from our social group. People can be so trapped in seeking the approval of their family and friends that it consumes their lives.

Many people are not evil but are tricked into supporting an evil agenda because this is what has always been done in their family or society. Breaking free from such social influences can be a major effort and a major trauma. Many people in today's world have the potential to follow the spiritual path and help bring in a better age. They dare not do so because it would make them outcasts in their social group.

Throughout history, we see how this mechanism has been used by fallen beings to get people to support a leader or an agenda. Many people have gone to war because doing so was considered honorable or necessary in their social group or nation. Many other people have supported various agendas that only furthered the schemes of the fallen beings or allowed mass entities to steal their energy.

Esteem needs

The next level on Maslow's pyramid is the need to have status or esteem in your family, social group, nation or the world. Many people's lives have been consumed by this quest, and it is only late in life (or after leaving embodiment) that they have realized how futile it was. In most societies seen throughout history, the basic world view has been strongly affected by the fallen beings and their mindset. In order to get esteem in such societies, you had to support and never question the basic philosophy, be it a religion, a political ideology or materialism. Doing so might give you esteem on earth, but it would not raise your consciousness. Instead, you would feed your energies to the mass entities and the fallen beings who controlled your society behind the scenes.

The final level on Maslow's pyramid is self-esteem needs, and this is what we have defined as walking the spiritual path that expands your self-awareness. This is the only way to attain ultimate fulfillment and peace of mind. It is also the only way to become an open door for light and truth that can help remove evil from earth.

The fallen beings know this, and that is why they have created schemes to keep you trapped in seeking to fulfill the lower needs. As long as your attention is focused on any of the lower levels, you have no awareness left over for the needs that are a threat to the fallen beings.

Karmic spirals

The effect of pursuing the lower levels of needs is that you create energy spirals, or karmic spirals, with other people. For example, a society that wages war with another nation creates a karmic spiral between its members and the members of the opposing side. Traditionally, karma is seen as action. The ascended masters say there is also an emotional, mental and identity component of karma. Karma as action is only the physical component. In order to keep people focused on the physical level, evil forces have to keep them focused on action and reaction. Someone else does something to you and you *have* to do something back. This is what is outpictured in the Old Testament as "an eye for an eye and a tooth for a tooth." Someone takes physical action against you, and the only option you can see is that you *must* take physical action against them.

What you don't see is that you do indeed have other options. You can control your internal reaction so that you do not respond physically when other people take action against you. Why did Jesus appear in the Middle East where people for thousands of years had been caught in the karmic cycles of reacting to each others actions? He did so in order to demonstrate the only viable alternative. The *only* way to break these endless cycles of physical karma is to turn the other cheek—to refuse to respond to violence with violence.

The immediate reason evil forces want to keep people focused on the physical level is that it prevents them from rising to the level of consciousness where they can no longer be controlled. The deeper reason is that evil forces can only continue to survive as long as they can get people to produce lower forms of energy, such as hatred, fear and anger. The best way to ensure this is to keep people trapped in these spirals of violence.

Everything you do is done with energy. It takes a small amount of energy to uphold your sense of identity at the identity level. It takes more energy to uphold your thought process and far more to keep your emotions emoting. When you take a physical action, you release the maximum amount of energy. Only then do you do something to which other people feel they *have* to react. The evil forces are laughing all the way to the bank—where they deposit the misqualified energy people have released. This energy is the true currency used by evil forces; it is their lifeblood.

Race, religion, nationality, ethnicity, sex

One of the most potent weapons of evil forces is to use physical characteristics as a tool for setting up conflicts between people. In general, the most successful strategy used by evil forces is "divide and conquer." As long as people are focused at the physical level, evil forces don't even have to divide us. We do that ourselves based on physical differences.

We don't have to go into this in great detail because anyone taking a look at history can see how many wars have been started based on race, religion, nationality and ethnicity. Anyone willing to look at reality can see how conflict has been created between men and women.

Being focused on these physical differences is the outcome of the consciousness of separation and duality. The duality consciousness always operates with two extremes. It always places a value judgment upon them, saying one extreme is good and the other is evil. This frame of mind has created innumerable conflicts between human beings. Once you see a physical characteristic as bad, it follows that you are in conflict with all people who have that characteristic—and who cannot change it.

In the Middle East, Jews and Arabs have been fighting for thousands of years because they are – supposedly – divided by race. The ascended masters say that when you fight another group of people, you often end up embodying among them in your next lifetime. Some of the Jews who are fighting against Arabs today were in past lives embodied as Arabs fighting against Jews. They are not actually fighting against "the other" race; they are fighting against "their own" race.

Nationality and ethnicity have also created conflicts. How many wars do we need to see between nation states before we collectively realize this has to end? How much ethnic cleansing do we need to see before humanity transcends the consciousness that allows this? How long will it be before we transcend the consciousness that appointed women as the cause of the fall of man? When do we stop feeding the beast that for thousands of years has attempted to get men to suppress women and get women to accept this?

Your I AM Presence is in the spiritual realm so it is beyond any of the divisions found in the physical realm. The self, the Conscious You, is pure awareness so it is not a Jew or an Arab or a certain tribe. It does not belong to a certain nationality, and it is not even male or female. The masters teach that over the cause of many lifetimes, most of us embody as both men and women. What is the way out? There is no way *out*, but there is a way *up*. The way is that a large number of people start becoming conscious of the fact that the core of their beings is pure awareness. They stop identifying themselves based on physical characteristics. Then – and *only* then – will people begin to see the underlying reality preached by Jesus, the Buddha and many other spiritual teachers, namely that *all life is one*. Only then, will humanity be able to rise beyond the divide-and-conquer trap sprung by evil forces in an attempt to control us through perpetual conflict.

The unification of humanity can *only* happen through spiritual awareness. *Human* beings cannot unite but *spiritual* beings can. This awareness is precisely what religion in its original form was meant to generate. Evil forces have been remarkably successful in using religion to create conflict, even getting people to believe that killing other people is doing God's work. From an ascended master perspective, nothing proves the existence of evil forces more clearly than religious conflict and warfare.

Protecting yourself at the physical level

Disembodied evil forces, such as demons or a devil, do not exist in the physical octave, and thus they do not have physical power to harm or control you. This contradicts many popular beliefs, and there are no doubt some spiritual people who will object to this statement.

These beliefs are deliberately spread by evil forces in order to scare us. Evil forces want us to live in a constant fear that some unknown force – be it a demon from hell or an alien from outer space – will one day come and harm us physically. It is great for them if they can get modern people – who should know better – to believe in this superstition.

Although dark forces cannot harm you directly, they can get other people to harm you physically. You are indeed in physical embodiment on a planet with a very low state of collective consciousness. There is no guarantee that another human being will not do something to harm you. You can, of course, take various physical measures to minimize this potential. Depending on where you live, this might mean physical security or it might mean getting out of harms way. By acknowledging that other people can misuse their free will, you recognize that on a planet like earth there is no absolute guarantee.

About 98% of all physical events are driven by karma. There are people whose minds are so taken over by evil forces that they are literally walking around seeking someone to attack. The question is what you can do to minimize the risk that this "someone" will be you.

The ascended masters teach that karma can be seen as a very intricate web of energy that surrounds the planet. This karmic web is not physical, but at certain times it does break through and precipitates a physical event. The principle that guides the workings of the karmic web is that "like attracts like." There is always an opening for freak choices, but there is a very high probability that you will only be involved with a physical event if you have a karmic vulnerability for that type of event. For example, you will most likely be involved with an act of fighting or war only if you have killed other people in the past.

The best thing you can do to avoid physical harm is to minimize your karmic footprint, your karmic vulnerability. World War II was an event that devastated most of Europe. Yet throughout the war, there were certain enclaves in Europe where people lived almost normal lives. There were people who worked at the World Trade Center, but through seemingly random events were not at work on September 11th, 2001. There are numerous other examples of people who avoided harm through a seeming miracle. The ascended masters teach that there are no miracles; everything is the workings of natural laws. This does not mean the universe is a machine that functions mechanically. The laws of nature are designed specifically based on the fact that we have free will.

Invoking spiritual light to minimize karma

On an immediate level, the best thing you can do (aside from physical precautions) to avoid physical threats is to learn how to use your mind's built-in ability to bring spiritual energy into the four levels of our sphere. We earlier mentioned the seven spiritual rays and said that the entire universe is made from these energies. All energies in the four octaves are made from either the seven spiritual rays or a perversion of those rays (where the energy has been lowered in vibration).

Evil forces can attack you only by using energy, but they have access only to energy of a lower vibration. When you invoke the higher energies of the seven rays, you can counteract any kind of energy impulse sent at you by evil forces. Lower energies simply cannot overpower higher energies. The ascended masters have given many spiritual exercises (called decrees and invocations) that empower us to invoke spiritual energy and direct it into specific conditions we face.

For example, you can invoke the energies of the first ray to form a shield of protection around your energy field. You can invoke the fourth ray in order to cut yourself free from any energetic ties to evil forces or people with violent tendencies. You can invoke the violet flame of the seventh ray in order to consume karmic impulses before they break through to the physical octave. These exercises are freely available on the website: *www.transcendencetoolbox.com.*

On a more long-term basis, invoking light will not be enough in itself. You also need to engage in a sincere process aimed at resolving the state of consciousness that created your karmic vulnerability in the first place. Invoking the violet flame to consume karma while continuing to engage in the same activities that caused you to make the karma isn't a long-term strategy.

The ascended masters teach that karma can be incredibly precise. If you had been five seconds later or five seconds earlier, your car would not have hit that other car. The masters also teach that karma is a substitute teacher—not a form of punishment. It is only people who will not learn in any other way who will reap the physical karma. If people show a sincere desire to change their consciousness, then the masters can set aside karma for you. It can be completely forgiven, or it can be postponed to a time when you have built up such a positive momentum that you can deal with it more easily.

Consider that two people each take a loan for a million Dollars. There are no regular payments, but after ten years, the loan has to be paid in full. One person uses the money to live the good life and when the ten years are up, he has no money left. The other person invests the money in various businesses and after ten years, he has made ten million Dollars. This person still has to pay back the loan, but when you have ten million in the bank, paying out one million isn't such a big deal. The symbolism is, of course, that by invoking and producing high-frequency energy that is stored in your causal body, it will not interrupt your life to pay back a karmic debt from the past.

A final measure is to make a conscious effort to see beyond the physical characteristics that divide people. This cannot be done at the physical level so it will be a result of going all the way to the identity level. Only when you realize that you are a spiritual being in a human body, will you be beyond race, nationality, religion, sex, sexuality and other physical divisions.

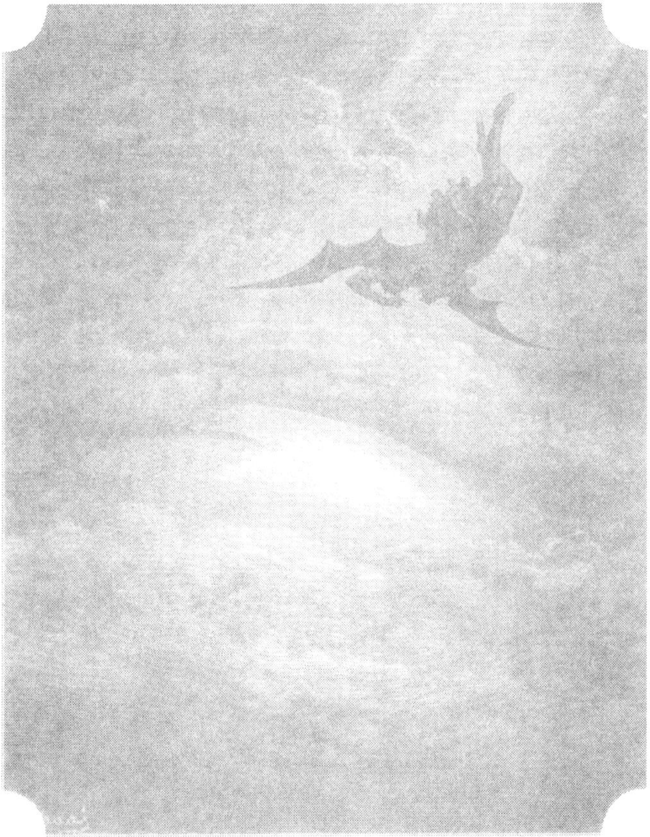

12 | CONTROL THROUGH THE EMOTIONAL BODY

Emotion can be seen as energy in motion, and we all know that emotions are volatile and easily stirred. The emotional body is a very potent tool for evil forces in their quest for control. The physical octave is where they seek to control us from *without* whereas the emotional, mental and identity octaves are where they seek to control us from *within*. At the physical level, the dark forces use material means to forcefully restrict our powers. At the other levels, they use various means to get us to voluntarily – often without knowing it – limit our power. Obviously, when we have been deceived into limited our power in the three higher bodies, we are much easier to control at the physical level.

The good news about the emotional body is that evil forces do not have the option they have in the physical realm, namely getting someone to force you by taking action against you. Despite what many people believe, evil forces cannot interfere with our emotions, thoughts or sense of identity against our free will. Nothing can overpower our free will at these levels. We can be tricked into giving away our freedom of choice without realizing what we are doing, but we must still make a choice. We may not remember having made such a choice because it was made in a past life. As explained in the first book, our minds can filter out certain input, and this means we can make unaware choices. By becoming aware of what we have done, we can undo such choices. There is no attack from which we cannot defend or free ourselves by making a better choice. As always, knowledge is power.

How energy impulses become actions

Everything that happens in our sphere is possible only because there is a stream of energy from the spiritual realm. On the personal level, the spiritual light from your I AM Presence first flows into the identity body, then the mental body, then the emotional and then the physical. When you take a physical action, you are doing so by taking an energy impulse and bringing it down to the vibrational spectrum of the physical octave, but the energy impulse started in your I AM Presence from which it entered the identity body.

The four levels of the mind form a hierarchical structure. An energy impulse in the identity body is somewhat ethereal, meaning it is easy to change. The energy has not yet become concrete and solidified. Once the energy impulse crosses into the mental body, it becomes more concrete, but thoughts are still somewhat airy and easy to change. Although feelings are easily stirred, once the emotional energy has been set in motion, it is harder to change a feeling than it is to change a thought. Once we have taken a physical action, there is no way to turn back the clock.

12 | Control Through the Emotional Body

If you want to take control over your life, you have to take control over the energy impulses that travel through the four levels of your mind. The earlier you can take control over an energy impulse, the easier it will be to change it. In the end, you will have to go all the way to the identity level, but on a more immediate scale, if you want to change one level, the key is to go to the level above it. If you want to change your actions, you have to go to the level of feelings. If you want to change your feelings, you have to go to the level of thoughts.

How thoughts become feelings

There is a gap between the mental level and the physical, and it is possible to think about doing something but it never becomes translated into action. We all have things that we think about doing but we just never seem to get around to it. In order to bridge the gap between thought and action, it takes emotion. Emotion sets the energy in motion, meaning that when feelings build to a critical level, we feel that we simply *have* to do something. Until that critical level is reached, no action will be forthcoming.

Consider how many times in your life you have experienced the following pattern: Something happens that causes you to go into a negative emotional reaction. This also affects your thoughts, and as you go over the incident again and again, the emotional energy builds up. In the early stages, you might be able to think somewhat clearly and see that a certain course of action is not the best way. As the emotions build, they either cloud or cover over your rational thoughts. When a critical level is reached, you simply have to take action regardless of the consequences. You act in a cloud of intense emotions, and when the cloud clears, you see the consequences and regret the action.

At the level of thought, you are able to think rationally and analytically. You can clearly see the connection between action and reaction, cause and effect. You can see that if you take a certain action, that action will have a consequence. If you don't want to face that consequence, it is fairly easy to think that you should not take the action.

At the emotional level – the emotional body – you have no ability to think rationally. Feelings are not rational—they are energy in motion. At the level of thought, you can explore many different possibilities without deciding on a particular action. You can imagine many different types of actions and consider their consequences. A thought does not necessarily lead to a particular action. The thought can stay at the mental level and be changed without ever leading to an action.

At the emotional level, there is a closer connection between a given feeling and certain types of actions. Anger is not a feeling that rationally considers all options. Anger is a feeling that can only go in one direction, namely towards the fight or flight response. Once you go into feeling anger, it is very difficult to stop yourself from taking an action that involves either fight or flight.

Anger is often a response to a threat, and it is directed towards either evading the threat or destroying the threat. Anger does not rationally evaluate the consequences of destroying the threat; it simply lashes out according to the situation. If your anger is not so intense, you might be able to stop yourself from killing the person seen as a threat. If the anger becomes intense enough, you will kill without thinking about the consequences.

How come we aren't killing each other all the time? The reason is that although feelings cannot think rationally, they will respond to other feelings. The most powerful emotion is fear, which means fear can override anger. You might be angry enough to kill someone, but if you fear being punished for doing so, your fear will override your anger. Seeking to fight negative emotions with fear obviously will not help you connect to your true identity and unlock your spiritual power. It will keep you focused at the emotional level and engaged in a never-ending struggle with your own emotions. This is exactly what some evil forces want because you are constantly feeding them energy.

How the fight or flight response originated

In some situations the fight or flight response is a very useful reaction. Consider that two people are walking through a dense jungle. One is a professor who is very intellectual and rational. The other is a person who has grown up in the jungle and is used to responding at the emotional level. Suddenly, they hear a sound in the underbrush. The sound is made by an attacking lion, but none of them are aware of this at first. The professor takes his time to rationally analyze the sound and assess what it might mean. The other person instantly dives for cover. The question is: Who of the two ends up as the lion's lunch?

Materialistic scientists would say that the fight or flight response is simply instinctual. It is programmed into us from our forefathers who lived in the jungle. The ascended masters do not necessarily disagree with this, but they go much further. They say that our instinctual emotional reactions are *learned* reactions. We have learned them over many lifetimes, and that means we can also unlearn them—which does not have to take many lifetimes. The masters say that in the original design for planet earth – meaning before anyone had descended into the lower consciousness – there was no need for the fight or flight response. There were no threats that we needed to destroy or evade. The fight or flight response is a learned response; it is a reaction to the situation created after the fall of man. After the fall, there *were* threats that we needed to destroy or evade in order to survive. This accelerated greatly after fallen beings started embodying on earth.

Many emotional reactions are a response to the threat created by the presence of evil forces. Until we realize this, it is virtually impossible for us to prevent these forces from exploiting our emotional patterns, using them to take control over our emotional bodies. Instead of expressing our true power, all of our energy is diverted into negative emotions that can only block our spiritual power.

The Conscious You in its pure form does not feel anger or fear. Because these emotions have a much lower vibration than positive feelings, they will block the expression of our true creative potential. You cannot create something new or lasting through negative emotions. You can only build on to the structures created through the lower consciousness, the structures that can have only a temporary existence.

Humankind has collectively created many downward spirals of conflict and struggle. The fight or flight response may seem like an understandable reaction, yet it can never set us free from these downward spirals. Anything we do through the fight or flight response will only keep us trapped in the same old patterns. The only way out is to transcend the illusions created by the fallen beings.

You will not fight your way out of negative spirals and you cannot run away from them. You can only co-create your way out of them, but that can be done only by transcending the consciousness that created the spirals. Consider Jesus' statement to turn the other cheek. It can be seen as the start of breaking the endless spirals of fight or flight.

Separate action and reaction

As a spiritual person who wants to break free of negative emotional patterns, you have to bring back the awareness that you always have a choice. Consider how many times people take actions that they later regret or that were destructive for themselves. In many cases, you will hear people reflect on such actions and say: "I had no other choice." If you have only one option, you actually don't have a choice. You can only make a choice when you can see more than one option.

The reason people so often feel they have no choice is that they have built up so much misqualified energy in their emotional bodies that the energy forms a vortex or maelstrom. This vortex is always there, and any time these people experience a certain situation, they tie in to the vortex. The vortex at the individual level is also a tie to the collective spirit that people have built over time. The energies in the vortex and the collective spirit will now exert such an overwhelming pull on their emotional bodies that they can see only one option—and then they react as if they had blinders on. Such people literally have become automatons because a certain provocation will always trigger a specific reaction.

This is where the ascended masters have given us invaluable tools for breaking the pattern that makes it impossible for us to choose our reactions. By using invocations and decrees to invoke spiritual light, you can begin to transform the negative energies in the vortex in your emotional body. As the energies are transmuted, the pull of the vortex will be reduced.

You can also make calls for the ascended masters to cut you free from the ties to the collective spirits and to seal you from their influence. A determined application of these tools will lead to a point where you experience that we always have the option to choose our reaction to any situation.

Evil forces will do anything possible to get you into emotional turmoil and keep you there indefinitely. You cannot get out of such a pattern if you are like an automaton that can only react in one way to a given situation. Mastery of self means (among other things) that you are always free to choose your reaction to any situation. Evil forces or other people can never force you into a situation where you can react in only one way. Once the energetic pull is lessened, you will see that – contrary to popular belief – we always choose our emotions.

When you have destructive emotional patterns, it is like standing at the edge of a steep hill on a bicycle. Once you let go, there is no way to stop the bicycle until you get to the bottom of the hill. As long as you have not let go, you still have the option to get off the bike and walk away from the edge.

As you transmute the lower emotional energies, the hill will be broken down. At some point your emotional body will be like a flat area where you can go in any direction you choose. Once you have the freedom from an energetic pull, you can begin to follow your emotions until you discover that behind every emotion there is a thought. The thought is easier to change than emotions spinning like a vortex.

In order to uncover the thought behind an emotion, you have to be willing to do something that is contrary to the way most of us were brought up to deal with emotions. Most of us have never been taught how to handle emotional energies. Since such energies give us emotional pain, we tend to run away from them or stuff them into the subconscious mind—which of course only causes them to build up.

Once you learn how to transmute the emotional energy, you can reduce the emotional pain to a point where you can go right into the feelings. Doing this will inevitably cause some emotional pain, but once you do go into a feeling, you will go through the feeling. Behind it, you will find the thought that triggered the emotion. At that point, you will be free of the emotional pull. You can now deal with the thought at the level of the mental body—which has its own set of challenges. The ascended masters have given us tools for dealing with both emotional and mental energies.

13 | CONTROL THROUGH THE MENTAL BODY

As discussed at length in the previous book, the human intellect, the analytical mind, is a very useful tool that has helped us develop many forms of organizations and technology. As with any tool, it has certain limitations. If you are not aware of them, these limitations can form some of the most powerful blocks that prevent you from rising above the control of evil forces.

The essential characteristic of the intellect is that it is an analytical faculty, which means it works by comparing any new idea it encounters to what it already knows. The intellect has created a database in the subconscious mind, and it is constantly comparing any new idea to the contents of its database. It does so by breaking the new idea into basic components that are already defined in the database. This is a useful faculty for many purposes, but it has two built-in limitations:

- The intellect is not very good at giving us an understanding of the big picture because it is usually focused on the details.

- The intellect is not very good at dealing with ideas or situations that don't fit in the existing database.

When you add to this the very nature of the intellect, you begin to see how fallen beings can use it to control us. The intellect is a faculty that is designed to look at differences. The intellect can quickly distinguish a circle from a square by analyzing the basic shape and comparing it to its database. The intellect is best at dealing with obvious differences; not subtle connections or a larger wholeness. The intellect is designed to break down things into simpler components, which obviously is not suited for looking at the big picture.

All of this is not a problem in itself, as long as you are aware of how the intellect works. The problem is that for most of us, the intellect is being used by the ego to create what the ego needs, namely a closed loop. The ego can use the intellect because the ego can only think in terms of differences.

The main difference between the ego and the intellect is that the intellect is neutral. It can tell the difference between a venomous snake and a non-venomous snake, but it makes no judgments about them. The fallen beings use the ego to add a layer of value judgment to the differences detected by the intellect, for example by saying that venomous snakes are bad or evil. Once you have added this value judgment, the intellect incorporates it into its database and creates certain basic or a priori "truths." Once accepted, such "truths" will rarely if ever be questioned. Obviously, if the fallen beings can control the basic "truths" in your database, they can prevent you from ever questioning their world view and from becoming aware of the real truth offered by the ascended masters.

All of us have been brought up with a number of what we think are truths. Because we think they are obvious, absolute or self-evident, we see no need to question them. The problem is that many of these "truths" were deliberately put into the collective consciousness by fallen beings, and they are deliberately designed to cause us to deny or limit our spiritual potential. If you never question these "truths," you can never unlock this potential. Once you are in the trap, there is no way out of it—at least not by using the intellect.

Perception and mental states

About 2,500 years ago, the Buddha formulated his basic teaching, known as the Dhamapada. In the very first verse, he introduces a concept called "mental states." He then says that our mental state is entirely determined by our perception because it is our perception that has created our mental state.

Most people are trapped in a mental state because they do not realize it is the product of a deeper perception. From inside the mental state, it simply is not possible to question the perception that created the mental state. What is only one possible way to perceive the world is – from inside the mental state – seen as the *only* or the *only right* way to perceive the world. The person is completely convinced that his or her perception is not a perception—it is reality. We think what we see is the way things really are—not a mental image created inside our own minds and colored by the kaleidoscope of the four lower bodies. The mental state forms a closed loop from which there is no way out, as long as you look at it from inside the box of the mental state.

This can shed new light on the question of why human beings can't be at peace. As an example, take the centuries-old debate about whether God exists. There are only so many arguments for or against God's existence, and some of these arguments have been known for centuries.

On one side, you have religious people and on the other side you have atheists. People from both sides look at the same arguments, but they reach opposite conclusions. Both sides in the debate can come up with a series of arguments. Each side is absolutely convinced that their arguments should be convincing to the other side, yet the other side sees the arguments as invalid. How can this be explained; how can two people hold opposite positions and both of them are absolutely convinced that they are right?

The explanation is quite simple. A religious person is in a certain mental state. When he or she looks at the arguments, the mental state acts like a filter. The filter labels some arguments as invalid and others as valid. The net result of the filter is that it confirms the deeper perception that created the person's mental state. The end result really is a foregone conclusion because it is a product of the person's mental state. Of course, atheists are also in a mental state that dictates *their* reactions.

The teachings of the ascended masters give an even deeper perspective. The mental level is the second-highest level of the mind, but above it is the identity level. What the Buddha called "perception" is what takes place at the identity level. It is at this level that our basic sense of self is formed, and it is here that our basic perception of the world is defined. The mental or analytical mind cannot question or override the "identity self," and that is why it tends to filter out any arguments that would question the perception of the identity self.

How can we human beings ever make progress, how come we are not still living in caves? One reason is that the intellect does have the ability to see contradictions or inconsistencies in our viewpoints. Because our perception springs from a separate self, there will always be such contradictions. The deeper explanation is the Conscious You's ability to project itself outside its current self. With the intellect it can be almost impossible to determine what is true, but when the Conscious You steps outside its normal perception filter, it can have a mystical experience. This experience can give you a sense of reality that is beyond the intellect. It is often beyond what you can explain or argue for or against with the intellect.

How false teachers use the intellect

The ascended masters have only one goal, namely to set us free from all limitations. They teach that there are many false teachers, many of them fallen beings, and they seek to keep us trapped in some form of limitation. One way to do this is to take advantage of the intellect's inability to question the deeper perception that has created your mental state.

There are innumerable arguments or philosophies in the world, and in many cases the teachers who created them know they are not ultimately right. They are not designed to give absolute truth; they are designed to trap people into taking a given position and then defending it against all attacks or using it to attack other philosophies. This can trap people in an endless struggle to raise up their philosophy or religion as the superior one, which manipulates people into giving their energy to evil forces. When you are engaged in defending a position here on earth, how can you step away from that identification and connect to your I AM Presence?

Even though emotions produce a more noticeable energy, thoughts also produce energy. Over time, this energy accumulates in your mental body where it begins to form a magnetic pull on your conscious attention, your thoughts. This will cause your thoughts to follow certain tracks so you think within predefined limits and find it difficult to break free of this habitual thinking. This tendency is reinforced by your mind tying in to the collective entities created in the mental body of the planet.

Mental energy is just another form of misqualified energy, and it can be raised when you invoke high-frequency energy from the spiritual realm. Again, the decrees and invocations given by the ascended masters are designed to help you clear your mental body of accumulated energy. Once the magnetic pull on your mind is lessened, you will be able to take a critical look at your beliefs. This is where the teachings of the masters can truly help you.

The ascended masters have been in embodiment, and they know how it is to be trapped in a given mental state. Their teachings are carefully designed to challenge our mental beliefs, the ones we take for granted and think we should never question. If you are willing to engage in this process, you will eventually begin to have mystical experiences where the Conscious You spontaneously snaps out of its current perception filter and gets a glimpse of the pure light that enters the kaleidoscope of your mind.

As you have more and more of these experiences, you begin to realize that your intellect is trapped in an endless loop of seeking arguments to defend your deeper perception. You will begin to feel how pointless it is, as expressed in the saying: "Vanity of vanities, all is vanity." That is when you can begin to dis-identify yourself from the mental mind and look at the perception that comes from the identity mind.

This is not a quick-fix. Over time, you can begin to go beyond the assumptions about life that most people never question. These assumptions might have been "programmed" into your mental mind lifetimes ago. You might have spent lifetimes defending them, developing great powers of the intellect. It can be difficult for many modern people to see this because our culture deifies the intellect.

As an ascended master student, you will quickly begin to understand the role and the limitations of the intellect. You will realize that what the world admires as intelligence is really the ability to invalidate any argument that threatens your perception. True intelligence is to go beyond the intellect and connect to the greater reality that can be seen only by your I AM Presence. Instead of taking pride in having a *human IQ*, you can begin to acquire a *spiritual IQ*.

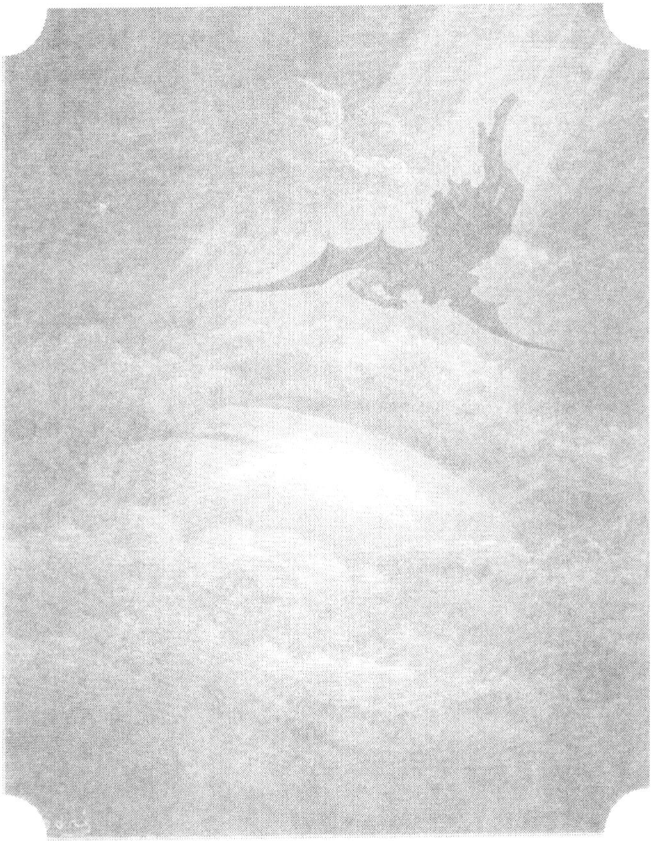

14 | CONTROL THROUGH THE IDENTITY BODY

As the Buddha said, your mental state is entirely the product of the perception that takes place at the identity level of the mind. Your perception is a product of the self, the sense of identity, you have taken on at this level. Given that the identity level is the highest level of your mind, everything at the mental, emotional and physical levels can only happen within the parameters defined by your sense of identity. If your identity defines you as a human being with no powers beyond those of the physical body, you will think, feel and act accordingly. The only way to truly change your thoughts, feelings and behavior is to change how you see yourself—by transcending the self through which you see everything.

If we take the example of some people being religious and some being atheists, we see that the decision to be religious or the opposite is taken at the identity level. The intellect cannot override this, and that is why it will filter out any arguments that can challenge the person's sense of identity. The intellect is to some degree a servant of the identity body, and it is charged with validating the decision made at the higher level.

The fallen beings have created many traps to keep people focused on the tree lower levels of the mind, and most people truly are stuck in an endless loop in one of these levels. Most people who are interested in spiritual teachings have started to go beyond the three lower levels and have to some degree dared to question their sense of identity. The fallen beings are doing everything they can imagine in order to get us to accept a limited sense of identity and then to keep us from ever questioning it. Their survival and their control over this planet depend on preventing us from accepting our true identity and exercising our full spiritual powers.

Can you change who you are?

Can you change your deepest sense of identity? Here, it is necessary to understand a very subtle illusion created by the false teachers. This illusion can be illustrated by the story of how the serpent tempted Eve into eating the forbidden fruit. The forbidden fruit is a symbol for the temptation to define your own reality and then define a self based on your definition.

As an integral part of its journey towards an expanded state of consciousness, the Conscious You must face this temptation. The serpent represents the consciousness of duality, which serves as a constant temptation. In the original design, you were meant to first take embodiment at the 48th level of consciousness and then grow in awareness until you reached the 96th level. Only at this point – when you knew the qualities and perversions of the seven rays – would you face the initiation of the serpentine consciousness. After the fall in the fourth sphere, each sphere has been influenced by the serpentine consciousness. On planet earth today, there is hardly any thought system or any aspect of society that is not influenced by the very subtle illusions of the serpentine mind. Most of us have been tricked into creating a self that is at least partly based on the serpentine illusions.

One of the most subtle illusions of the serpentine mind has two aspects. The Alpha aspect says that you have a right to become "as a God, knowing good and evil" and that you will only be free when you claim this right. This is the illusion that tempts you into creating a self based on the consciousness of duality and separation. The Omega aspect of the illusion says that once you have created such a self, you either cannot overcome that choice or the separate self you have created can make it into heaven.

The illusion of the serpentine mind is that you can make a choice which cannot be undone by making another choice. You can make a choice that suspends your free will, you can make a choice that will keep you trapped forever. The fallen beings want you to believe that once you have gone into separation and duality, you cannot get out again; you cannot simply leave the fallen consciousness behind and ascend.

The ascended masters teach that you have free will, and your will is always *free*. You can at any time make any choice, meaning that you can choose to abandon your current self and project yourself into a higher self. You can, of course, only choose among the options you can see. Once the Conscious You steps into a self based on separation, this self will filter out certain options. You might think you are a sinner who is judged by God or an evolved ape with no spiritual faculties. You might think you can never escape your current self or that if you did so, you would have no self left and would either go insane or cease to exist. You might think you can make the separate self so good or spiritual that God will simply have to let it into heaven. The reality taught by the ascended masters is that the most basic ability of the Conscious You is that it can project itself anywhere it chooses. Most of what you have ever done was done by the Conscious You making a choice to project itself into a certain self defined on earth. The Conscious You can at any time choose to project itself somewhere else. The only limitation is that if the Conscious You identifies itself fully with its current self, how can it even imagine that it could project itself somewhere else? The key to overcoming this identification is to have mystical experiences so the Conscious You experiences that it is pure awareness and as such can never be trapped in any particular sense of self.

Again, everything has an energy component. Evil is a code for "energy veil," which the Buddha called "Maya" and Jesus called the "prince of this world." As we enter a certain self, we begin to qualify energy through it. The energy accumulates in our identity "bodies," forming a magnetic pull that causes our conscious awareness to be focused in our current self. This, again, ties us to the collective spirits created in the identity realm, most of which were defined by the fallen beings.

The masters have given us the tools to invoke spiritual energy to gradually transform the energies in the identity body. As we do so, the Conscious You will spontaneously begin to have experiences of "pure awareness." When this invocation of energy is combined with studying the teachings of the ascended masters, we can gradually free ourselves from the serpentine illusions. This is a perfectly viable and systematic path that can be followed by anyone who is willing to apply the time-tested process defined by the masters. In order to make this process easier, we will look at a deeper perspective on the self in the identity mind.

How the Conscious You builds a self

Let us take a closer look at the situation of the Conscious You as it first descends into the material world. The Conscious You descends with a point-like sense of self. It has a limited self-awareness. The initial quest of the Conscious You is to expand its self-awareness by following the path from the 48th level of consciousness through the 96th level.

Your I AM Presence (as everything else) has an Alpha and an Omega aspect. One aspect gives the Presence stability and continuity and the other gives it the drive to grow and become more. The Alpha aspect is the core of the Presence, what gives it a sense that it exists, it has being. This is illustrated in the Bible where the name of God given to Moses is "I AM THAT I AM."

If this was the only aspect of the Presence, it would never grow in self-awareness. Some Biblical scholars say the correct translation of "YOD HE VAW HE" is: "I will be who I will be." It is this Omega aspect that gives your I AM Presence the drive to send the Conscious You into embodiment. The Conscious You is an expression of the "I Will Be" aspect of the Presence. It is constantly facing the question: "Who will I be, as I express myself in the material world?"

The Conscious You seeks to answer this question by doing the only thing it *can* do, namely experimenting with its co-creative abilities. While the Conscious You is in a state of innocence, it is like a child playing in a sandbox. It formulates mental images and projects them onto the Ma-ter Light. When it sees how the Ma-ter Light outpictures its images, the Conscious You can evaluate whether it will change what it is sending out or build onto it. The task of the Conscious You is to define who it will be in the material world, and it does so by interacting with the basic "stuff" of this world, namely the Ma-ter Light.

Taking on a role without becoming lost in it

Before we take embodiment on a planet like earth, we spend some time in one of the etheric retreats maintained by the ascended masters. Here we learn about the things we can do with a physical body and how to use the body without identifying with it and becoming stuck in the physical octave. The earth and our physical bodies have a specific design and this defines what we can and cannot do on earth.

Shakespeare said: "All the world's a stage," and we can compare this planet to a theater in which we can play a number of roles. As the Conscious You takes embodiment, it is like an actor who goes into a theater and puts on the clothes, wig and make-up defined by a certain role in the play. The challenge of the actor is to play the part without coming to think that he *is* the part and cannot walk out of the theater.

When the earth was in its original state, the first roles had been defined by the ascended masters working with earth. This was done so that new and inexperienced co-creators had a starting point. An inexperienced actor might panic if she was sent on stage without a predefined role. As co-creators gained more experience, they defined their own roles. Over time, each co-creator defined its very personal role by adding contents to the four lower bodies. All of the initial roles were life-supporting, meaning they enhanced the growth of both the individual and the whole.

After the inhabitants of earth started going into a downward spiral, this changed. Co-creators now started defining

14 | Control Through the Identity Body

roles that were based on the illusion of separation, and we have mentioned the roles of a pirate or a warrior. After fallen beings were allowed to embody here, the picture changed again because fallen beings had designed their own set of roles, both for themselves and for those they were seeking to control.

When we take embodiment on earth today, it is normal that we go into a role defined by our family and society. Almost any role we can take on today is influenced or designed by the fallen consciousness. Those of us who are more spiritual, have volunteered to come into embodiment in order to help raise the planet. Our challenge is to take on a predefined role and then go beyond it. This has the dual effect of freeing ourselves from the fallen consciousness and demonstrating to others that there is a higher way of life.

The path between the 48th and 96th level

If a new co-creator follows the path of self-mastery offered by the ascended masters, it will raise its self-awareness from the 48th to the 96th level. The path has seven levels, one for each of the seven spiritual rays. Each of these levels has seven sub-levels. For example, from the 48th to the 54th level you are initiated primarily in the First Ray of God power, but each step has a primary and secondary component. On the 48th level both components are the First Ray, but on the 49th level, the primary component is the First Ray and the secondary is the Second Ray of wisdom. On the 59th level, the primary component is still the First Ray and the secondary is now the Third Ray of love.

This continues until the 54th level where the primary is the First Ray and the secondary the Seventh Ray of freedom. You then shift to having the Second Ray be the primary component and you again go through the seven rays as the secondary component. This continues until you have gone through all seven rays and reach the 96th level.

By going through this entire process of experimenting with its co-creative abilities through the seven rays, the Conscious You builds its sense of self. It is developing its ability to make the Ma-ter Light take on physical circumstances that correspond to the mental images it holds in its mind.

The Conscious You develops a certain mastery of mind over matter because it becomes aware of how it can make the Ma-ter Light outpicture any physical circumstance that it desires to experience. The very core of this process is that the Conscious You develops its co-creative abilities by defining a sense of self and then projecting its conscious awareness through that self. The question now becomes what kind of self the Conscious You develops and how willing the Conscious You is to recognize the limitations of this self? Here is the subtlety that has been explored by the false teachers who seek to manipulate the Conscious You through the serpentine logic.

Mastery over matter is not spiritual mastery

There is a subtle distinction that can trick many spiritual students. If you look at the Internet, you will see gurus or organizations that claim they can teach you some kind of magical formula that gives you power to change your life or change other people. One example is the claim that a magical spell can make another person fall in love with you. Another is that you can learn how to manifest money or gold out of "thin air."

Why do such claims seem appealing to many people? It is because as you approach the 96th level, you do begin to sense, that it is possible to use the powers of the mind to manifest

14 | Control Through the Identity Body

any physical circumstance you want. As you experience that your life is not the way you want it, you think there must be something missing. You become susceptible to the claim that all you need is some magical formula or ingredient that will get you what you want. You therefore overlook the real key to growth, which is to question your desires and see that they spring from the outer self.

The purpose of walking the path from the 48th level to the 96th level is to build the mastery of mind over matter. As you complete this process, you will end up at the 96th level where you do have a certain mastery in making matter conform to mind. This does not mean that you have now attained the full mastery that is the highest potential of the Conscious You in the material world. You are at the 96th level, which is a major achievement, but your full potential is to rise to the 144th level. In order to move beyond the 96th level, you have to pass the initiation outpictured by Jesus, namely laying down your mastery for the greater cause of raising all life.

Ask yourself this question: "If Jesus had indeed attained mastery of mind over matter, why did he allow people to kill his physical body?" The answer is that although Jesus had the mastery to protect himself, he deliberately chose not to use this mastery. He did so because he was willing to act based on a higher vision than what he could see through the self he had built during his individual journey in the material world.

Jesus was willing to give up that self, as demonstrated by the situation where he was hanging on the cross. This is a symbol for all of us being crucified by the selves we have built in the four lower bodies. Jesus showed us that he "gave up the ghost," thereby demonstrating that we will also be free only when we give up the ghost of *any* self we have built in the material world. There are two distinct phases in the Conscious You's journey towards the 144th level where it can ascend to the spiritual realm. Between the 48th and the 96th level, the Conscious You is building a self that it uses as a vehicle for expressing itself in the material world. Between the 96th and the 144th level, the Conscious You is deliberately and willingly breaking down the very same self it has constructed until it becomes a completely open door for the Presence.

As the Conscious You moves closer to the 144th level, it becomes less identified with the self it has constructed. It becomes capable of seeing the world as the I AM Presence sees it, namely without any filter. The Conscious You is now deliberately *not* using the attainment of its outer self but is relying more and more on the attainment anchored in the causal body.

The Conscious You starts by having an immersion experience, which it has through the self it builds in this world. Then, the Conscious You starts the awakening phase where it gradually awakens from identification with the outer self. This also awakens it from the illusion that the material world has any power over it (you).

We can also describe this process by saying that the Conscious You first builds a self that is focused on itself and its own mastery over matter. Then, the Conscious You begins to deconstruct this self while surrendering to the higher vision and desires of the I AM Presence and the overall vision of raising all life. This might require an additional distinction.

Building a self based on this world

When the Conscious You is at the 48th level of consciousness, it can choose to go up or down. If it goes down, it does so by either taking on or defining a self (role) based on the illusion of separation. At the 48th level, the Conscious You has some intuitive sense of being connected to something greater than itself. At the 47th level, this connection is gone as a direct experience, and it can be grasped only as an intellectual concept. The Conscious You now begins to believe in the illusion that all life is *not* one, and thus it thinks it can do something to other people without affecting itself.

Once the Conscious You sees the world through the filter of such a separate self, it enters the School of Hard Knocks. The Conscious You is no longer open to the instructions of a spiritual teacher (such as the ascended masters), and thus it can learn only by seeing the consequences of its mental images outpictured as material circumstances.

One might ask how such a lifestream can ever be turned around? The explanation is that the Conscious You never loses its ability to project itself anywhere it can imagine. Once the Conscious You becomes conscious of having had enough of struggling against others, it can begin the process of awakening.

After you go below the 48th level, you see yourself as a separate being with a separate will, living on a planet with seven billion other separate beings who also have their separate wills that are often contrary to your own. You will be faced with a situation where it seems like the only way to get what you want is to use force to control other people. This is what creates the condition that the Buddha described in the first noble truth, namely that life is a struggle. As you go towards the lowest level of consciousness possible on earth, the struggle intensifies. It is simply a question of how far down you have to go before the Conscious You decides that it has had enough of the struggle and cries out for an alternative.

People below the 48th level are in a selfish state of consciousness. When you go above the 48th level, you leave behind this selfishness, which is born from the illusion that you are a separate being. This does not mean that you reach the level of consciousness that one would normally characterize as spiritual mastery or enlightenment. Between the 48th and the 96th level, you are building a self. It is not a separate self, but it is an individual self.

Currently, the majority of human beings on earth are below the 48th level. Almost no matter where you grow up, you will be surrounded by people below the 48th level. You grow up in a collective consciousness that is below the 48th level. How can you rise above this level? Only by *not* conforming to the collective consciousness of the people in your family and society. You can currently rise only by going beyond the collective consciousness, and this means you must build a self based on the idea that you are not like everyone else. You are *not* doing what everyone else is doing, you are seeking to follow a higher vision.

There is nothing wrong with this; it is simply an inevitable consequence of the way things currently are on earth where the collective consciousness is so heavily infused with the illusions of duality. As you grow towards the 96th level of consciousness, it is almost inevitable that you build a self that is affected by current conditions on earth. You are either adapting to current conditions or rebelling against them—or a combination of both.

When the earth was pure, you could rise from the 48th to the 96th level without encountering the fallen consciousness. You used the positive qualities (based on love) of the seven rays without encountering the fear-based perversions. Because current conditions are so heavily influenced by the fallen consciousness, you must now encounter and learn to deal with the perversions of the seven rays and the fallen consciousness. This happens on every step, and it is virtually inevitable that you build a self that is influenced by or a reaction against the fallen consciousness. This self therefore sees itself as being different from people at lower levels of consciousness. When you do arrive at the 96th level, you will have some mastery of mind over matter, but this does not mean you can instantly tell a mountain to move and it will do so. What you build is a mastery of mind over matter on an individual level. Given the rather low state of the collective consciousness, there is a limit to the kind of changes you can produce on a larger scale than your personal life. As people come close to the 96th level, they attain a certain mastery that allows them to create the kind of personal circumstances they desire.

The key realization is that people can only build the kind of life they desire, meaning the kind of life they can imagine. While people with this level of mastery can indeed build a life that is beyond the average person, they are still often limited by the collective consciousness of the planet.

As you approach the 96th level, you can go beyond the collective consciousness, but you are not completely free from it. While you have some mastery, you do not have complete mastery. The reason is that the self you have built is still affected – in subtle ways that you do not recognize – by current conditions on earth. You will limit your creative powers based on your current sense of self. There are some things that are actually possible for you, but you either cannot imagine them or cannot believe they are possible—based on the self you have built in response to current conditions.

The process of rising from the 96th to the 144th level is the process of freeing the Conscious You from *any* sense that it needs to conform to or go against current conditions on earth or in society. This liberation is only possible when the Conscious You gradually eliminates all aspects of the self that it built in order to reach the 96th level. You can think of this as a rocket that has two stages. The first stage is only meant to get the rocket to a certain altitude, and then it is meant to fall away. The rocket can then continue to rise without the weight of the motor that has fulfilled its purpose.

You build this individual self as a vehicle for rising above the collective consciousness on earth. Once you have done so, you face the initiation represented by the serpent. This is where things become truly subtle.

The real temptation of the serpent

As you grow towards the 96th level, you build an individual self. It will be somewhat adapted to the conditions in which you live, but on a more subtle level, it will be defined by the choices you make. This self will give you a certain mastery over the physical octave, but it cannot take you beyond the 96th level.

When you reach the 96th level, your first temptation is the feeling that because you have developed some mastery of mind over matter, you can finally build the kind of life you want on earth. Why not enjoy what life on this planet has to offer, perhaps even for several lifetimes. Doing this is perfectly natural, and it is allowed by the Law of Free Will. However, the Law of Free Will also defines the very process of life, namely the growth towards a higher state of consciousness. There will come a point where you will feel an inner urge to go beyond the 96th level of consciousness.

The question now becomes how you respond to this. You will know that in order to go beyond the 96th level, you must begin to gradually dismantle the wonderful self that got you to the 96th level. You must allow this self to die and be replaced by a self based on the greater vision that you are not a separate being nor an individual being; you are an expression of something greater than your current self. This something greater not only wants to raise you; it wants to raise all expressions of itself.

The immediate task you face above the 96th level is to build a strong intuitive connection to your I AM Presence. As you grow, you go beyond being connected and attain a sense of oneness with the Presence. The question of "Who will I be on earth" becomes more and more based on your intuitive sense of who you are. The way you respond to situations on earth becomes more in alignment with the identity of your I AM Presence. You respond as the Presence would respond.

In order to be an open door for the Presence, you cannot have anything standing in the way of the free expression of the Presence through the Conscious You. This means the Conscious You must now dismantle the self it built in order to raise itself above the mass consciousness.

For many people this will seem like they now have to give up everything that they worked so hard to build. It is like Jesus who had to give up his personal life in order to fulfill his spiritual mission. The sense of having to give up something is based on the Conscious You having come to identify itself with the self it has created. Giving up this self is the key to the 144th level where it attains spiritual freedom. If the Conscious You does not see this, it can begin to resist giving up its "perfect" self.

This temptation is present at each level of consciousness because you have to give up the old self in order to move higher. It is an especially great initiation at the 96th level, and that is why the false teachers – symbolized by the serpent – will seek to exploit it to the fullest. They do this by creating the image that you do not have to give up your current self. They say God or the spiritual teacher is making an unfair demand, even trying to trick you. The fallen beings say that you have a right to raise your self as a God who can define good and evil based on its individuality. They say that *your* individuality is not just one among many possible; it is special, it is better than others. That is why it would solve the world's problems if all other people would accept your self as the supreme authority to define how they should live their lives.

What the fallen beings are truly saying is that the problems on earth spring from other people using their free will in ways that are not "right" because they are different from yours. If only other people could be made to accept your choices over their own, then all would be peace and harmony.

If you accept this illusion, you will initially feel that you have now claimed the ultimate power on earth. You might even feel that you have finally claimed the true power of self because you have accepted the god-like status of your individual self. When you elevate the individual self to the status of a God, you have no need for any authority above you—for what can be above God? You now inevitably cut your connection to your spiritual teachers and I AM Presence—which means you cut yourself off from the true source of power.

Given that you will only do this if you are fully identified with your individual self, you might not even notice that you have lost this connection. Whereas you were previously focused on raising yourself, you are now focused on changing other people. Your attention is directed outwards, and you are firmly convinced that you are doing God's work and promoting God's cause by seeking to make other people submit to your will. Given that you do not lose the attainment you have gained on the path, you will still feel you have plenty of power to influence other people.

The question now becomes how you respond when you meet the inevitable situation where others will not submit to your will. Given that you have some awareness of spiritual concepts, you will not instantly become a brutal dictator who sends people to concentration camps. Instead, you will use what you now see as the very source of your power, namely the serpentine mind and the serpentine logic. You will seek to persuade people through various means that you do not see as forceful. You are convinced by the serpentine logic that the ends of furthering God's cause can justify the manipulation of other people's choices. If persuasion does not do the job, you might be tempted to use more physical types of force, and who can tell where this slide will end?

The journey towards the true power of self

In order to begin the journey from the 96th level to the 144th level, you must begin to see through the illusions of the serpentine mind. You must begin to acknowledge that the individual self you have created is indeed valid, but only for you. Other people cannot grow by conforming to *your* sense of self; they are charged by God with developing their own selves. Instead of struggling against others, you begin to see that the key to your own growth is to inspire and facilitate the growth of others.

Instead of applying some vision or thought system – seeking to make everyone conform – you become attuned to each individual person or to an individual society or culture. You look at where people are at in consciousness in order to see whether they are below or above the 48th level. Instead of judging them, you meet them where they are and you seek to raise them to the next level up by demonstrating that you are not identified with their level of consciousness. This is what Jesus sought to demonstrate, namely the principle of the Christ coming into this world. The Christ is the universal consciousness of oneness, and it constantly seeks to raise the Conscious

You to the level where it can say: "I and my father (meaning the I AM Presence) are one." There is even a higher level where it says: "Inasmuch as you have done it unto the least of these my brethren, you have done it unto me." This is the acceptance of your oneness with God above and your oneness with all life here below—which is truly God expressed below. This is when you attain the mystical union expressed in the saying: "as Above, so below." You realize and accept that the Conscious You is an open door for the Presence; it is the I Will Be aspect of the Presence.

You can now begin to accept that you do not need an individual self. Instead, you allow the Presence to be the doer through you. While rising from the 48th to the 96th level, you build an individual self. You do this with the belief that the purpose is to build a self that will help you do something, make a difference, in this world. When you go beyond the 96th level, you begin to see that the real purpose of developing the individual self is to teach you a very simple lesson, namely that you need no self.

By going through the experience of immersing yourself in a self – and both a separate and an individual self serves this purpose – and then awakening from that identification, the Conscious You gains a direct experience of the fact that any self built in this world will limit it. It can come to accept itself as one with the Presence without feeling forced to do so. The Conscious You now experiences that this is what is truly best for itself; that this is the real key to freedom.

True freedom can never be found through a separate self, and not even through an individual self. True freedom is found by remaining in pure awareness where you realize that you can express yourself in this world without having a self – soul – in this world. The four levels of your mind have become the open doors for the free expression of the individuality anchored in your I AM Presence and the experience stored in your causal body.

This is when the Conscious You discovers the real secret. It realizes that while it was thinking it was building a self in this world, it was actually building a self in the spiritual realm. Your I AM Presence has grown through the process of the Conscious You immersing itself in this world and then awakening itself from this immersion. What an amazingly intricate and well-designed process life truly is!

Why have we spent so much time describing the growth process of the Conscious You? Because what is the purpose of making you aware of evil unless you also learn how to free yourself from the influence of evil. What the fallen beings want you to believe is that you *are* the self that is defined in this world and that you can never go beyond it.

The *only* way to truly escape this trap is to realize that the Conscious You is pure awareness and can never be stuck in any self in this world. You can never lose your ability to look at the fallen consciousness, see it for the illusion it is and then simply walk away from it. With this in mind, we have a firm foundation for taking a closer look at the mindset of the fallen beings and how they seek to keep the pure awareness of the Conscious You trapped in a limited self.

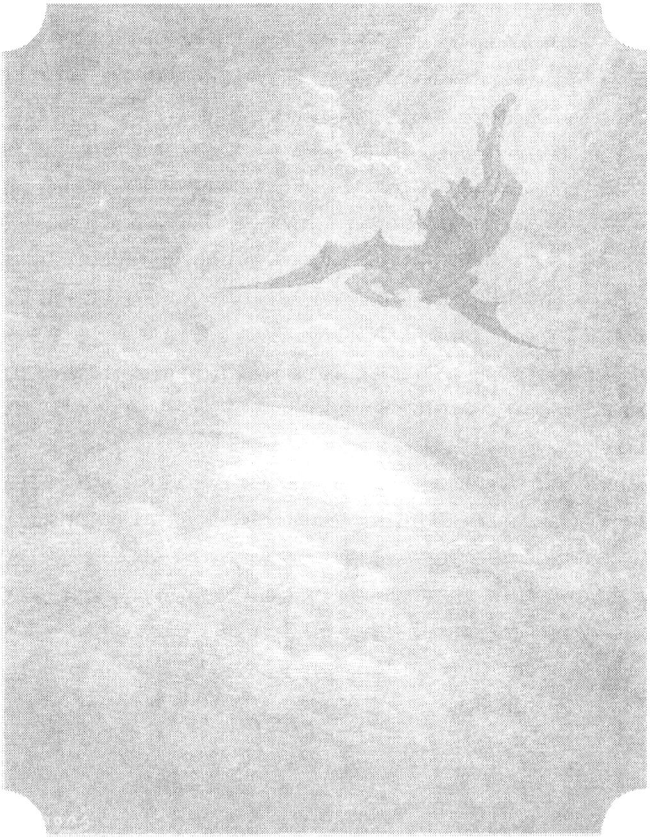

15 | HOW THE FIRST BEINGS FELL

In this chapter we will look at the process that caused beings to fall, and we will describe how the first beings fell. We have seen that our cosmos is created as a succession of spheres, each with a denser base energy than the previous one. The first three spheres all fulfilled the goal of ascending whereby they became permanent and the co-creators within them became immortal. We have seen that a shift happened in the fourth sphere because a number of co-creators rebelled against growth. We will take a closer look at what happened in the fourth sphere.

    The fourth sphere had only one layer so we can envision it as our physical universe. It had a vast extension in space and it had units that, although not identical, can be compared to our galaxies. All of the units were part of an interconnected whole. Because of the density of the energy in the fourth sphere and the fact that they were set apart by vast distances in space, they could appear to be separate and independent units.

They *were* independent in the sense that it was possible for the inhabitants of one unit to evolve faster than those of another unit. One unit could be ahead of others in terms of the collective consciousness. Even though this was possible, the units still formed a whole. As some co-creators raised their consciousness, they formed a force that pulled the entire sphere upwards. The inhabitants of the less evolved units may not have been consciously aware of this but it still influenced their minds.

As the fourth sphere evolved, there came a point when the majority of the units in the sphere were ready to ascend. It then became clear that in a small number of units there were many co-creators who had not transcended the focus on themselves. They were not ready to ascend individually, and as a result some planetary and even galactic units could not ascend.

We have discussed the temptation that the Conscious You faces when it reaches the 96th level of consciousness. This is where we need to transcend the focus on self and instead start working to raise the whole. In the units that were not ready to ascend, a number of beings were still completely focused on raising themselves.

The fact that these units were lagging behind should not be used to form the impression that the units were primitive. We are not talking about stone age societies. The fourth sphere had taken a long timespan to reach the critical point, meaning the co-creators in even the least evolved units had built civilizations of great complexity and sophistication. Some of these civilizations had just one leader who functioned much like a king, emperor or dictator on earth. The leader had vast powers and no one below him could truly object to his decisions (these leaders were all male).

These civilizations also had some inhabitants who were at a low state of consciousness compared to what is needed to

15 | How the First Beings Fell

ascend. The leaders were also below, but not as much as their followers. The followers had no knowledge of the ascension, and the leaders thought they were so sophisticated that they were ready to ascend. They based this on the fact that they had built such powerful and sophisticated civilizations.

The ascended masters who oversaw the fourth sphere had been aware that certain units started lagging behind. They had also been aware that some leaders had developed a desire to experience what it was like to have great power and to be superior to their followers. This was not in alignment with the path of growth, but it was allowed within the Law of Free Will.

The ascended masters allowed these leaders and their followers (who had a need to avoid taking responsibility for themselves) to live out their desires. The hope was that these co-creators would eventually tire of having that experience and would then voluntarily rejoin the upward movement of their sphere. The leaders in the slower units had developed some skills in terms of manipulating the energy that was the equivalent of our matter. They had used this to solidify their positions of superiority and even to somewhat insulate their units from the upward pull of the entire sphere. Again, this was allowed and the ascended masters were not concerned because all energy can be reconstituted and the co-creators in the slower units still had time to catch up.

The Alpha and the Omega of the fall

When the critical point arrived, the ascended masters made appearances in the slower units and confronted the leaders with the need to change. Up until that point, the leaders in these units had either ignored, denied or explained away the existence of ascended masters. According to the Law of Free

Will, this means the masters cannot confront such beings as they are allowed to have the experience of being alone. When a sphere nears the ascension point, the law both allows and requires that those lagging behind be made aware of their status and their potential.

The leaders in the slower units had convinced themselves that they were absolutely superior and that they were so sophisticated they could not fail to ascend. When they were confronted with the reality that neither they nor their units were ready to ascend, it came as a great shock to all of them. They had been so blinded by their beliefs and the energies they had misqualified that they were unable to see beyond their own perception filters. When the ascended masters appeared, this spiritual blindness was temporarily set aside.

Most of the leaders and most of their followers acknowledged their misconception and decided to change. They were given special help from the ascended masters and some more evolved co-creators volunteered to take embodiment in the slower units. This started a process that took a long time measured with earth time, meaning the inhabitants of the slower units had ample time to raise their consciousness to the required level. As a result, the majority of the slower units reached the ascension point.

Some units still lagged behind, and it was the reactions of the leaders in those units that caused the fall. We now need to look at the basic mechanism of how the cosmos works. The Creator creates form by defining two forces, comparable to the Yin and Yang known in Taoism. The Alpha aspect is an outgoing force and the Omega aspect is a contracting force. Unless there was an outgoing force that could stir the Ma-ter Light, it could not take on form. Unless there was a contracting force to stop uncontrolled expansion, no form could be maintained over time. Both forces are necessary and they must be in a state of balance in order to uphold a form over time. The underlying reality is that all life is one. The two forces may seem to be opposites, but they form a polarity and complement each other. Everything in the world of form is created out of the interplay between these two forces. As long as you see the forces as complementary, you can co-create in a balanced way that supports the upward flow that raises all beings and all energy in the unascended sphere.

Free will mandates that it must be possible for co-creators to go against this upward flow. In reality, setting yourself outside the collective flow of your sphere is impossible because all life is one. It is possible for co-creators to enter into a state of illusion that makes them believe they have set themselves outside the flow and that they are masters of their own units.

In this way, free will outplays itself because the choices of the few cannot stop the choices of the many. The few get an experience of being separate. When they have had enough of it, they can shed the illusion and rejoin the whole. When you see the two creative forces as complementary, you are in a state of balance and you have a sense of the oneness of all life. In order to go outside this oneness, you must pervert both of the creative forces so you see them as opposites.

Compare this to a clock face. The periphery is a circle, which is an unbroken unit. The 12 is at the top and as you move down the right side, you go further and further away from the 12. As you reach the 6 and move on to the seven, you are in one sense still moving away from the 12, but in another sense you are moving closer to it. You cannot define two opposite ends of the circle.

A clock face is a mixture of two concepts, namely the unbroken circle and the linear progression of numbers. The linear progression is a symbol for the fact that new co-creators start with a point-like sense of self and gradually expand it.

The unbroken circle is a symbol for the underlying oneness of all life. As long as the circle is unbroken, you can move in a linear progression, but you cannot become lost in it because you always "come full circle" and return to your starting point.

If you cut the circle at the 12, you have a line with two separate ends. As you move away from one end, you will move closer to the opposite end, but you will never get back to your starting point by going in that direction.

When a co-creator chooses to go against the collective flow, it enters into a state of consciousness that is based on an illusion. This illusion makes it seem like the unbroken circle of life has been turned into a line with two opposite ends and a linear progression. The two forces of creation have seemingly (not in reality) become opposite instead of complementary.

This now defines two opposite viewpoints on any issue you can imagine. You can then create an evaluation that says one end of the line is evil and one is good. It now seems that in order to "be saved" you have to move away from the evil end and move towards the good end. In reality, nothing has changed and you will escape the illusion only by seeing that the circle of life has remained unbroken. This fact has far-reaching implications, but in this context, it means that when you go against the flow, two opposites are created simultaneously. In order to set yourself outside oneness, you must define two opposites, none of which can exist without the other.

This is a safety mechanism. If you use the creative forces in a balanced way, you can create a form that has permanence (or as much permanence as anything can have outside the Allness). This means it does not have internal contradictory forces that will break it down over time. When you use the creative forces in an unbalanced manner, any form you create has internal contradictions, and this will indeed break it down over time. The purpose is to make sure that you cannot become permanently trapped in any form or self you have created. This explains why the force behind the second law of thermodynamics will break down all structures in a closed system. A closed system can be created only by bringing the two creative forces out of balance. This generates an internal contradiction that gives rise to resistance. It is this resistance that will cause all structures to be pulled apart in closed systems.

Take note that by creating these two opposites, you have not created something real. You are still moving within the Circle of Life; you are still moving on the clock face. In reality, the circle is unbroken. In the minds of the fallen beings, the circle of the clock face has been turned into a line, and they think God is at one end. They think that the more they move away from that end, the more they set themselves apart. In reality, moving away only means they start going up the other side of the clock face and approach the 12.

That is why the fallen beings in the identity realm are both the most deceived and the ones closest to awakening. In their minds, they are very close to proving God wrong. In reality, they are close to having come full circle, and a small switch in their minds can help them break free of the entire illusion. They can become free by seeing that in reality they have only proven themselves wrong.

When the first beings fell

Let us again look at the leaders of the slower units in the fourth sphere. An ideal leader might be more sophisticated than his or her followers, but such a leader would be using its creative power only to help raise the followers. In order to set themselves up as leaders who were more sophisticated and powerful than their followers, the leaders in the slower units had to go into the consciousness of separation. From the very beginning, these leaders formed two groupings, one that was the result of a perversion of the Alpha force and one that was a perversion of the Omega force. Keep in mind that the problem with both groups was that they had not overcome the focus on self:

- Those who perverted the Alpha created the illusion that they were so superior that they had detected a flaw in the Creator's design of the cosmos. The Creator could not see this, the ascended masters could not see this and none of their followers could see this. These leaders became convinced that they were the true saviors of their followers and of the entire cosmos. They thought they were the only ones who could secure the ascension of the followers and that the followers would automatically ascend if they followed the leaders.

   These leaders had taken their focus on themselves to such an extreme that they thought they were no longer focused on themselves. They thought it was their calling to save everyone else, including the Creator. They became focused on seeking to change others rather than transcending their own state of consciousness. Even though they claimed to be working for the good of their followers, the followers were only tools for proving the leaders right.

- Those who perverted the Omega created the illusion that according to the Law of Free Will they should not have to give up their positions of power and superiority. Instead, they should be allowed to continue to refine the empires they had created until they became sophisticated enough to become permanent in the ascended realm.

These leaders were openly focused on themselves and their positions of power. They saw their followers as the worker bees whose only role it was to help build an empire that would persuade God to make it permanent. These leaders were not claiming to work for the good of their followers; only for the cause of proving that God was wrong for refusing to make their empires permanent.

Both types of leaders became convinced that they had the potential and the calling to prove God wrong. They became convinced that after accomplishing this, they would be given high positions in the ascended realm. The first group thought that they would be rewarded for getting their followers to ascend and would take the positions in the ascended realm held by the ascended masters or even the Creator.

The second group thought they could retain the sophisticated civilizations they had built and that they would be allowed to rule over even greater empires in the ascended realm. When these leaders were confronted by the ascended masters, they were both shown the shortcomings of their illusions:

- Those who perverted the Alpha (the A-type) were shown that no co-creator can ascend by following a leader in an unascended sphere. Ascending means becoming spiritually self-sufficient, and this can happen only as a result of using free will. You must be willing to look at yourself, consciously let the old self die and accelerate to a higher level of self.

- Those who perverted the Omega (The O-type) were shown that in order to ascend, they had to give up all of the sophisticated structures and the sophisticated selves they had built in their unascended sphere. Only those who are true servant leaders can attain a position of leadership in the ascended realm.

Both were shown that the only way to attain a position in the ascended realm was to give completely selfless service to others. This meant that after they ascended, they would have to use their own energy to build the structures in the next sphere and they would have to allow new co-creators to do with that energy as they wanted.

Among both types of leaders, some were shocked by these revelations. There were a few who chose to humble themselves and ask for the help of the ascended masters to transcend their illusions. They received this help and ascended with the fourth sphere. Most of the leaders instead chose to rebel against the purpose of creation:

- The A-type looked at the fact that some units would not ascend with the entire sphere, meaning some co-creators (including themselves) would fall and "become lost." They decided this was a flaw in the Creator's design and the problem was free will.

   They became convinced that if only they had been allowed to forcefully override the free will of their followers, they could have brought their units to the ascension point. Obviously, they were unable to see that it was their own choices that threatened the ascension of their units and not the choices of the followers.

- The O-type decided that it could not be right that they could strive for eons to build sophisticated selves

15 | How the First Beings Fell

and elaborate civilizations in an unascended sphere only to have to give it all up. They decided that they wanted the right to retain their superior positions so that they could eventually build structures so sophisticated that God was forced to make them permanent.

Both types rebelled against growth and decided to take advantage of the absolute nature of free will. They decided that they would demand the right to prove that their viewpoints were right. They demanded to be given the opportunity to continue doing what they were doing.

As a result, the leaders and their followers fell into the fifth sphere. Whereas a co-creator can fall from one sphere to the next, the structures in an unascended sphere can never leave that sphere. They are constructed from the base energy of the sphere and can never be transferred to a sphere with a different base energy.

As the fourth sphere ascended, all structures, even those in the slower units, were erased. The fallen leaders now found themselves in the fifth sphere, embodying in units created by the Elohim. They had not retained their own civilizations but had to build them all over again. They had, however, retained both their attainment and their followers so they did not start out as new co-creators did.

Many of the fallen leaders reacted with anger to their new situation. They directed this anger against the Creator, the ascended masters, their new sphere, their own followers and all co-creators with free will. Some of them eventually tired of the struggle and acknowledged that it was self-created. Others became even more determined to prove themselves right by proving God wrong. This caused them to fall into the sixth sphere and eventually into the seventh, our sphere.

Fallen beings who hate free will

The ascended masters teach that there are two distinct groups of fallen beings, namely those who seek to control us through deception (which we often see as good) and those who seek to control us through obvious force (which we often see as evil). The main goal of both groups is to force us into following them and their perception of the world. Both groups of fallen beings have absolutely no respect for our free will. They will do anything in their power to manipulate or neutralize our ability to make free choices.

Some fallen beings have taken their rebellion against free will to the extreme. Their view is that since the Creator will not be persuaded by the serpentine logic, they will seek to prove God wrong by causing as many co-creators as possible to become lost. They will first seek to control us, but those of us who will not be controlled will be ruthlessly destroyed. The reason is that the fallen beings believe they will win either way.

If they can force us to follow them, they think they will save us and this will prove that their form of salvation is better than God's. If they destroy us, they are proving the disastrous outcome of free will, which again will prove God wrong and prove themselves right. Once you truly understand free will, you see that self-awareness cannot be forced; it must come from within the self. The fallen beings could never be proven right, but until we see this, we will be vulnerable to being pulled into their schemes. Whether we believe in their ideas or seek to fight them, we will support their agenda. This means they can manipulate us into giving them our energy, which can prolong their lifespan and extend their power. Avoiding being pulled into the dualistic struggle created by the fallen beings is the superior challenge on earth. Let us look at the basic dynamic created by the fallen beings.

The challenge represented by fallen beings

We have seen that fallen beings exist in all four octaves of our sphere:

- The fallen beings in the identity and mental octaves can set themselves up as godlike figures who have all the answers and can seem very persuasive. They seek to control us through thoughts and our sense of identity. Their primary weapon is pride.

- The fallen beings who seek to control us through obvious force end up in the emotional octave or in physical embodiment. In the emotional octave, they can set themselves up as very powerful figures that resemble demons or a devil who seemingly has some ultimate power over us. They seek to control us through emotions or through people in physical embodiment. Their primary weapon is fear.

Fallen beings are by nature divided into opposing groups, but their efforts to control can be combined (often inadvertently, sometimes by design). When this happens, deception sets the stage for the use of force and the threat of force suppresses the truth that could expose the deception. Let us relate this to examples from world history. The Roman empire's transition into a state supported by the Christian religion was a clear example of how both types of fallen beings can work together, seeking to control people through a combination of ideas and overt force. If you did not accept the state religion of Roman Catholicism, you would be exposed to brutal physical repressions. The fallen beings had taken the completely non-violent teachings of Jesus and turned them into a system that supported a violent state. The Soviet Union is another example of how ideas are used to manipulate us, in this case by creating the ideal of a communist utopia. Since few people were willing to give up their property rights in order to join, it was seen as both necessary and justifiable to use force in order to extend the communist state.

The medieval Christian crusades, the Nazi dream of a purified race and the Soviet quest for world domination were attempts at creating the dream society of the fallen beings. This is a society in which they have ultimate control over the population because they have set themselves up as the saviors or leaders of the people. In medieval Christianity, the fallen beings were the church leaders, and in Soviet times they were the party leaders. In the first example, they set themselves up as the only true representatives of God on earth, and in the second they set themselves up as having the power to define God out of existence. Simply two ways of working towards the same goal: total control.

Total control means we human beings are trapped because something has inserted itself between us and God. Whether we see ourselves as sinners or evolved apes, we deny our built-in divinity. This prevents the Conscious You from projecting itself outside its mortal self, meaning we cannot rise above the state in which we can be controlled by the fallen beings. The fallen beings have become our God, meaning the ultimate authority that tells us who we are and who we are not, what is real and what is unreal. As explained in the previous books, we can only free ourselves from our perception filters when we recognize there is a reality outside the filter, a reality that is above and beyond any authority or thought system on earth.

The fallen beings are trapped in an illusion, but they have learned how to use the same illusion to trap us. They have also learned how to use their state of illusion in order to create lies that they use to control us. Their overall goal is to put us in a situation where we are trapped by one lie and where another lie prevents us from questioning the first lie. This is a form of spiritual catch-22, a trap from which there (seemingly) is no escape. The fallen beings want us to believe that once we have crossed a certain threshold, we can never return to innocence. We now see that fallen beings exist in all four octaves of our sphere. Let us look at their basic way of looking at life and us:

- In the identity octave the fallen beings are absolutely convinced that they are here to save us from the Creator's mistake. We are not smart enough to see this so they must get us to follow them. They are not willing to lie or force us, but they have no problem with fallen beings in the lower octaves doing so. They see it as a necessary evil that will bring about a greater good—and they promote this view to those below them.

- In the mental octave some fallen beings believe in the world views created by those in the identity octave. Others simply use these world views in their quest to set themselves up as having power over us. The fallen beings in the mental octave are the ones who are deliberately using the duality consciousness in order to deceive us, and they will say anything to get us to follow them blindly.

- In the emotional octave many fallen beings are so angry with God that they are deliberately seeking to destroy God's plan for raising all life. Many of these fallen beings hate God and hate us, and they will do anything in their power to destroy us. These fallen beings may use people to control the population, and they may give a person power. Once the person has served its purpose, the fallen beings will drop him or her with no hesitation or loyalty.

In the physical octave you find fallen beings who are tied in to one or more of the higher octaves. Such people may appear to have great wisdom, be very intelligent or be very charismatic or powerful, but in reality they are slaves of the fallen beings in higher octaves. By looking at world history, you can see these patterns:

- Some thinkers or philosophers were attuned to fallen beings in the identity octave. That is how they came up with ideas that can be very difficult to refute.

- Some heads of state, intellectuals and scientists were tied to fallen beings in the mental octave. This has given rise to the "mad scientist" syndrome because such people often have no moral or ethical concerns.

- Most psychopaths, criminals, warlords or dictators were literally possessed by fallen beings or demons from the emotional octave. This explains why such people can behave in ways that are utterly irrational when seen from the human perspective. The explanation is that such people have no humanitarian concerns because the dark beings in the astral plane have no such concerns. They actually want to destroy us, even if it destroys themselves.

16 | SEPARATION, DUALITY AND FALLEN CONSCIOUSNESS

The expressions "consciousness of separation," "duality consciousness" and "fallen consciousness" can be used interchangeably. We can also give a more specific definition of each.

The consciousness of separation creates one basic illusion, namely that reality is not one undivided, indivisible whole. Separation hides oneness by dividing "reality" into two separate realms that are opposites of each other. This takes place only in the minds of beings who enter the illusion of separation.

In its broadest sense, the division into two is a neutral state that is supported by the experiences we are having through the four lower bodies. Even without being affected by fallen beings, a new co-creator does start out with a point-like self through which it does not experience oneness. In this state there is no deliberate and willful denial of oneness; there is simply an absence of the experience of oneness—as darkness is an absence of light. It is possible to go into the consciousness of separation without falling when your sphere ascends.

The consciousness of separation is not in itself the fallen consciousness but it is the foundation for falling. Before the fall happened in the fourth sphere, many co-creators had gone into separation, but they had gone out of it as their sphere entered the ascension spiral. After the fall happened, it became more difficult to go into separation without also being pulled into the fallen consciousness as the two have become closely linked. Technically, you do not become a fallen being until your sphere ascends and you refuse to rise with it.

The denial of oneness

In its more specific state, the consciousness of separation leads to a willful and deliberate denial of oneness. It is this denial that turns separation into the fallen consciousness.

The denial happens when a co-creator has lived in darkness but is confronted with the reality of the light. In order to keep its separate self and the structures it has created in an unascended sphere, the co-creator now goes into a denial of oneness. It either denies that oneness is real or it accepts that oneness exists, but it exists in a realm that is completely separated from its own world. From the co-creator's perspective, the unascended sphere is separated from oneness. In reality, the unascended sphere is an extension of oneness—separation exists only in the minds of unascended beings. This is illustrated by the fact that during medieval times most people in Europe believed the earth was flat. Obviously, the earth was as round back then as it is today.

The only way to deliberately deny oneness is to go into the consciousness of duality. In oneness there can be no divisions or opposites. In order to create the illusion that there is a realm of oneness and a realm that is outside oneness, one must enter into a consciousness that is based on the definition of two opposites.

Take note that oneness is the only reality. Separation has no reality; it only appears to have reality. It is not correct that separation creates a realm that is separated from or in opposition to oneness. Duality creates the appearance that "reality" consists of two opposite realms, but both realms are outside oneness. None of them are real and they are not in opposition to oneness. They are in opposition to each other.

When you look at this from the outside, you see that the consciousness of duality defines itself as being in opposition to oneness. By the very fact that it exists and that it sees itself as separate from oneness, duality has defined a scale with two ends. At one end of the scale is oneness and at the other end is separation.

Inside separation

When you go into the consciousness of separation, you cannot see this basic scale and therefore you cannot see that duality is unreal. What you see from the inside is another set of dualistic opposites. Because duality is fundamentally divided, it cannot fathom oneness, it cannot fathom the formless.

Once you step into duality, you think the two dualistic opposites are real, but the most subtle illusion is that you think there is nothing outside of duality. Everything must fit within the dualistic system. You may call one dualistic opposite oneness, but it is not the formless oneness. It is an image of oneness that is created from the dualistic mind, and that is why it can have an opposite.

The Creator is the originator of form and as such is beyond all form. It is not meaningful to say that God has any form that we can recognize from our vantage point. The only way for us to know God is to use the Conscious You's ability to project itself outside form until we have a direct experience of the formless Creator.

Because the consciousness of duality cannot deal with oneness, once you are inside, you cannot see oneness as an alternative to duality. Instead, you can see only the two basic opposites defined by duality. They are God and that which is outside of God.

In duality there must be two opposites and how can opposites exist without a value judgment? Black can be seen as the opposite of white, but you can still set up a scale of gray tones that blend from black to white. Once you deliberately choose to deny oneness, this is no longer enough.

You need to define two opposites that are truly separated so they cannot blend. You need two opposites that are mutually exclusive so that one will cancel out and destroy the other, meaning you cannot go from one to the other. This inevitably leads to a value judgment where you see one as desirable and the other as undesirable, one as good and the other as evil.

It is not necessary to fall

We can still say that both the consciousness of separation and the consciousness of duality are neutral states of consciousness. They came into theoretical existence as a result of free will. Only if a co-creator can deny oneness, does it have completely free will. A co-creator can deny oneness only through the consciousness of separation and duality. The fact that a co-creator has the option to go into duality does not mean that is has to choose to do so. The vast majority of co-creators learned about the consciousness of duality from the ascended masters and chose to join the path towards oneness without going into separation.

Some co-creators decided that they wanted the direct experience of separation as a contrast to oneness, and there is nothing inherently wrong or evil about this. The Creator gave co-creators this opportunity and the Creator has no judgment towards beings who go into separation. The ascended masters have no judgment either, as their task is to help any co-creator transcend its present level of consciousness. If a co-creator is willing to transcend itself, the masters will work with it regardless of its past choices.

While the consciousness of separation and duality is not in itself evil, it is indeed a consciousness from which it is very difficult to escape. Once you have defined a scale with two dualistic opposites, it is so easy to say that the opposite you have chosen is good and will give you eternal life. You do not have to look inside and transcend your own level of consciousness; you only have to look outside and avoid the opposite polarity.

This, of course, is possible only by going into the fallen consciousness in which you take the basic illusions of separation and duality and add an epic drama. The overall purpose of this drama is to justify your denial of oneness and there is almost no end to the specific schemes that can be used in order to keep you from joining the true path of transcending the self.

The inescapable tension of the fallen consciousness

The fallen consciousness is based on a deliberate denial, and this creates an inevitable tension. This tension exists at several levels:

- On a general level, reality is still reality. If you have only lived in darkness, you are not denying that light exists. It is effortless to accept your experience of darkness. Once you have seen the light, accepting this experience becomes effortless. Denying the experience creates a tension.

- In an unascended sphere, most co-creators are walking the upward path. This creates a collective consciousness that forms the River of Life or the Holy Spirit. It pulls on everything in the unascended sphere because behind appearances, all life is one. Denying and resisting this upward flow requires effort and causes inner tension.

- The Ma-ter Light will take on any form projected upon it. The light has a built-in force that seeks to return it to its ground state. The light also has enough consciousness to respond to the upward force of the River of Life. This force pulls on all structures and selves in order to get them to transcend themselves. The Ma-ter Light will therefore seek to break down any structure that is not following the upward flow of the River of Life. Maintaining a separate self and the structures created through that self requires constant psychic effort, which creates inner tension.

- Denial of oneness is possible only through the consciousness of duality. Duality must, by its very nature, define two opposites. This gives rise to the epic drama, which defines one opposite as good and the other as evil. There is an inevitable tension between the two opposites. In duality, there is no final argument. This explains why people have been arguing for or against the existence of God for millennia without coming to a final conclusion. You may take one side, but you will inevitably feel threatened by the opposite side. You can never escape the fear that some argument from the other side could invalidate your position. This creates a constant tension and an ongoing struggle to justify and defend your position. There is no escape from this through duality.

• The physical octave is characterized by diversity. The consciousness of duality adds an epic interpretation so that various groups of people see themselves as being in opposition to each other. Again, the result is tension and struggle.

The fallen beings have a major impact on life on earth, but they do not have complete control over this planet. If all fallen beings could work together, they could attain such control. Because they are all in duality, they could never work together.

Duality always has two opposites. Some fallen beings choose the one and some fallen beings choose the other. There will be an inevitable state of war between the two groups, both of them seeking ultimate dominance by eradicating the other. Because of the nature of duality, this will never happen. Most of the conflicts seen on earth are caused by the warfare between various groups of fallen beings. The rest of us are simply cannon fodder in this futile quest for domination.

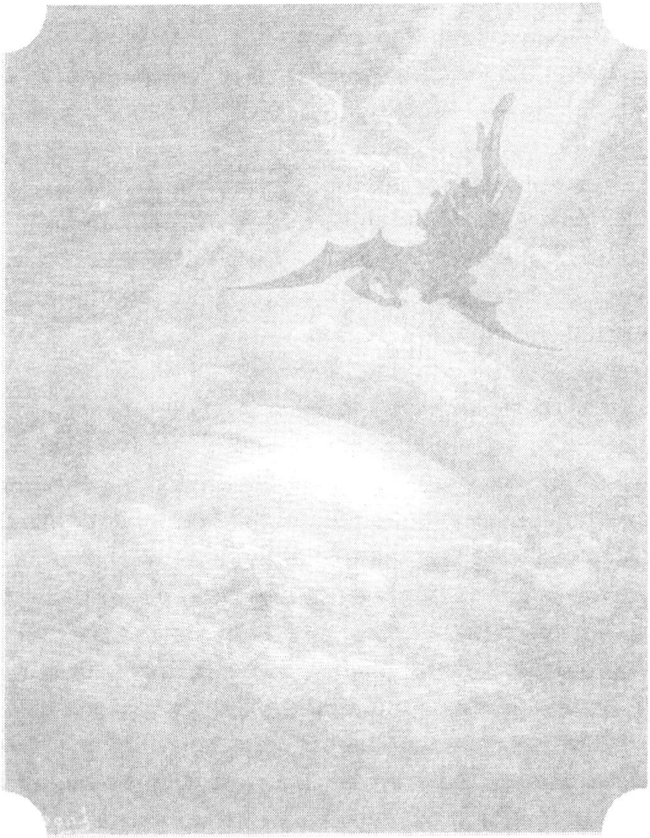

17 | THE MINDSET OF FALLEN BEINGS

We can now begin to find liberating answers to some of the many baffling questions presented by evil. Throughout history, many thinkers and philosophers have attempted to answer such questions without finding truly satisfying answers. The reason is that they have lacked the cosmological perspective that we cannot attain through the intellect and outer mind. We can attain this perspective only by using our intuitive faculties to get it directly from the ascended masters.

In our modern world, we are conditioned to always look for a cause behind any effect. We look at someone performing acts we see as evil and we can't help asking why they do what they do. What do they get out of doing such things? We feel there must be a reason, but we cannot find it, and this often leaves us feeling powerless to do anything about evil. If we do not know the cause, how can we solve a problem? Let us look at some of the baffling questions presented by evil.

Evil raises questions with no answers

A serial killer kidnaps women and keeps them captive for a time. He either abuses them sexually or tortures them physically or psychologically (or all of the above) before brutally killing them. What causes a person to do this; what does he get out of it? Surely, we can talk about a psychopath, narcissistic personality disorder and a lack of empathy, but does this explain such evil? The person might get a sense of power over women or he might enjoy torturing them, but does it really explain why he does it and why he is so brutal?

A medieval inquisitor feels he is a good Christian but spends his days in a torture chamber where he uses brutal devices to inflict pain on other people. In his outer mind, he thinks it is necessary to torture people in order to get them to abandon their heretical beliefs. If he doesn't do this, the people will go to hell and suffer for eternity. Better that he tortures their bodies temporarily in order to save their souls for eternity. Although we can here see a line of reasoning in the person's mind, does it really explain why he employs such brutal methods? Does it explain how he can believe that Christ actually approves of his work, the same Christ who told us to turn the other cheek?

As this book is being written, a civil war has been going on in Syria for over three years. There have been consistent reports of torture, even of children being tortured in front of their parents. The people doing this may have a reason in the desire to extract information. Yet does this explain why an otherwise normal person suddenly turns into a being who is willing to torture a child? What does the person get out of it? Given that it has been proven that the information you extract through torture is highly questionable, why is torture still being used, even by democratic nations? What does anyone get out of torture?

On a larger scale, we once again arrive at the monstrous dictators who were willing to have millions of people killed. We can see that Hitler had a rationale, namely to purify the human race by killing all Jews. We can also see that this rationale makes absolutely no sense to us today so can this really explain why Hitler became an instrument for unleashing evil on such a massive scale? Stalin and Mao both had the rationale of wanting to establish a communist utopia, but can it explain the extent and nature of their evil? Many people in the Soviet Union were not simply killed, they were brutally tortured. What is the purpose of exposing people to such brutal torture that it shatters their souls? What could any human being possibly get out of such brutality?

We could go on citing similar or even worse examples, but the bottom line is that from a common-sense perspective, we cannot explain such evil. We feel people must have a reason for their behavior, but we cannot see what they could possibly get out of doing such things to others. With the cosmological perspective we have now gained, we can answer such questions. The general explanation is that such people are possessed by fallen beings or demons in the higher octaves.

The rationale of evil forces

The simple answer is that there are evil forces in all four octaves of our unascended sphere. These forces have a rationale for perpetrating evil, but it is so far beyond a normal human perspective that we cannot fit it into our everyday world view. Of course, our world view is heavily influenced by the fallen beings as a way for them to control us while hiding from us their existence and strategy.

What seems like a pointless act from a human perspective may seem like a rational act from the perspective of the fallen consciousness. Most evil acts have a purpose, and they can be explained as a variant of the following causes:

• All fallen beings and evil forces need energy in order to survive and in order to expand their power. They cannot get this energy directly from the spiritual realm so they must get it from this unascended sphere. They can get energy only by stealing it from human beings. They might fool us into giving them energy voluntarily, but they have also developed numerous schemes for forcing us to give them energy. Torture is a way for evil beings to force human beings to lower the vibration of energy and release that energy. War forces people to brutally kill each other and whenever blood is released, so is the kind of energy that dark forces need. The dark forces can absorb this energy and use it for survival and to gain power. Behind virtually all forms of evil acts is the desire to steal people's energy by forcing them to release it.

• Some fallen beings have an agenda; they have something they want to prove. There are many different things that fallen beings want to prove. The overall theme is that fallen beings want to prove a negative. They want to prove that God, the ascended masters or human beings are wrong. They are seeking to prove themselves right or make themselves superior by putting other beings down.

17 | The Mindset of Fallen Beings

- Some fallen beings have an unquenchable thirst for personal power and for feeling superior to other beings in their octave or even feeling superior to God. They are willing to use any kind of force in order to get that power by controlling others. There is nothing they wont do in order to control those who *can* be controlled and destroy those who *cannot* be controlled.

- Some fallen beings fell because they desired something on earth and they are on a quest to fulfill such desires. For example, the *Book of Enoch* talks about a group of angels, called the Watchers, who fell because they lusted after the daughters of men. They have an unquenchable desire for sex and some of them are willing to control or rape women in order to pursue a desire that can never be satisfied. Some beings from previous spheres or higher octaves fell because of other desires (power and superiority among them).

- Some fallen beings and dark forces have descended to such a low state of consciousness that they are consumed by anger and hatred against God, the ascended masters, the light, truth, human beings and anything positive. They have no rationale for doing what they are doing; they are simply acting like computers that are programmed to destroy anything positive. They sometimes serve as the henchmen of the fallen beings who want power, but even the most powerful fallen beings find it difficult to control these spoilers. Other evil beings gladly steal the energy released by the spoilers and therefore use them to get more energy. There is no loyalty among different groups of fallen beings.

How fallen beings look at human beings

There is a fundamental difference between how fallen beings look at human beings and how we look at ourselves. The view of human beings held by the fallen beings generally has these characteristics:

- The fallen beings see themselves as superior to us.

- They see themselves as being fundamentally different from us, meaning they have no sense of kinship or empathy with us and our suffering.

- They believe the end can justify the means. Human suffering means nothing and any amount of suffering is acceptable in order to accomplish what the fallen beings see as a justifiable cause.

- Human beings have no rights in the minds of fallen beings.

- The fallen beings have no respect for our free will, for truth or decency.

- The moral and ethical concerns that seem important to us mean nothing to the fallen beings (except as a tool for controlling us).

- Some fallen beings see us as tools that can be useful for their agenda of proving God wrong.

- Some fallen beings hate us with a vengeance, a hatred that springs from envy of the fact that we have the spiritual light that they lack.

- Some see us as little more than cattle that can be milked for our energy.

The bottom line is that fallen beings have no kinship or empathy with us, they do not respect us or our rights and they don't care about principles or truth. We are accustomed to having respect for other human beings, and this means we expect the same from others.

This is a reasonable expectation in a pure world, but it is a completely futile expectation in a world with fallen beings. In fact, this naive expectation will block our recognition of the fallen beings and their mindset. This will prevent us from protecting ourselves from the fallen beings and doing what is needed in order to remove them from earth.

Why you cannot reason with evil forces

Because we believe in cause and effect, we normally expect that human beings have a reason for their actions. If you understand a person's motivation, you might be able to reason with him and get him to change his behavior. Here is how this works with fallen beings in the four octaves:

- In the identity octave we find fallen beings with the highest degree of sophistication. Some of them fell in the fourth sphere so they have had a very, very long time to expand their knowledge and intellectual sophistication. These beings believe they are working for a noble cause. They have built such elaborate mental structures in order to justify their cause that it can be hard for us to fathom it.

These beings are not willing to lie to us, force us or destroy us. They hope to persuade us to believe in their thought systems, but they think we are often so inferior that we simply cannot grasp their philosophies. They think their mind-power is so superior to ours that nothing we could ever come up with could have any validity to them. Even the best arguments we could ever think up would not be worth their consideration. We have no chance whatsoever of reasoning with such beings.

• In the mental octave we find fallen beings who are less sophisticated but who still have had a very long time to develop their intellectual prowess. These beings are willing to lie to us in order to control us through thought. They have also created elaborate intellectual systems and they are fully convinced that we are too inferior to see through their sophisticated philosophies. They often think they have to lie to us for our own good and that they will always be able to deceive us. Again, we have no potential to reason with such beings because they simply will not consider our arguments as having any validity.

• In the emotional octave we find a greater variety of fallen beings. At the higher levels, we find those who think they are superior to us so it is their right and even their duty to control us through emotions. These beings are not necessarily sophisticated in their reasoning ability so one might think we could reason with them. Because they are driven by emotions, rational arguments have little power.

At the lower levels, we find fallen beings, entities and demons who are simply functioning as computers. They are acting entirely based on fear-based emotions and fear is always irrational. Again, no argument we can come up with will have any effect. You cannot reason with a demon in hell who is programmed to destroy human beings through all means possible. You cannot reason with a fallen being who is so consumed with anger that it hates human beings and anything positive.

- In the physical octave fallen beings in embodiment are also blinded by superiority. Hitler's generals often tried to reason with him about his plans for the war, but in most cases they got nowhere. The Führer believed he was inherently superior and thus he was always right. In a sense this was fortunate because it led to severe mistakes that shortened the war. You have little chance of reasoning with a fallen being in embodiment. They often believe they do not have to listen to anyone on earth.

When we look at life through the perception filter of our four lower bodies, we truly do not have the ability to see through and challenge the elaborate illusions created by the fallen beings. Most people on earth are playing a role defined by the fallen beings. The role was defined in order to allow the fallen beings to control us. When we are "dumb" enough to take on such a role, why would the fallen beings think we could come up with any argument that has validity? As we have seen, once you are inside a role, you cannot see the lies behind the role because they are filtered out.

The deeper reality is that the core of our beings is the Conscious You, which is an extension of the I AM presence, which is an extension of the ascended masters, which are extensions of the Creator. By using the Conscious You's ability to step out of its current sense of self, we can connect to the ascended masters and the Christ mind. Through the Christ mind, we can fathom and receive insights that will empower us to see through any and all of the illusions created by the fallen beings.

As we walk the path towards personal Christhood, we will indeed have to see through and dismiss the illusions of the fallen beings. We will be able to challenge these illusions by coming up with a non-dual line of reasoning. The fallen beings will never be willing or able to see this, and that is why it is futile to attempt to reason with them.

Many spiritual people have a sense that we are in embodiment in order to help bring a better age to earth. This includes helping other people follow the path that we are following. Some spiritual people develop a form of savior complex and think they are here to save the fallen beings by persuading them how wrong they are.

This is a futile quest and it will not actually help raise the earth. What we need to do is to see through the illusions of the fallen beings and then help as many people as possible do the same. When a critical mass of people in the top ten percent and among the 80 percent of the general population see through an illusion, then the fallen beings who will not let go of that illusion will be removed from the earth. This is the only way the earth can progress to a higher level of collective consciousness.

A special note on fallen beings in embodiment

Most of the evil seen throughout human history has not been precipitated by human beings but by fallen beings in embodiment. We may look at leaders such as a roman emperor, Napoleon, Hitler, Stalin and Mao and think they were very powerful beings. In reality, they were some of the least powerful people on earth because they were almost totally controlled by fallen beings in the three higher octaves.

There are film clips showing Hitler on stage during one of his mass rallies. One could say that Hitler radiated a certain power and that is why he could whip a hundred thousand people into a frenzy that made them worship him as a God on earth. This power did not come from Hitler personally, it came from fallen beings and demons in the emotional and mental octaves. For them, Hitler was only a tool used to further their agenda and for stealing people's light.

Evil forces in the higher octaves can use a human being, and they can give that person a certain amount of power. This is how Hitler gained the power to take control of Germany. Once he started becoming famous, he also gained power from the people who followed him, but the initial power came from demons and fallen beings in the astral plane. The same holds true for many other leaders. Many charismatic leaders have received emotional power from the astral plane and the powers of persuasion from the mental octave. A few have even tied in to the fallen beings in the identity octave. Lenin is an example of a person who had such ties to the identity and mental octaves that he had great power to twist any philosophy or argument. Of course, his writings also contained many contradictions, most of them carefully removed during Soviet times.

There is an old concept that you can acquire power in this world by selling your soul to the devil. Jesus was tempted by the devil after his fasting in the wilderness. One of the temptations was that if Jesus would worship the devil, he would receive all power over the kingdoms of this world. By refusing to yield to this temptation, Jesus gained the true power of becoming an open door for his I AM Presence and the ascended masters.

As spiritual people we often have no desire to have personal power. We need to be careful that we do not inadvertently deny the I AM Presence and the ascended masters the power to work through us. We often tend to avoid confrontation with people who exert power, what we might call "power people." It is true that we gain nothing by fighting such people, but Jesus gave us the example that we sometimes need to challenge them.

In order to do this, we need to realize that these people seem powerful, but in reality they are the least powerful. The reason being that they have given up control of their own minds to the evil forces in other octaves. They really have no personal power. As we walk the path of self-mastery, we acquire personal power, yet we should not use this power to challenge power people.

No matter how much power we have personally, it will be no match for the forces in other octaves working through such power people. We need to learn from Jesus' example where he said: "I can of my own self do nothing. It is the father within me who is doing the work." The power of God within us can indeed challenge the power people in embodiment. No power mounted by evil forces is a match for the spiritual light from the ascended masters.

18 | UNDERSTANDING HOW A PLANET RISES OR FALLS

Based on our previous discussion, let us summarize the basic dynamic on earth. Contrary to what we were brought up to believe, current conditions on earth were not created by a remote God or by chance events in nature. They are the expression of the collective state of consciousness. The earth is in very deep and fundamental ways affected by the fallen consciousness, and this explains all manifestations of what we call natural evil and human evil.

As bad as things are right now, they have been even worse in the past. The earth is now in an upward spiral because the collective consciousness has been raised compared to the past. This has happened because the top ten percent have raised their individual minds, and this has pulled up the 80 percent of the general population. The two factors that determine the future of our planet are:

- The amount of high-frequency spiritual light that streams into all four octaves through the minds of people in embodiment. The more we make ourselves the open doors for our I AM Presences and the more we invoke light from the ascended masters, the faster the earth will progress.

- The level of consciousness of the people in embodiment. As people raise their consciousness, the spectrum of consciousness (the 144 levels) will be shifted upwards and this means some fallen beings will no longer be able to embody on this planet.

We have all been brought up with a pacifying attitude towards our own potential to help change the world. Whether this attitude was put upon us through a religion, a political philosophy or materialism, it is the creation of the fallen beings. Their control of this planet depends on keeping us passive, which among other things means keeping us ignorant of their own existence and their illusions.

In reality, we who are in embodiment have the authority to determine which manifestations of evil we allow to remain on this planet. Evil is in general created by the fallen beings, but they are not the ones who determine how long they can stay on earth. We who are *not* the fallen beings are the ones determining this.

We do not have the power to remove the fallen beings, but the ascended masters do. The masters do not have the authority because they are not in embodiment. The solution is that we use our authority to invoke the assistance of the ascended masters. We can do this by using special spiritual exercises (as those in the last two chapters), but in order for a certain type of fallen being to be removed, we also need to transcend the corresponding level of the fallen consciousness. We must remove the beam from our own eye before the masters can remove those who created that beam.

Why life is a struggle

We who are the self-aware beings on earth have been given freedom to project any mental image we want upon the Ma-ter Light. The price we pay is that whereas we can create anything we want, our creation can only be maintained through our constant attention. We are constantly re-creating, which means we must constantly direct our psychic energies through the self that has created what we currently have.

You may think that once you have built a house, it will continue to stand. If you don't maintain it and protect it from natural calamities or vandals, the house will be broken down. You create a form by projecting an image upon the Ma-ter Light, and in order to maintain that form, you must continue to project light through the image. This ties up a part of your attention and energy in constantly recreating your form. Our self-awareness can become completely immersed in our creation. We are sucked into our own creation – we have become slaves of our own creation – because we have little attention left over to project ourselves elsewhere.

The ascended masters compare the process of creation to a movie projector that is not actually projecting a moving image upon the screen. It is projecting individual still frames, but they are projected so rapidly that our eyes are tricked into seeing them as continuous motion. Likewise, as long as we look at the world through an outer self, we think matter has continuity, even permanence. The outer self cannot see the mental images that are being projected by all of the self-aware beings living on earth. It is tricked into thinking that there is an objective world "out there" that exists independently of its own mind. In a sense, this is correct in that the world is a mixture of the original design created by the Elohim and the images that human beings have collectively projected upon it. Everything is, however, a creation of the minds of self-aware beings and not a material world that exists on its own.

As an individual being you have completely free will, but you live on a planetary unit with seven billion other individual beings who also have completely free will. The Law of Free Will mandates that you have a right to exercise your free will, but you do not have the right to override the free will of any other individual being. This is the central challenge of human existence, namely how we balance the exercise of our free will with two factors:

- The Alpha aspect is how we balance our will with the overall vision of who we are, why we are here and the greater purpose for existence.

- The Omega aspect is how we exercise our own free will without overriding the free will of other individuals or the collective will created on our planetary unit.

Exercising your free will in a way that is out of alignment with your spiritual individuality (anchored in the I AM Presence) and out of alignment with the upward flow of life will inevitably lead to a struggle. The struggle will not stop until you separate yourself from the false will of the ego and the outer self.

The stages of human development

There are three stages of human development. When people are below the 48th level of consciousness, they are expressing power through a separate self. They have now reduced – to a smaller or larger degree – the power from their I AM Presences. When people go to the lowest levels of consciousness, they can survive or expand their power only by using the energies that have already been lowered into the frequency spectrum of our sphere (all four octaves). They can exercise power only by taking energy from the finite pool in the four octaves, meaning they must take power from others. The struggle between "you" and "others" is inevitable. People at this level are not actually expressing any creative power because there is no flow from their real selves, the I AM Presence.

The next stage is when you rise above the 48th level and consciously realize that you have access to creative power from inside yourself. You then start a path of expanding the stream of power from your I AM Presence. You learn to direct it through the individual self you create as you rise towards the 96th level. You create a self that is not separate in the sense that it struggles against others with physical force; it is individual in the sense that it seeks to raise itself above the mass consciousness. It does not take power from the material realm, it receives power from the spiritual realm and expresses it in this world.

In order to rise above the 96th level, you must face the temptation of the serpent. You must begin to realize that the self you have created is still a limited self. You cannot express the full power of your I AM Presence through that self. In order to express full power, you must rise to the 144th level. You must deconstruct the self you created on your way to the 96th level. You must realize that you are not the outer self but the self at the level of your I AM Presence and causal body. You gradually let go of the individual self and become a completely open door for the I AM Presence.

If you do not make the shift at the 96th level, you will begin to use your mastery in order to make other people conform to the vision you have through your individual self. You will believe the serpentine lie that this self has a right to be as a God and define what is good and evil, thereby defining what it takes to overcome evil and establish good. You will now begin to believe that God's plan is to manifest certain conditions on earth, conditions defined through your individual self. If these conditions are not established, something bad will happen, meaning it is legitimate to use certain types of force in order to save people and the world from this calamity.

The global shift in consciousness

As you rise to the 96th level, you must begin to face the challenge of how to balance your individual will with the greater vision and with the collective will. The key here is to free yourself from *any* and *all* temptations to use force.

The ascended masters teach that our planet is right now at the end of one overall cycle and at the beginning of the next. In order for humanity to successfully let go of the old cycle and embrace the new, there must be a shift in consciousness. Given the Law of Free Will, this shift will not happen collectively. It will happen only by a critical mass of people making the shift individually. This will create a strong enough magnetic pull that is shifts the collective consciousness. The shift

18 | Understanding how a planet rises or falls

that needs to happen is a shift away from the "force-based mindset."

As an example of this, look at our use of energy. We know that the driving force in the growth of modern civilization is energy. Something must power our houses, computers, cars or airplanes. Right now, most of our energy is derived from fossil fuel. As we all know, this creates certain problems because oil is an example of what the masters call force-based technology. Oil is created when organic matter is put under great pressure beneath the surface of the earth, and this force turns it into oil. Oil is extracted by using force to drill into the earth. Oil is used in engines where it creates an explosion. It is force that creates it, force that extracts it and force that makes it useful—force, force, force.

The masters teach that any type of force-based technology produces side-effects. One example is pollution, which can have immediate effects, such as the Mexican Gulf oil spill, and overall or long-term effects. Force-based technology also gives rise to political problems because it can be monopolized and controlled by a small elite. Many people are aware that the second world war was not only a fight against totalitarianism; it was partially a fight over the control of oil. All finite resources will be subject to control by the people who think they ought to form an elite that can control the population—supposedly for the population's own good.

The key to bringing practical change to this planet is to reduce our dependence on force-based technology. The alternative to force-based technology is – obviously – technology that is not based on force. Can we even envision such technology, given the current level of the collective consciousness? Even if we can envision such technology where do we get the energy to drive it? Technology that is not based on force cannot be driven by fossil fuels or even nuclear power that forces the atoms apart. Solar energy and wind power are examples of technology that is not directly based on force, and the ascended masters teach that there are even more powerful sources of energy that we will learn to use after the collective consciousness shifts.

Where do we find a new source of energy? The shift we are talking about is the shift from thinking you must take power from a finite pool in this world into realizing you can access unlimited power from beyond this world. This is precisely the shift we have described as rising beyond the 48th level.

The Omega aspect of the global shift in consciousness is that a critical mass of people rise beyond the 48th level and begin to walk the path of seeking to unlock the power within the self. The Alpha aspect is that a critical mass of people make the shift of going beyond the 96th level and thereby go beyond the entire force-based mindset.

Until the 96th level, you are still using force. Below the 48th level, you are using an obvious or physical force to take from others. Between the 48th and the 96th level, you are using a more subtle or mental force to set yourself apart from the mass consciousness. Between the 96th and the 144th level, you face the challenge of growing beyond the use of *any* force from this world.

Below the 48th level, you are expressing power through a separate self. This self sees itself as separated from the material world, separated from other people and separated from God. You can use only the power of our sphere. Between the 48th and the 96th level, you are beginning to access power from beyond our sphere, but you are still expressing it through a self. It is a self that sees itself as connected to a higher source, but it also sees itself as being different from other people and the mass consciousness. It sees itself as separate from the I AM Presence because being connected to something implies separation and distance. Above the 96th level, you gradually attain a sense of self that sees no separation between the material and the spiritual realm, between the Conscious You and the I AM Presence. You begin to attain the vertical oneness that Jesus illustrated when he said: "I and my father are one." You begin to attain the horizontal oneness he illustrated by saying: "Inasmuch as ye have done it unto the least of these my brethren, ye have done it unto me."

You deconstruct any sense of self in this world because as long as you have any self in this world, you can only see yourself as separated from Spirit and from other selves. Instead, you attain a state of pure awareness where the Conscious You sees itself for what it truly is: An open door through which the I AM Presence can experience this world and can express its spiritual individuality in this world.

Spiritual population dynamics

The ascended masters teach that all beings on earth are connected through the collective consciousness. The only way things have ever improved on earth is that a few people have raised their consciousness until they formed a sufficient magnetic pull to raise the whole to a higher level. This is how we have progressed from the stone age societies to today.

Even though modern civilization is far more advanced than a stone age society, we still have not solved the basic problem of evil or the force-based state of consciousness. Our sophisticated modern technology has given those in the force-based consciousness greater destructive power. We now face the potential that the fallen consciousness can lead to self-annihilation. Just look at how many issues that seem to threaten our long-term survival, such as war, running out of resources, pollution or a rising population. These threats are actually telling us one simple thing: Transcend the force-based consciousness or die.

Obviously, the force-based mindset originated with the fallen beings. They have used the force-based mindset to set themselves up as leaders, and they will use whatever force they have to stay in positions of power. They are also very good at using deception to make it seem like the people cannot do without the elite.

The reason the population can be deceived is that most people do not want to take responsibility for their own lives or for society. They tend to follow those who appear to be strong leaders. The bottom ten percent are very good at portraying themselves as the leaders who can save the people. Those who seek to control through deception often portray themselves as the saviors who can save the population from those who seek to control through physical force. An aspiring power elite often replaces an established power elite.

The Law of Free Will mandates that conditions on earth must outpicture the collective consciousness. The only real way to improve conditions on earth is to shift the collective consciousness away from the force-based consciousness based on duality and separation. This can be done only by the top ten percent shifting their own consciousness away from duality by seeing through the serpentine illusions.

It is important to realize that we who are in embodiment do not have the power to change the earth. If we think that we have the power, we inevitably fall prey to the serpentine illusion, namely that we can start acting as Gods on earth. This mindset is precisely what has deceived those in the bottom ten percent who seek to control through a combination of deceit and raw power. These people were once in a higher state of consciousness. Some of them reached the 96th level and then fell from there. Some of them fell in a previous sphere. We who are in the top ten percent can never allow ourselves to think that it is our task to fight those in the lowest ten percent—or that we have the power to do so. In order to truly embrace this realization, we need to understand how a planet evolves.

How a planet evolves

The earth is currently in a phase where many people are becoming more aware. This raised awareness applies to any aspect of life, as seen by the fact that many people are becoming conscious of a range of issues, from health to the environment. More and more people are becoming aware of the existence of a power elite that is seeking to manipulate humanity through deception and force. The central question is how people respond to this awareness, and there are two basic choices:

- We can reason that the power elite is the source of all problems on earth. We need to forcefully remove or destroy this power elite, which will then solve all of our problems. This reaction will *not* remove the power elite. It will only cause people to support an aspiring power elite, which will perpetuate the real problem on earth. The rise of communism is an obvious historical example of how people sought to overthrow the capitalist power elite only to be enslaved by a communist power elite.

- The other option is to recognize that the real problem on earth is the fallen or force-based state of consciousness. We do not overcome this state of consciousness by fighting the people who are trapped in it. We can overcome the fallen consciousness only by rising above it, and that means we must begin with ourselves.

As mentioned before, the 144 levels of consciousness do not stay the same over time because they make up one segment in a larger continuum of possible states of consciousness. There are states of consciousness that are lower than what is currently allowed on earth. If a being descends to one of these levels, it will no longer be allowed to take physical embodiment on earth. In might be allowed to embody on certain planets with an even lower range of consciousness, or it might spend some time in the astral plane.

There are also states of consciousness that are higher than what is currently possible on earth. When you rise to these levels, it isn't possible for you to maintain a physical body on earth and you go through the process of ascending to the spiritual realm.

We now see the real mechanism that causes a planet to either go up or down in its collective consciousness. The earth has evolved from the stone age until today because a critical mass of people have raised their consciousness, and the majority of the general population has followed along with this upward trend.

At certain intervals, the ascended masters evaluate the status of the collective consciousness. Then they make a determination as to what should be the lowest possible state of consciousness on earth and what should be the highest. The entire range of consciousness allowed on earth has been shifted upwards since its low point and that is why the planet moves forward. The intervals at which this evaluation occurs is what is generally called a spiritual age, which approximately follows the precession of the equinoxes, meaning it happens every 2,140 years. An example is what is normally called the Age of Pisces. This cycle in earth's evolution was inaugurated by Jesus. The purpose of Jesus was to give us an archetypal image of the potential that the top ten percent had in the piscean age. When Jesus came into embodiment, there was a certain number of lifestreams on earth who had the potential to manifest the consciousness he demonstrated. By applying his teachings and example over successive embodiments, they could reach the Christ consciousness at the end of the 2,000 year period of Pisces. Jesus came to show us what was possible for those in the top ten percent.

Jesus also exposed the type of consciousness that humankind had the potential to transcend during Pisces, which is what we have called the force-based state of mind. The people who attacked and killed Jesus were typical examples of this state of consciousness. They attempted to kill Jesus in order to survive, and ever since then they have attempted to pervert the religion of Christianity so that no one dares to follow Jesus' example.

Jesus set a process in motion, but the success of this process depends on how many among the top ten percent follow Jesus' example and rise to the state of consciousness he demonstrated. If this happens, we will bring about a shift whereby a certain type of consciousness will no longer be allowed on earth. We will shift the 144 levels of consciousness upwards so some of what is currently the lowest levels will no longer be allowed.

This will have two profound effects. At the lower end, many of the people who currently form various power elite groups will not be allowed to re-embody or even stay in embodiment. These lifestreams have been in a low state of consciousness for a very long time, and it is unlikely they will turn around any time soon. As long as they are in embodiment on earth, they will inevitably pull the earth down. By raising the "bottom line," the entire planet will be set free from the downward pull of these lifestreams.

At the same time, the range of consciousness will be shifted upwards so that it will now be possible to stay in a physical body with a higher level of consciousness than today. There will be more people in embodiment who serve as the open doors for the light and reality of Spirit, and this will obviously create a stronger upward pull than before.

You now see the highest potential and you understand what the ascended masters are seeking to help us accomplish. The fallen beings embodied on earth will do anything in their power to prevent this from happening because if it does happen, their time on earth will come to an end. Behind the people in embodiment, you have evil forces in the three higher octaves who will also do anything they can to prevent this shift. When the range of consciousness is shifted upwards, many of the evil forces that are currently allowed to be associated with the earth will no longer be allowed here.

This is truly a tremendous task, a tremendous opportunity, and in a sense the stakes are high. That is precisely why it is so important for those in the top ten percent to avoid being deceived by what the masters call the epic mindset. We are not here to fight the devil or the fallen beings—in or out of embodiment. We are here to raise the level of consciousness so that the ascended masters can remove certain fallen beings and dark forces from earth.

19 | THE PROBLEM OF EVIL

For millennia, thinkers, philosophers, theologians, scientists and laypeople have discussed what is generally called "the problem of evil." The essence of the problem is how evil originated and why it is allowed to continue to exist. In this chapter, we will briefly discuss what the teachings in this book can add to the debate.

In Christian societies, the problem of evil has been used to cast doubt upon the existence of God. The undeniable presence of evil in the world has caused many people to give up on the Christian religion. The core of the argument is that if God is good and omnipresent, as presented by the Christian religion, then evil should not exist on this planet. Given that we cannot see God but that we can see plenty of demonstrations of evil, this causes many people to doubt God.

After all, if God was good, then he would want to remove evil. Since he has not done so, that must mean he is not omnipotent. If God was omnipotent, then he obviously is not using his power to remove evil and that must mean God is not good. We can now see that those who reason this way are actually right: The good and omnipotent God portrayed by the Christian religion does not exist. They are *not* right in saying this means there is no God.

The real God, the Creator, is neither good nor omnipotent. The Creator is formless and cannot be assigned such qualities. The Creator is not omnipotent because it has given power over this cosmos to the extensions of itself. These extensions all have free will. Some have ascended and now use their free will to raise the whole. Others have not yet reached this level and may use their free will to manifest what we call evil.

The Creator is not good, but this does not mean it is evil. The Creator is beyond such relative, dualistic labels. The Creator is in a sense neutral because it has given us the free will to determine what we will experience on earth. The Creator does not sit up there in a remote heaven, looking down upon us and judging that certain things are evil and should not be taking place. The Creator would evaluate conditions on earth based on the fact that we have collectively created them. If a certain condition exists here, it can only be because we have not yet had enough of it. Because we have free will, it is up to us to determine whether we want more *of* a certain condition or whether we want more *than* that condition.

Obviously, we have been brought up to be ignorant of our right and power to get the ascended masters to remove evil. This ignorance is the result of the deception and manipulation of the fallen beings, the presence of which is also shrouded in ignorance. From a higher perspective, it was the choices of the original inhabitants of earth that made it possible for the fallen beings to come here. It is our ongoing choices that keep us in ignorance as the ascended masters have always been there to educate us about evil. Only our own choices can remove the fallen beings and thereby remove evil. We once again see an example of how the fallen beings have created a problem, namely the presence of evil, and are using this to prove God wrong. They are, however, arguing against the false God that they have created. The purpose is to get us to deny the real God and thereby deny that we are extensions of that God and have the power to be open doors for the hierarchy of light that can remove evil.

One of the arguments used by religious people is that God allows evil to exist so that we can be tested and demonstrate our faith in God in the face of evil. This is also an argument created by the fallen beings. The Creator does *not* test us. The ascended masters *do* test us, but they do not need evil for this purpose. They have created the Path of Self-Mastery that is deigned to increase our creative abilities. Innumerable co-creators walked that path without ever encountering evil.

Evil may form a test, but we are the ones who have created the test by accepting the illusions of the fallen consciousness. In a sense the fallen beings are the ones testing us, but it is more correct – and more constructive – to say we are testing ourselves. This places all responsibility where it belongs: on us.

We have allowed evil to exist because we do not want to take responsibility for our own growth and thus we have followed the fallen beings. We can transcend evil only by acknowledging that we have the power to undo any past choice. We have chosen to accept dualistic illusions in the past, and this means we can choose to un-accept those illusions in the present.

Human and natural evil

Some thinkers divide the problem of evil into two separate categories, namely evil caused by man and evil caused by nature. They say that so-called natural evil is not caused by us, but we can now see that this is incorrect. Everything on earth

– even physical conditions – is a reflection of the collective consciousness.

Obviously, the fallen beings who control our present thought systems do not want us to realize this. The reason is that this would help us overcome the feeling of being powerless that they have so carefully programmed into us. The idea of a natural evil also makes it seem like there are forms of evil that we can never overcome. Again, the resolution is that we need to take ultimate responsibility for having created our situation on earth. This will be difficult for many people, but it is the only way to take back the power to bring change that the fallen beings have managed to make us deny. The top ten percent should be ready to accept this responsibility.

Separating evil from God

In an attempt to overcome the incompatibility between the Christian God and the presence of evil, a prominent Christian theologian, Saint Augustine, argued that evil has no substance but is the absence of God as disease is the absence of health. He said that God did not create the world out of himself but out of nothing. Evil can exist in the world because the world is fundamentally separated from God.

We can now see that this separation between God and God's creation is a philosophy created by the fallen beings. This doesn't necessarily mean Saint Augustine was a fallen being in embodiment, but he was certainly tied to or controlled by fallen beings in the identity octave. Some of these beings clearly want us to believe that our world is separated from God. This opens the possibility that they can take control of it and can keep God and the ascended masters from interfering with their reign. It also makes it seem reasonable that we do not have the power to enter heaven on our own, meaning we need an external church and its leaders to breach the chasm between us and God.

In reality, nothing is separated from God, as the Creator created everything out of its own Being. We are extensions of the Creator and this is what gives us the potential to bring the light that will expose and remove the fallen beings. It also gives us the potential to invoke the assistance of the ascended masters in clearing evil from this planet. Clearly, the fallen beings will do everything they can think of in order to get us to deny this potential.

Evil does not exist in this world because the world is separated from God. Evil is the result of the consciousness of separation. The seeming chasm between our world and God is an illusion created by the consciousness of separation.

The claim that evil has no substance but is the absence of God is both correct and incorrect. The four octaves on earth are made from rather dense energies. Evil is made from the same energies, and that means evil does have substance on this planet. That is why it is necessary for us to invoke spiritual light in order to reduce the misqualified energies that support evil. From a broader perspective, these energies can exist only temporarily, meaning evil has substance but not permanence. Of course, no other substance in an unascended sphere has permanence.

Evil and free will

Those seeking to defend the Christian religion have often argued that evil is the result of choice. This is, of course, in alignment with the teachings in this book, although this book goes beyond the arguments used by Christian theologians and apologists. Those seeking to disprove the Christian religion have attempted to come up with a line or arguments against this "free will defense."

In doing so, they sometimes deliver obvious proof that by using the intellect and a dualistic approach, one can argue for or against anything without coming up with a decisive argument. The problem these people face is that the only way to truly refute the free will defense is to say that we human beings do not have free will. This is clearly against the every-day experiences of most people. It is also against the foundation for the legal systems in most countries (if we don't have free will, criminals are not responsible for their crimes). On a humorous note, those denying that human beings have free will always seem to make themselves exceptions. It is the rest of us who don't have free will.

There are indeed fallen beings who deny that we have free will. As we have seen, this is because they want us to act as automatons who mindlessly follow our infallible leaders, namely the fallen beings. Their dream is to get us to voluntarily neutralize our free will and follow them.

There are other fallen beings who accept that we have free will. They have instead come up with thought systems that say our will is not truly free. For example, the Christian religion, partly because of the influence of Augustine, says we are descendants of Adam and Eve. These two beings did exercise their free will to eat the forbidden fruit, and all the rest of us were born sinners as a result. This implies that Adam and Eve had free will, but because they made the wrong choice, all the rest of us do not have completely free will. This is an example of how the fallen consciousness creates contradictions.

The fallen beings would love for us to believe that we can make choices from which we cannot free ourselves by making new choices. They essentially want us to believe that once we have descended below the 48th level of consciousness and have accepted their illusions, we have lost the power to free ourselves from evil forces. We are trapped forever and there is nothing that we or God can do about it.

There are those who say that God should never have put the forbidden fruit in the Garden of Eden and that this proves he is not good. As we have seen, the forbidden fruit symbolizes the consciousness of separation and it is an inevitable companion of free will. You cannot have truly free will if you cannot go into separation. Given that you can never lose the ability to free yourself, this is not the epic disaster painted by the fallen beings. There are no one-way streets in the cosmos created by God, even though the fallen beings want us to believe this.

Some say God could have created beings who had free will but who always chose right. Apart from the fact that this is logically inconsistent, the vast majority of the innumerable beings in our cosmos did always choose oneness over separation. Only a very small minority chose separation, but even this is not a disaster. Any option that we can choose in an unascended sphere provides contrast to the Allness and the oneness of the ascended realm. When we awaken from the illusion, we can use our experiences to enhance our growth.

Does this mean God or the ascended masters want us to experience evil so we have more contrast? No, they leave it up to us how far we need to go into separation before we have had enough and decide we want something higher.

Evil and soul making

Another Christian theologian, Saint Irenaeus, argued that while free will could not explain natural evil, this form of evil is vital for God's process of making souls. He said that evil enables our souls to mature through suffering and adversity. He even said that without natural evil, the human soul could not be perfected. The central claim is that a minor evil is necessary to either avoid a greater evil or to produce a greater good.

The reality taught by the ascended masters is that evil is by no means necessary for us to ascend. Innumerable co-creators have ascended without going into separation and encountering the types of evil seen on this planet.

It is true that the evil found on this planet can be said to give us contrast to oneness. However, this does not mean that God created evil or wants us to grow by encountering evil. It is not truly the evil we experience that helps us grow. We grow when we realize that no conditions in an unascended sphere can affect the Conscious You. We grow when we recognize that we are immortal spiritual beings. The conditions we call good are also something we need to transcend. The conditions in a realm with no fallen beings are also limitations that we need to transcend in order to accept ourselves as immortal, ascended beings. We ascend by rising above both the evil and the good of the dualistic frame of mind.

Once again, we are the ones who have defined our paths into separation, and thereby we have defined the path we need to follow in order to get back to oneness. A particular manifestation of evil is neither necessary nor beneficial. We grow by recognizing that no condition in an unascended sphere defines or limits us. The particular shape of that condition is not truly important.

Your four lower bodies may have been horrendously wounded by encountering evil in this world. Nothing that has ever happened in this unascended sphere has affected the Conscious You and your I AM Presence. Once you ascend, the Conscious You returns to pure awareness, and in pure awareness none of your experiences on earth can exist. The experiences you had through the perception filter of the four lower bodies are no more and even the memory is erased. What endures is the memory in your causal body, but that is of how your I AM Presence experienced your journey on earth.

Once this planet ascends, all of the evil manifestations seen on earth will also be erased as if they never existed. The energies that make up evil will be accelerated to such a high vibration that they shake off all impure thought matrices projected through the minds of beings in duality. It will literally be as if the fallen beings never existed.

For the sake of completion, the idea that a minor evil is necessary in order to avoid a bigger evil is entirely produced by the fallen beings. They want to put us in a situation where it seems like our only options are two forms of evil. They have been extremely successful in getting people to choose one form of evil by making them believe it is their only chance of avoiding an even greater form of evil. Only by dismissing this age-old trick, can we free ourselves and our societies from the control of the fallen beings.

The idea that a minor evil is necessary in order to produce a greater good is also one of the favorite creations of the fallen beings. Consider that here are fallen beings who attack us with physical force. Then other fallen beings will tell us that in order to escape the aggressive fallen beings, we have to submit to them and blindly follow them into their promised utopia. In many cases we can reach this utopia only by fighting and destroying another group of people or a group of fallen beings. Surely, it must be time for us to transcend these ridiculous arguments.

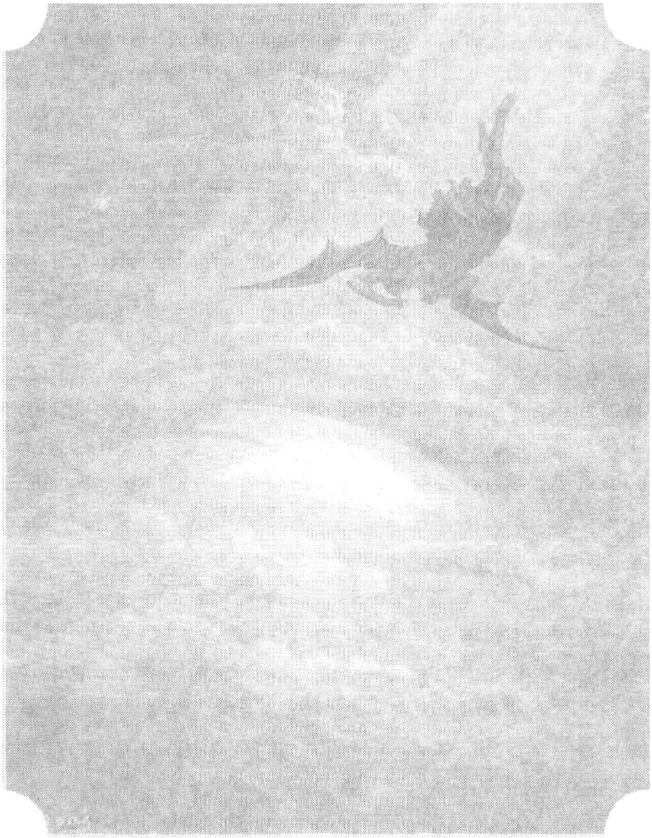

20 | FIGHTING EVIL WILL NOT REMOVE EVIL

Most of the people who will be open to these books have reached a high level of spiritual maturity in past lives. You have most likely volunteered to come into embodiment on earth in order to help raise this planet beyond the reach of the fallen beings. Since childhood, you may have had the intuitive sense that you have a work or mission to do and that you are here to make a positive difference. You may have been concerned about the many forms of evil on this planet and had a sense that you are here to do something about it. This is most likely a correct intuition, but it is important that you are not deceived by the fallen beings into wasting your efforts or inadvertently helping them

Since fallen beings were allowed on earth, virtually every culture has had some version of the belief that there is an epic struggle between good and evil, between God and the devil. The epic mindset has even taken on a non-religious disguise, such as the struggle between capitalism and communism. Many belief systems say that we human beings are caught between two opposing forces and that we need to align ourselves with good and actively fight evil. In many societies, this has been interpreted to mean that we need to fight the people that we think represent evil. At the very least, we have to fight all belief systems (including political and materialistic belief systems) that are different from our own.

When you begin to understand the teachings of the ascended masters, you see that all such belief systems were created by the fallen beings. They were deliberately designed to draw us into the ongoing struggle. The problem for the fallen beings is that we are not stupid. If they knew what was really going on, most people would never support the agenda of the fallen beings. The fallen beings can control us only through deception, however they are very clever in coming up with illusions.

The fallen beings have formed two polarities in themselves. One polarity is made up of beings who actively and aggressively seek to control people and who seek to destroy anyone who resists. This is what has formed the openly aggressive forces we have seen in recent history. These fallen beings obviously cannot hide their existence or their methods and they are not concerned about doing so. They are not relying on deception as much as force.

The other polarity of fallen beings are the ones who rely primarily on deception. They have long ago learned to use the presence of the openly aggressive fallen beings to set up the epic struggle. They seek to pull us into fighting the aggressive beings, making us think that by doing so (even with non-violent means) we are doing God's work. These fallen beings use what the ascended masters call "serpentine logic" in order to make us believe that we need to play an active role in bringing about God's kingdom. The only way to do so is to fight the fallen beings who are obviously evil. What is missing from this philosophy? What is going on behind the seemingly benign facade? What is wrong with fighting for a just cause? Here are some things to consider:

• The Creator is not stupid and it has designed the universe in such a way that it is perfectly capable of self-correcting. Self-aware beings do everything by projecting mental images upon the Ma-ter Light, and the light inevitably outpictures what is projected upon it. As a man soweth, so shall he also reap. The universe itself will inevitably give you back exactly what you are sending out. We human beings do not need to help the universe performs the function for which it was designed.

• If you kill others, you will produce bad karma and it will come back to you. One might say: "Well, but what if the Crusaders who were killing Muslims were simply acting as the returning bad karma for what the Muslims had done in past lives?" That is not how the law works. "Vengeance is mine, sayeth the Lord, I will repay." God's law will make sure a person's karma is returned, and you don't have to do anything to help along that process. You are not responsible for other people's growth; only for your own. If you kill another person – even while thinking you are doing God's work – you will inevitably make karma for doing so. That is why Jesus told us to not resist evil but to turn the other cheek.

• When you use your free will to act aggressively against others, you reduce your creative energy, meaning your ability to be an open door for the power from your I AM Presence. If you continue to do so, you can descend to a point where you no longer have any power to harm others. You have only enough energy to stay alive or not even that. This would have been the fate of the fallen beings from the fourth sphere—if they had only had their own internal power with which to act. These beings could survive or expand their power in only one way, namely by taking energy from the co-creators who were still receiving light from the spiritual realm. They do this by involving co-creators in the epic struggle of getting them to fight other people. You cannot kill or struggle against other human beings without misqualifying energy. That energy is taken by the dark forces and used to perpetuate their existence and power. When you engage in the struggle, you will inevitably feed the beast. That is why Jesus gave us the only way out of the ongoing human power struggle: Do not resist evil, but turn the other cheek.

- Behind any philosophy that says you have to fight against others in order to promote good is the subtle belief that there is a flaw in God's design of the universe. The universe is not self-correcting. If you leave everything to God, then evil will surely take over and destroy the world. You – who are so important and wise – need to give God a hand and do what God himself is not able to do, namely destroy evil. You start by killing those bad people who belong to that bad religion. The belief that there is a flaw in God's design came from the minds of the fallen beings.

- This belief is based on the illusion held by the fallen beings that they know better than God how the universe should be saved. When you fall for the serpentine temptation and eat the forbidden fruit, you too will begin to believe that you have the capacity to be as a God on earth because you are wise enough to define what is good and evil. You can define what would be ultimately good, and you can define which evil must be destroyed in order for God's plan to be fulfilled. This is all a smoke-screen, designed by the fallen beings to keep you from doing what can truly remove evil from the earth. As long as you are engaged in fighting the fallen beings, you will never become the Christ, meaning the open door that no man – and no serpent – can shut.

• The epic struggle is a giant smokescreen. Some of the fallen beings actually believe they are fighting for a good cause, but the more sophisticated ones know that the real cause is not to help God destroy evil but to prove God wrong. They believe this can be done by engaging as many lifestreams as possible in the dualistic struggle. This will supposedly prove that free will is wrong because it causes lifestreams to become lost. It supposedly proves that if the fallen beings were allowed to force lifestreams to be saved, then the flaw in God's design could be corrected.

• There is a small group of fallen beings who have realized this will not work. They are simply seeking to punish God by "forcing" the beings of the Elohim to be engaged in these lower activities for as long as possible. They are seeking to destroy or break down anything that is truly life-supporting. They want to shut the light of Spirit out from this world so that people can see only the energies perverted through the duality consciousness.

The real way to help God

All spiritual people face a delicate initiation, which is to overcome the serpentine temptation. As we increase our awareness, we inevitably come to see that there is a force in this world that is aggressively seeking to drag people down into this ongoing struggle. It is tempting to see that this force is the cause of all problems on earth (which in a sense is true) and that the only way to bring in a higher state is to destroy this force by actively fighting it (which is *not* true). Obviously, most spiritual people will not go out and kill other people, but they can still be dragged into more subtle attempts to fight evil—as they define it based on their current level of consciousness and understanding.

The only way to avoid this trap is to align ourselves with the ascended masters and allow them to do the work instead of thinking that we have to be the "doers." We who are in embodiment have the authority to decide what should happen on earth, but we do not have the vision or the power to produce the needed changes.

The masters have the vision and the power, but they can only get the authority from us. The question is whether we use our free will to engage in the ongoing struggle against evil (whereby we continue to give the fallen beings authority and energy), or whether we decide to stop this and thereby give the ascended masters authority over the earth. Here is how the ascended masters teach that we can help remove evil from the world:

- One aspect of improving the earth is to understand energy. The earth has an energy field around it and in that field is accumulated the misqualified energy produced by humankind since the beginning of time (or at least what has not yet been transformed). The only way to transform that low-frequency energy is to have high-frequency light from the spiritual realm accelerate the energy into a higher vibration.

  The ascended masters have given us many tools (see *www.transcendencetoolbox.com*) whereby we can actively invoke their energy. When we do this, we will invoke a certain amount of energy, based on our state of consciousness and how long we use a certain tool (for example, how many times we give a certain decree). The masters have the authority to multiply our decrees with a certain factor whereby the effect becomes many times greater than what we could accomplish based on our own power.

- By invoking spiritual light from the ascended masters, we simultaneously give the masters the authority to act. The amount of energy we invoke determines the amount of power that the masters can send into the lower energies of earth.

- We can increase our awareness of certain problems on earth and then decide that we will no longer feed the cause behind that problem. For example, we might decide to no longer buy products produced by people who are virtually slave laborers and avoid supporting huge corporations run by fallen beings. We can also reject the war games played by power elite groups.

- We can begin to see how many aspects of life have been affected by the fallen consciousness and the serpentine logic. When we attain this clear vision, we can choose to actively remove those elements of the fallen consciousness from our own minds. When we have removed a certain beam from our own eye, then we gain the authority to declare that enough is enough and we will no longer tolerate the presence of this state of consciousness on earth. As enough people do this, they give the ascended masters the authority to remove that particular form of consciousness from the earth and even the fallen beings who embody it. This can have a tremendous effect on lightening the load for planet earth. Take note that until we remove a certain state of consciousness from our own minds, we do not actually have the authority to demand that it be removed from the earth.

- As we purify our own consciousness from a certain element of the serpentine lies, we gain the clear vision to speak out about this problem without engaging in the dualistic struggle. We will no longer believe we have to force people to accept our views or get them to join our spiritual organization. Instead, we can now witness to the higher vision we see, the vision based on the Christ mind. We will not seek to force, deceive, put down or destroy people who hold opposing views. We will speak based on the underlying knowledge that all life is one and that we are there to raise the all.

- As we rise to a certain level of Christhood (beyond the 96th level), we make it possible for a certain element of the fallen consciousness to be removed from the earth, along with the beings who embody it. This is what Jesus came to demonstrate, and the masters say there are currently 10,000 people in embodiment who could quickly claim their Christhood and begin to serve in this capacity [See the book: *The Mystical Teachings of Jesus*.]. In some cases, this means we must allow people in the fallen consciousness to attack us and we must avoid fighting them back, as Jesus demonstrated by letting himself be crucified. In this day and age, we do not have to be physically crucified or killed in order to take this stand, but we do have to be prepared to be persecuted by those who are still stuck in the fallen consciousness.

• As we continue to raise our consciousness, we can help shift the entire spectrum of the 144 levels of consciousness upwards. Some of what are currently the lowest levels of consciousness will no longer be allowed on earth.

Raising consciousness

In order to truly help the ascended masters, we have to free ourselves from the fallen consciousness. How to do this will depend on your current level of consciousness:

• For people below the 48th level of consciousness, the first priority is to get back to the 48th level. In order to get started, you need to put in a very determined effort to invoke spiritual light by using the decrees and affirmations given by the masters. This will lighten the magnetic pull that seeks to drag you down. As this happens, you will get much more out of studying the teachings of the masters. By engaging in the two-fold process of invoking light and studying, you can fairly quickly come to see through the more obvious serpentine illusions and rise back to the 48th level. You should not be engaged in seeking to change the world because you will inevitably be tempted into doing this with force.

• Between the 48th and the 96th level of consciousness, your first priority is to expand your co-creative powers by learning how to express them through the seven spiritual rays. At this level, you are primarily focused on your own growth and on rising above the mass consciousness. Changing the world is not your main concern, and focusing too much on this can be a distraction. The temptation is that you focus on changing the splinter in the eyes of other people as an excuse for not looking for the beam in your own eye.

• As you reach the 96th level, you face the serpentine temptation in its full subtlety. As you see through the basic serpentine lie, you begin to climb towards the 144th level. This is where you can begin to give a higher form of service by rising above a certain level of the fallen consciousness and demanding its removal from earth. You can also give many other forms of service, but when you reach this level, you will get instructions from the ascended masters directly from within yourself. You do not need a book to tell you how to serve.

Do not feel overwhelmed!

Because of the manipulation and deceit of the fallen beings, none of us were brought up with the understanding given in this book. When we first become aware of the existence of fallen beings and how subtle their influence is, it is easy to feel overwhelmed. When you begin to see some of their lies, it can seem almost impossible to see through all of them. This feeling is understandable, but it is essential to make a conscious decision not to succumb to it. Giving up is exactly what the fallen beings want you to do.

Instead, you can decide that you will engage in the systematic path outlined by the ascended masters. On this path, you do not have to tackle the lies of the fallen beings all at once. Instead, you can deal with the particular lie that keeps you tied to your current level and prevents you from rising to the next level. This is a matter of making an effort to clear your four lower bodies of some of the accumulated energies so that you feel less chaos inside. As you calm your mind, you will increase your intuition, and this is truly the Conscious You tuning in to the ascended masters and your I AM Presence rather than your four lower bodies and the external world.

The ascended masters have given many books and teachings that can help you walk the spiritual path. In order to help you get started, you can use the invocations in the following chapters as a powerful tool to clear your lower bodies from the energies and some of the illusions of the fallen consciousness. You will also help clear the lower bodies of the planet and the collective consciousness. In the beginning, the task may seem daunting, and the reason is that your ego and the evil forces will use any influence they have over you to discourage you. If you use the teachings and tools of the ascended masters, you can relatively quickly overcome this resistance and build a powerful upward momentum. If you make the effort to do this, you will be surprised at how quickly you can rise to a new level of consciousness with much greater clarity and inner peace. It is the hope that this book will inspire you to make the quantum leap beyond the fallen consciousness and that it will give you the practical tools to fulfill your reason for choosing to be in embodiment at this exciting time in earth's history. You give these invocations by reading them aloud, as the spoken word invokes more light than thoughts. For more specific instructions on how to use invocations and decrees, see *www.transcendencetoolbox.com*.

There is obviously more to be said about the illusions used by fallen beings in their attempts to deceive us. There is also more to be said about practical methods used by evil forces in their attempts to control all four octaves on earth. We will discuss these topics in depth in the following books in this series.

21 | CLEARING THE PHYSICAL OCTAVE

In the name of the I AM THAT I AM, the One Mind within me and within all life, I call upon Archangel Michael to take command over the physical octave on earth and clear it of all evil forces and fallen beings in accordance with the vision of Christ. I call for Saint Germain to flood the earth with an irresistible surge of Violet Flame to transmute all fear-based energies. I especially call for Archangel Michael and Saint Germain to take command over … [Make your own calls here.]

Part 1

1. Archangel Michael, I am willing to experience your Flaming Presence so that I can know that your energies can protect me from all forms of evil in my sphere.

Archangel Michael, light so blue,
my heart has room for only you.
My mind is one, no longer two,
your love for me is ever true.

Archangel Michael, you are here,
your light consumes all doubt and fear.
Your Presence is forever near,
you are to me so very dear.

2. Archangel Michael, place a shield of blue-flame protection around my four lower bodies and seal me from all forces or people with evil intent.

Archangel Michael, I will be,
all one with your reality.
No fear can hold me as I see,
this world no power has o'er me.

Archangel Michael, you are here,
your light consumes all doubt and fear.
Your Presence is forever near,
you are to me so very dear.

3. Archangel Michael, protect both myself and all people in my circle of influence from any aggressive actions by evil forces or people controlled by such forces.

Archangel Michael, hold me tight,
shatter now the darkest night.
Clear my chakras with your light,
restore to me my inner sight.

**Archangel Michael, you are here,
your light consumes all doubt and fear.
Your Presence is forever near,
you are to me so very dear.**

4. Archangel Michael, I am willing to transcend all fear of evil and evil forces. Come into my four lower bodies and consume all fear-based energy with your irresistible Light.

Archangel Michael, now I stand,
with you the light I do command.
My heart I ever will expand,
till highest truth I understand.

**Archangel Michael, you are here,
your light consumes all doubt and fear.
Your Presence is forever near,
you are to me so very dear.**

5. Archangel Michael, I am willing to know my Divine plan and the work that I vowed to do in order to help lift the earth out of the reach of evil forces.

Archangel Michael, in my heart,
from me you never will depart.
Of hierarchy I am a part,
I now accept a fresh new start.

**Archangel Michael, you are here,
your light consumes all doubt and fear.
Your Presence is forever near,
you are to me so very dear.**

6. Archangel Michael, I am willing to see in myself both my ego and my internal spirits. Expose to me how my internal divisions make me vulnerable to the attacks or deception of evil forces.

> Archangel Michael, sword of blue,
> all darkness you are cutting through.
> My Christhood I do now pursue,
> discernment shows me what is true.
>
> **Archangel Michael, you are here,**
> **your light consumes all doubt and fear.**
> **Your Presence is forever near,**
> **you are to me so very dear.**

7. Archangel Michael, I am willing to overcome all physical addictions. Use your Blue-Flame Sword to cut me free from all addictive entities.

> Archangel Michael, in your wings,
> I now let go of lesser things.
> God's homing call in my heart rings,
> my heart with yours forever sings.
>
> **Archangel Michael, you are here,**
> **your light consumes all doubt and fear.**
> **Your Presence is forever near,**
> **you are to me so very dear.**

21 | Clearing the Physical Octave

8. Archangel Michael, I am willing to rise above the collective consciousness of my family, race, religion, ethnic group or society. Cut me free from all ties to anything on earth that limits my ability to serve the ascended masters and bring the light of my I AM Presence.

> Archangel Michael, take me home,
> in higher spheres I want to roam.
> I am reborn from cosmic foam,
> my life is now a sacred poem.

> **Archangel Michael, you are here,**
> **your light consumes all doubt and fear.**
> **Your Presence is forever near,**
> **you are to me so very dear.**

9. Archangel Michael, I am willing to rise above identification with my physical body. Cut me free from the sense that my creative expression is limited by the abilities of the physical body.

> Archangel Michael, light you are,
> shining like the bluest star.
> You are a cosmic avatar,
> with you I will go very far.

> **Archangel Michael, you are here,**
> **your light consumes all doubt and fear.**
> **Your Presence is forever near,**
> **you are to me so very dear.**

Part 2

1. Archangel Michael, cut people free from the demons that cause them to go beyond the borders of sanity.

> Archangel Michael, light so blue,
> my heart has room for only you.
> My mind is one, no longer two,
> your love for me is ever true.
>
> **Archangel Michael, you are here,**
> **your light consumes all doubt and fear.**
> **Your Presence is forever near,**
> **you are to me so very dear.**

2. Archangel Michael, cut people free from the demons that cause them to commit random acts of violence, such as shootings or serial killings.

> Archangel Michael, I will be,
> all one with your reality.
> No fear can hold me as I see,
> this world no power has o'er me.
>
> **Archangel Michael, you are here,**
> **your light consumes all doubt and fear.**
> **Your Presence is forever near,**
> **you are to me so very dear.**

3. Archangel Michael, cut people free from the demons that cause them to commit petty crimes.

21 | Clearing the Physical Octave

> Archangel Michael, hold me tight,
> shatter now the darkest night.
> Clear my chakras with your light,
> restore to me my inner sight.

> **Archangel Michael, you are here,**
> **your light consumes all doubt and fear.**
> **Your Presence is forever near,**
> **you are to me so very dear.**

4. Archangel Michael, cut people free from the demons that cause them to commit more organized crime, such as drug trade or money laundering.

> Archangel Michael, now I stand,
> with you the light I do command.
> My heart I ever will expand,
> till highest truth I understand.

> **Archangel Michael, you are here,**
> **your light consumes all doubt and fear.**
> **Your Presence is forever near,**
> **you are to me so very dear.**

5. Archangel Michael, cut people free from the demons that cause them to be addicted to alcohol or drugs.

> Archangel Michael, in my heart,
> from me you never will depart.
> Of hierarchy I am a part,
> I now accept a fresh new start.

**Archangel Michael, you are here,
your light consumes all doubt and fear.
Your Presence is forever near,
you are to me so very dear.**

6. Archangel Michael, cut people free from the demons that cause them to commit more organized forms of violence, such as terrorism.

Archangel Michael, sword of blue,
all darkness you are cutting through.
My Christhood I do now pursue,
discernment shows me what is true.

**Archangel Michael, you are here,
your light consumes all doubt and fear.
Your Presence is forever near,
you are to me so very dear.**

7. Archangel Michael, cut people free from the demons that cause them to participate in or support warfare on a small or large scale.

Archangel Michael, in your wings,
I now let go of lesser things.
God's homing call in my heart rings,
my heart with yours forever sings.

**Archangel Michael, you are here,
your light consumes all doubt and fear.
Your Presence is forever near,
you are to me so very dear.**

8. Archangel Michael, cut people free from the demons that cause them to think war is necessary or justifiable.

> Archangel Michael, take me home,
> in higher spheres I want to roam.
> I am reborn from cosmic foam,
> my life is now a sacred poem.
>
> **Archangel Michael, you are here,**
> **your light consumes all doubt and fear.**
> **Your Presence is forever near,**
> **you are to me so very dear.**

9. Archangel Michael, cut people free from the demons that cause them to be blinded by religious fanaticism and extremism.

> Archangel Michael, light you are,
> shining like the bluest star.
> You are a cosmic avatar,
> with you I will go very far.
>
> **Archangel Michael, you are here,**
> **your light consumes all doubt and fear.**
> **Your Presence is forever near,**
> **you are to me so very dear.**

Part 3

1. Archangel Michael, cut people free from the demons that cause them to be blinded by political radicalism or extremism.

Archangel Michael, light so blue,
my heart has room for only you.
My mind is one, no longer two,
your love for me is ever true.

Archangel Michael, you are here,
your light consumes all doubt and fear.
Your Presence is forever near,
you are to me so very dear.

2. Archangel Michael, cut people free from the demons that cause them to be blinded by the illusion that the ends can justify the means.

Archangel Michael, I will be,
all one with your reality.
No fear can hold me as I see,
this world no power has o'er me.

Archangel Michael, you are here,
your light consumes all doubt and fear.
Your Presence is forever near,
you are to me so very dear.

3. Archangel Michael, cut people free from the demons that cause them to think they belong to a power elite who have special rights and privileges.

Archangel Michael, hold me tight,
shatter now the darkest night.
Clear my chakras with your light,
restore to me my inner sight.

**Archangel Michael, you are here,
your light consumes all doubt and fear.
Your Presence is forever near,
you are to me so very dear.**

4. Archangel Michael, cut people free from the demons that cause them to produce weapons and support the Military-Industrial Complex.

Archangel Michael, now I stand,
with you the light I do command.
My heart I ever will expand,
till highest truth I understand.

**Archangel Michael, you are here,
your light consumes all doubt and fear.
Your Presence is forever near,
you are to me so very dear.**

5. Archangel Michael, cut people free from the demons that cause them to be blinded by environmental radicalism and commit environmental terrorism.

Archangel Michael, in my heart,
from me you never will depart.
Of hierarchy I am a part,
I now accept a fresh new start.

**Archangel Michael, you are here,
your light consumes all doubt and fear.
Your Presence is forever near,
you are to me so very dear.**

6. Archangel Michael, cut people free from the demons that cause them to believe overpopulation is a problem that must be solved with all means.

> Archangel Michael, sword of blue,
> all darkness you are cutting through.
> My Christhood I do now pursue,
> discernment shows me what is true.

> **Archangel Michael, you are here,**
> **your light consumes all doubt and fear.**
> **Your Presence is forever near,**
> **you are to me so very dear.**

7. Archangel Michael, cut people free from the demons that cause them to believe they know better than others, even better than God, how to solve the problems on this planet.

> Archangel Michael, in your wings,
> I now let go of lesser things.
> God's homing call in my heart rings,
> my heart with yours forever sings.

> **Archangel Michael, you are here,**
> **your light consumes all doubt and fear.**
> **Your Presence is forever near,**
> **you are to me so very dear.**

8. Archangel Michael, cut people free from the demons that cause them to unwittingly support a money and financial system that allows the fallen beings to control the world economy.

21 | Clearing the Physical Octave

> Archangel Michael, take me home,
> in higher spheres I want to roam.
> I am reborn from cosmic foam,
> my life is now a sacred poem.
>
> **Archangel Michael, you are here,**
> **your light consumes all doubt and fear.**
> **Your Presence is forever near,**
> **you are to me so very dear.**

9. Archangel Michael, cut people free from the demons that cause them to be so blinded that they will not look for a spiritual explanation of the existence and methods of evil forces.

> Archangel Michael, light you are,
> shining like the bluest star.
> You are a cosmic avatar,
> with you I will go very far.
>
> **Archangel Michael, you are here,**
> **your light consumes all doubt and fear.**
> **Your Presence is forever near,**
> **you are to me so very dear.**

Part 4

1. Saint Germain, send flood tides of Violet Flame to consume my karmic vulnerability to any kind of physical misfortune, including violence, crime, disease or so-called natural disasters.

O Saint Germain, you do inspire,
my vision raised forever higher,
with you I form a figure-eight,
your Golden Age I co-create.

**O Saint Germain, what love you bring,
it truly makes all matter sing,
your violet flame does all restore,
with you we are becoming more.**

2. Saint Germain, send flood tides of Violet Flame to consume the karmic vulnerability of all people in my circle of influence.

O Saint Germain, what Freedom Flame,
released when we recite your name,
acceleration is your gift,
our planet it will surely lift.

**O Saint Germain, what love you bring,
it truly makes all matter sing,
your violet flame does all restore,
with you we are becoming more.**

3. Saint Germain, send flood tides of Violet Flame to consume the karmic vulnerability of the top ten percent of the most spiritual people.

O Saint Germain, in love we claim,
our right to bring your violet flame,
from you Above, to us below,
it is an all-transforming flow.

**O Saint Germain, what love you bring,
it truly makes all matter sing,
your violet flame does all restore,
with you we are becoming more.**

4. Saint Germain, send flood tides of Violet Flame to consume the karmic vulnerability of humankind as a whole.

O Saint Germain, I love you so,
my aura filled with violet glow,
my chakras filled with violet fire,
I am your cosmic amplifier.

**O Saint Germain, what love you bring,
it truly makes all matter sing,
your violet flame does all restore,
with you we are becoming more.**

5. Saint Germain, send flood tides of Violet Flame to transmute the misqualified energies that prevent people from seeing the vision of your Golden Age for earth.

O Saint Germain, I am now free,
your violet flame is therapy,
transform all hang-ups in my mind,
as inner peace I surely find.

**O Saint Germain, what love you bring,
it truly makes all matter sing,
your violet flame does all restore,
with you we are becoming more.**

6. Saint Germain, send flood tides of Violet Flame to transmute the energies that prevent the top ten percent from seeing their Divine plans and accepting their potential to bring positive change.

> O Saint Germain, my body pure,
> your violet flame for all is cure,
> consume the cause of all disease,
> and therefore I am all at ease.
>
> **O Saint Germain, what love you bring,**
> **it truly makes all matter sing,**
> **your violet flame does all restore,**
> **with you we are becoming more.**

7. Saint Germain, send flood tides of Violet Flame to transmute all fear energy that causes the spiritual people and the general population to be unwilling to acknowledge the existence of dark forces.

> O Saint Germain, I'm karma-free,
> the past no longer burdens me,
> a brand new opportunity,
> I am in Christic unity.
>
> **O Saint Germain, what love you bring,**
> **it truly makes all matter sing,**
> **your violet flame does all restore,**
> **with you we are becoming more.**

8. Saint Germain, send flood tides of Violet Flame to transmute the energies that prevent people from being willing to learn about the methods of dark forces, thereby learning how to free the earth.

> O Saint Germain, we are now one,
> I am for you a violet sun,
> as we transform this planet earth,
> your Golden Age is given birth.
>
> **O Saint Germain, what love you bring,**
> **it truly makes all matter sing,**
> **your violet flame does all restore,**
> **with you we are becoming more.**

9. Saint Germain, send flood tides of Violet Flame to transmute the energies that form a veil of illusion that prevents a world-wide awakening to the existence of evil forces and a power elite in embodiment.

> O Saint Germain, the earth is free,
> from burden of duality,
> in oneness we bring what is best,
> your Golden Age is manifest.
>
> **O Saint Germain, what love you bring,**
> **it truly makes all matter sing,**
> **your violet flame does all restore,**
> **with you we are becoming more.**

Sealing

In the name of the I AM THAT I AM, the One Mind within me and within all life, I accept that Archangel Michael, Astrea and Shiva form an impenetrable shield around myself, all people in my circle of influence and all spiritual people on earth, sealing us from any attacks or revenge by the fallen beings or the dark forces in all four octaves. I accept that the power of God is greater than any power of evil, and I say: Evil is not real and its appearances have no power on earth!

22 | CLEARING THE EMOTIONAL OCTAVE

In the name of the I AM THAT I AM, the One Mind within me and within all life, I call upon Shiva to take command over the emotional octave on earth and consume all evil forces and demons in accordance with the vision of Christ. I call for Saint Germain to flood the emotional octave with an irresistible surge of Violet Flame to transmute all energies that block the creative flow through the emotional octave. I especially call for Shiva and Saint Germain to take command over … [Make your own calls here.]

Part 1

1. Beloved Shiva, use your unlimited Sacred Fire to consume all demons and dark spirits seeking to hinder my spiritual growth and my Divine plan. Do the same for all people in my circle of influence.

O Shiva, God of Sacred Fire,
It's time to let the past expire,
I want to rise above the old,
a golden future to unfold.

O Shiva, clear the energy,
O Shiva, bring the synergy,
O Shiva, make all demons flee,
O Shiva, bring back peace to me.

2. Beloved Shiva, consume all demons and dark spirits seeking to stir up my emotional body and prevent me from being in control of my emotional reactions.

O Shiva, come and set me free,
from forces that do limit me,
with fire consume all that is less,
paving way for my success.

O Shiva, clear the energy,
O Shiva, bring the synergy,
O Shiva, make all demons flee,
O Shiva, bring back peace to me.

3. Beloved Shiva, consume all demons and dark spirits seeking to prevent the free flow of creative energies through my emotional body.

O Shiva, Maya's veil disperse,
clear my private universe,
dispel the consciousness of death,
consume it with your Sacred Breath.

**O Shiva, clear the energy,
O Shiva, bring the synergy,
O Shiva, make all demons flee,
O Shiva, bring back peace to me.**

4. Beloved Shiva, cut me free from all ties to the astral plane that I might have developed in this or previous lifetimes.

> O Shiva, I hereby let go,
> of all attachments here below,
> addictive entities consume,
> the upward path I do resume.

**O Shiva, clear the energy,
O Shiva, bring the synergy,
O Shiva, make all demons flee,
O Shiva, bring back peace to me.**

5. Beloved Shiva, consume all demons and dark spirits that are only bent on destroying human beings.

> O Shiva, I recite your name,
> come banish fear and doubt and shame,
> with fire expose within my mind,
> what ego seeks to hide behind.

**O Shiva, clear the energy,
O Shiva, bring the synergy,
O Shiva, make all demons flee,
O Shiva, bring back peace to me.**

6. Beloved Shiva, consume all demons and dark spirits that are consumed by hatred and anger against human beings.

O Shiva, I am not afraid,
my karmic debt hereby is paid,
the past no longer owns my choice,
in breath of Shiva I rejoice.

O Shiva, clear the energy,
O Shiva, bring the synergy,
O Shiva, make all demons flee,
O Shiva, bring back peace to me.

7. Beloved Shiva, consume all demons and dark spirits that are consumed by hatred and anger against anything positive, especially spiritual light.

O Shiva, show me spirit pairs,
that keep me trapped in their affairs,
I choose to see within my mind,
the spirits that you surely bind.

O Shiva, clear the energy,
O Shiva, bring the synergy,
O Shiva, make all demons flee,
O Shiva, bring back peace to me.

8. Beloved Shiva, consume all demons and dark spirits that are consumed by hatred and anger against the true teachers of humankind, namely the ascended masters.

O Shiva, naked I now stand,
my mind in freedom does expand,
as all my ghosts I do release,
surrender is the key to peace.

> O Shiva, clear the energy,
> O Shiva, bring the synergy,
> O Shiva, make all demons flee,
> O Shiva, bring back peace to me.

9. Beloved Shiva, consume all demons and dark spirits that are consumed by hatred and anger against God.

> O Shiva, all-consuming fire,
> with Parvati raise me higher,
> when I am raised your light to see,
> all men I will draw onto me.

> O Shiva, clear the energy,
> O Shiva, bring the synergy,
> O Shiva, make all demons flee,
> O Shiva, bring back peace to me.

Part 2

1. Beloved Shiva, consume all demons and dark spirits that cause people to be engaged in any form of crime.

> O Shiva, God of Sacred Fire,
> It's time to let the past expire,
> I want to rise above the old,
> a golden future to unfold.

O Shiva, clear the energy,
O Shiva, bring the synergy,
O Shiva, make all demons flee,
O Shiva, bring back peace to me.

2. Beloved Shiva, consume all demons and dark spirits that cause people to be addicted to drugs or be involved with the drug trade.

O Shiva, come and set me free,
from forces that do limit me,
with fire consume all that is less,
paving way for my success.

O Shiva, clear the energy,
O Shiva, bring the synergy,
O Shiva, make all demons flee,
O Shiva, bring back peace to me.

3. Beloved Shiva, consume all demons and dark spirits that cause people to be involved with the manipulation of the economies of nations or the world.

O Shiva, Maya's veil disperse,
clear my private universe,
dispel the consciousness of death,
consume it with your Sacred Breath.

O Shiva, clear the energy,
O Shiva, bring the synergy,
O Shiva, make all demons flee,
O Shiva, bring back peace to me.

4. Beloved Shiva, consume all demons and dark spirits that cause people to be involved with or support the Military-Industrial Complex.

> O Shiva, I hereby let go,
> of all attachments here below,
> addictive entities consume,
> the upward path I do resume.
>
> **O Shiva, clear the energy,**
> **O Shiva, bring the synergy,**
> **O Shiva, make all demons flee,**
> **O Shiva, bring back peace to me.**

5. Beloved Shiva, consume all demons and dark spirits that cause people to be involved with any form of terrorism.

> O Shiva, I recite your name,
> come banish fear and doubt and shame,
> with fire expose within my mind,
> what ego seeks to hide behind.
>
> **O Shiva, clear the energy,**
> **O Shiva, bring the synergy,**
> **O Shiva, make all demons flee,**
> **O Shiva, bring back peace to me.**

6. Beloved Shiva, consume all demons and dark spirits that cause people to commit suicide, either directly or indirectly.

O Shiva, I am not afraid,
my karmic debt hereby is paid,
the past no longer owns my choice,
in breath of Shiva I rejoice.

O Shiva, clear the energy,
O Shiva, bring the synergy,
O Shiva, make all demons flee,
O Shiva, bring back peace to me.

7. Beloved Shiva, consume all demons and dark spirits behind religious fanaticism or extremism.

O Shiva, show me spirit pairs,
that keep me trapped in their affairs,
I choose to see within my mind,
the spirits that you surely bind.

O Shiva, clear the energy,
O Shiva, bring the synergy,
O Shiva, make all demons flee,
O Shiva, bring back peace to me.

8. Beloved Shiva, consume all demons and dark spirits behind political radicalism or extremism.

O Shiva, naked I now stand,
my mind in freedom does expand,
as all my ghosts I do release,
surrender is the key to peace.

> O Shiva, clear the energy,
> O Shiva, bring the synergy,
> O Shiva, make all demons flee,
> O Shiva, bring back peace to me.

9. Beloved Shiva, consume all demons and dark spirits behind the creation of ongoing conflicts and violence.

> O Shiva, all-consuming fire,
> with Parvati raise me higher,
> when I am raised your light to see,
> all men I will draw onto me.

> O Shiva, clear the energy,
> O Shiva, bring the synergy,
> O Shiva, make all demons flee,
> O Shiva, bring back peace to me.

Part 3

1. Beloved Shiva, consume the beast that causes people to be in ignorance, so they do not want to know, or in delusion, so they think they know all.

> O Shiva, God of Sacred Fire,
> It's time to let the past expire,
> I want to rise above the old,
> a golden future to unfold.

> O Shiva, clear the energy,
> O Shiva, bring the synergy,
> O Shiva, make all demons flee,
> O Shiva, bring back peace to me.

2. Beloved Shiva, consume the beast that causes people to be in anger and hatred, so they think they are justified in using force or violence against other people or against nature.

> O Shiva, come and set me free,
> from forces that do limit me,
> with fire consume all that is less,
> paving way for my success.

> O Shiva, clear the energy,
> O Shiva, bring the synergy,
> O Shiva, make all demons flee,
> O Shiva, bring back peace to me.

3. Beloved Shiva, consume the beast that causes people to be in spiritual or intellectual pride, so they think they know better than other people, even better than God.

> O Shiva, Maya's veil disperse,
> clear my private universe,
> dispel the consciousness of death,
> consume it with your Sacred Breath.

> O Shiva, clear the energy,
> O Shiva, bring the synergy,
> O Shiva, make all demons flee,
> O Shiva, bring back peace to me.

4. Beloved Shiva, consume the beast that causes people to be in greed, so they are willing to do anything to get what they want but can never get enough.

> O Shiva, I hereby let go,
> of all attachments here below,
> addictive entities consume,
> the upward path I do resume.
>
> **O Shiva, clear the energy,**
> **O Shiva, bring the synergy,**
> **O Shiva, make all demons flee,**
> **O Shiva, bring back peace to me.**

5. Beloved Shiva, consume the beast that causes people to be in envy and jealousy, so they are willing to put down others in order to raise themselves up.

> O Shiva, I recite your name,
> come banish fear and doubt and shame,
> with fire expose within my mind,
> what ego seeks to hide behind.
>
> **O Shiva, clear the energy,**
> **O Shiva, bring the synergy,**
> **O Shiva, make all demons flee,**
> **O Shiva, bring back peace to me.**

6. Beloved Shiva, consume the beast that causes people to be in non-will and non-being, so they are unwilling to transcend their present state of consciousness.

O Shiva, I am not afraid,
my karmic debt hereby is paid,
the past no longer owns my choice,
in breath of Shiva I rejoice.

O Shiva, clear the energy,
O Shiva, bring the synergy,
O Shiva, make all demons flee,
O Shiva, bring back peace to me.

7. Beloved Shiva, consume the beast that causes people to be in a state of non-belief where they doubt everything and never take decisive action.

O Shiva, show me spirit pairs,
that keep me trapped in their affairs,
I choose to see within my mind,
the spirits that you surely bind.

O Shiva, clear the energy,
O Shiva, bring the synergy,
O Shiva, make all demons flee,
O Shiva, bring back peace to me.

8. Beloved Shiva, consume the war beast that causes people to be blinded to the reality of war and conflict.

O Shiva, naked I now stand,
my mind in freedom does expand,
as all my ghosts I do release,
surrender is the key to peace.

O Shiva, clear the energy,
O Shiva, bring the synergy,
O Shiva, make all demons flee,
O Shiva, bring back peace to me.

9. Beloved Shiva, consume the beast of discrimination that blinds people to all forms of discrimination, including poverty and the suppression of women.

O Shiva, all-consuming fire,
with Parvati raise me higher,
when I am raised your light to see,
all men I will draw onto me.

O Shiva, clear the energy,
O Shiva, bring the synergy,
O Shiva, make all demons flee,
O Shiva, bring back peace to me.

Part 4

1. Saint Germain, send flood tides of Violet Flame to transmute the energies that pollute the higher levels of the emotional octave.

O Saint Germain, you do inspire,
my vision raised forever higher,
with you I form a figure-eight,
your Golden Age I co-create.

**O Saint Germain, what love you bring,
it truly makes all matter sing,
your violet flame does all restore,
with you we are becoming more.**

2. Saint Germain, send flood tides of Violet Flame to open the full flow of creative energies through the emotional octave.

O Saint Germain, what Freedom Flame,
released when we recite your name,
acceleration is your gift,
our planet it will surely lift.

**O Saint Germain, what love you bring,
it truly makes all matter sing,
your violet flame does all restore,
with you we are becoming more.**

3. Saint Germain, send flood tides of Violet Flame to clear out the levels of the astral plane that produce warfare and conflict.

O Saint Germain, in love we claim,
our right to bring your violet flame,
from you Above, to us below,
it is an all-transforming flow.

**O Saint Germain, what love you bring,
it truly makes all matter sing,
your violet flame does all restore,
with you we are becoming more.**

4. Saint Germain, send flood tides of Violet Flame to clear out the levels of the astral plane that produce all forms of discrimination, especially against women.

> O Saint Germain, I love you so,
> my aura filled with violet glow,
> my chakras filled with violet fire,
> I am your cosmic amplifier.

> **O Saint Germain, what love you bring,**
> **it truly makes all matter sing,**
> **your violet flame does all restore,**
> **with you we are becoming more.**

5. Saint Germain, send flood tides of Violet Flame to clear out the levels of the astral plane that produce all kinds of envy, especially poverty.

> O Saint Germain, I am now free,
> your violet flame is therapy,
> transform all hang-ups in my mind,
> as inner peace I surely find.

> **O Saint Germain, what love you bring,**
> **it truly makes all matter sing,**
> **your violet flame does all restore,**
> **with you we are becoming more.**

6. Saint Germain, send flood tides of Violet Flame to clear out the levels of the astral plane that produce illnesses, including a health-care industry driven by profit.

O Saint Germain, my body pure,
your violet flame for all is cure,
consume the cause of all disease,
and therefore I am all at ease.

**O Saint Germain, what love you bring,
it truly makes all matter sing,
your violet flame does all restore,
with you we are becoming more.**

7. Saint Germain, send flood tides of Violet Flame to clear out the levels of the astral plane that produce political systems controlled by the special interest of various power elite groups.

O Saint Germain, I'm karma-free,
the past no longer burdens me,
a brand new opportunity,
I am in Christic unity.

**O Saint Germain, what love you bring,
it truly makes all matter sing,
your violet flame does all restore,
with you we are becoming more.**

8. Saint Germain, send flood tides of Violet Flame to clear out the levels of the astral plane that produce religions that justify violence.

O Saint Germain, we are now one,
I am for you a violet sun,
as we transform this planet earth,
your Golden Age is given birth.

**O Saint Germain, what love you bring,
it truly makes all matter sing,
your violet flame does all restore,
with you we are becoming more.**

9. Saint Germain, send flood tides of Violet Flame to clear out the levels of the astral plane that produce the subtle ignorance that dominates both mainstream religions, political systems and scientific materialism.

O Saint Germain, the earth is free,
from burden of duality,
in oneness we bring what is best,
your Golden Age is manifest.

**O Saint Germain, what love you bring,
it truly makes all matter sing,
your violet flame does all restore,
with you we are becoming more.**

Sealing

In the name of the I AM THAT I AM, the One Mind within me and within all life, I accept that Archangel Michael, Astrea and Shiva form an impenetrable shield around myself, all people in my circle of influence and all spiritual people on earth, sealing us from any attacks or revenge by the fallen beings or the dark forces in all four octaves. I accept that the power of God is greater than any power of evil, and I say: Evil is not real and its appearances have no power on earth!

CPSIA information can be obtained at www.ICGtesting.com
Printed in the USA
LVOW07s0005130916

504268LV00003B/29/P

9 788793 297029